Wild
Things

Perverse
Modernities

A series
edited by

Jack
Halberstam
+
Lisa Lowe

Wild Things

the disorder of desire

Jack Halberstam

Duke University Press   Durham and London   2020

Printed and bound by CPI Group (UK) Ltd, Croydon, CR0 4YY

Designed by Aimee C. Harrison and Drew Sisk
Typeset in Garamond Premier Pro and Neuzeit Std Book
by Copperline Book Services

Library of Congress Cataloging-in-Publication Data
Names: Halberstam, Jack, [date] author.
Title: Wild things : the disorder of desire / Jack Halberstam.
Other titles: Perverse modernities.
Description: Durham : Duke University Press, 2020. |
Series: Perverse modernities | Includes bibliographical
references and index.
Identifiers: LCCN 2020008115 (print)
LCCN 2020008116 (ebook)
ISBN 9781478010036 (hardcover)
ISBN 9781478011088 (paperback)
ISBN 9781478012627 (ebook)
Subjects: LCSH: Queer theory. | Gender identity. | Sex. |
Heterosexuality. | Homosexuality. | Desire.
Classification: LCC HQ76.25 .H353 2020 (print) |
LCC HQ76.25 (ebook) | DDC 306.7601—dc23
LC record available at https://lccn.loc.gov/2020008115
LC ebook record available at https://lccn.loc.gov/2020008116

Cover art: Candice Lin, *Petrification*, 2016. Mixed media.
Courtesy of the artist and Ghebaly Gallery, Los Angeles.

For José

CONTENTS

ALEX THE LION: The wild? Are you nuts? That is the worst idea I have ever heard!
MELMAN THE GIRAFFE: It's unsanitary!
MARTY THE ZEBRA: The penguins are going, so why can't I?
ALEX THE LION: The penguins are psychotic.

—*Madagascar* (2005)

Many a book on the wild begins with a backward glance at the youth of the author, when times were different, when black-bellied dippers, red squirrels, or natterjack toads still roamed the woods and valleys, and when mankind had not yet begun to circle the drain in the universal pool of life. I am tempted to tell you about the hedgehogs that were easily spotted on my lawn in the mornings of my youth and that have now declined in numbers in the United Kingdom from 36 million in 1961 to 1 million today. I am, like so many of my generation, amazed at how much has been lost, how little we have to show for it, and how quickly we have embraced a world largely cleansed of all connections to wildness. And yet, like many others, I come not only to mourn wildness but also to rediscover it, to track its path from there to here, to find my way through and with, and to take walks into the woods, into the streets, and into other less obvious dark and deep places of the wild. However, we must not imagine that the wild is ours to discover or rediscover; we should resist the temptation to believe that it once existed and now has gone; and we must find a way around the treacherous binary logics that set the wild in opposition to the modern, the *civilized*, the cultivated, and the real. And, while the wild is tethered to nature in our imaginations, or to one particular version of nature, wildness is not limited to the natural world, and it has an extensive life elsewhere too—in aesthetics, politics, theory, and desire.

Our notions of the wild do still largely derive from nineteenth- and early twentieth-century naturalists like Thoreau ("How near to good is what is wild") or John Muir ("I never saw a discontented tree"). And despite rigorous analyses of the colonial production of distinctions between the domestic/tame/civilized and the foreign/wild/barbaric, we still, in literature and film, subscribe to such distinctions, leaving their imperial heritages untouched and contributing anew to the romance of going back to some mystical unsullied land (Jon Krakauer's *Into the Wild*), on the one hand, or discovering our real selves in the nakedness of nature (Cheryl Strayed's *Wild*), on the other. But perhaps the wild is better described nowadays by the melancholic words of Alex the Lion in the animated classic *Madagascar*, for whom the wild is "the worst idea I ever heard," suitable only for the psychotic penguins, and representative of a fantasy of freedom that the zoo itself maintains and stokes. And so, this book cautions against investments in a wildness that lies in a distant past never to come again or in a future of restored wildness that will be delivered through science and conservation. This book takes the wild instead as an epistemology, a terrain of alternative formulations that resist the orderly impulses of modernity and as a merging of anticolonial, anticapitalist, and radical queer interests. As in *The Queer Art of Failure*, I chart here a meandering road through counterintuitive terrain, and as in earlier work of mine on gothic monstrosity, queer time and space, and subjugated knowledge and archives, this book looks to what the culture has discarded for clues to new wild logics of being and doing.

But before we take a leap into that kind of wildness, I must, for once in my life, obey the law of genre and tell you one of the stories that brought me to the wild. The story that stays with me, even more than the missing hedgehogs, as an indicator of a wildness manqué concerns a cuter and even more elusive creature. Although I have been known, on occasion, to accept invitations to talk at somewhat remote places (*remote* is a relative term here, relative to my permanent location at the time) on the basis of being promised a sighting of endangered or just odd animals like yellow-eyed penguins in Dunedin, New Zealand, quetzals in Costa Rica, and koalas in Brisbane, Australia, this was not one of those occasions. I had, perhaps foolishly, agreed to speak at a conference on "remote sexualities" to be held in one of the truly remote and wild places in Europe—the Faroe Islands—not in search of a creature, but just to see a place I knew I would otherwise never visit. The Faroe Islands have to be accessed through Denmark since they hold the status of an autonomous country within the Kingdom of Denmark, but they sit in a bleak and stormy spot between the Norwegian Sea and the North Atlantic. The Faroe Islands are 200 miles north-northwest of Scotland and cover only 540 square miles, their total population numbering less than ten thousand.

Traveling to the Faroe Islands took on a host of symbolic meanings, as it was at a difficult time in my life. I was in the process of a breakup with a partner, and we began to feel like bit players in an epic tale of struggle and adversity as one leg after another of a very long and elaborate itinerary carrying us from California to an island north of Scotland was canceled or late. Why we persevered in our efforts to get to the islands was not clear to either of us. Nonetheless, after a protracted travel experience lasting almost two days, we disembarked from a small plane into a forlorn airport in the Faroe capital of Tórshavn (*capital* being a rather fancy word for this tiny area of land). Almost upon arrival we both felt some combination of claustrophobia and agoraphobia. The islands were too small, the sky was too big, and there was simply nowhere to hide from the weather, the climate, space, light, dark, water, sadness, and remoteness of all kinds. From every spot on the main island you could see the ocean, terrifying and gray, turbulent and menacing. It was summer, so the nights were very short and the light was almost oppressive in its persistence. We holed up in our hotel and tried to block the light and the views in order to sleep.

The next day, after the conference—a fascinating event which, as a city-person, I bluffed my way through—we agreed to go on a boat trip around the islands looking for the mating puffins that the islands were known for. The puffin is often misidentified as being a cousin of the penguin, but the two species are not related, despite the fact that both their names mean fat or swollen (puffed). We knew the puffins were here somewhere because Tórshavn was full of reminders in the form of sad taxidermic specimens—"stuffed puffs" as we quickly dubbed them. Puffins were also, even more sadly perhaps, on a few menus and were considered a local delicacy. The stuffed puffs stared at us in cafés, in the hotel, and adorned publicity posters, postcards, tourist publications, menus, and so on. I can attest that, in their stuffed form, puffins quickly lose their charm; rather than presenting us with the slightly cheeky demeanor of a puffy, paddling pelagic, the stuffed puffs looked more like discarded toys from an era lacking both comfort and imagination.

Despite the creepy omnipresence of stuffed puffins, or maybe because of it, we set out enthusiastically to encounter the real thing. The little boat that was to take us around the islands did not inspire trust in its seaworthiness, and the water was inevitably rougher than we would have liked. As we rounded small islands, we heard from the captain/guide that some of the islands in this archipelago were home to only two people—a mating pair, I suppose—for whom the solitude was unfathomably (to us at least) alluring. Finally, we came to a stretch of rocky cliffs. The captain explained that they had to airlift sheep into and out of these stretches of land in order to give them access to grazing land.

I struggled to picture a helicopter lowering bewildered sheep onto these small strips of green. But the main attraction of these rocks were not the odd sheep that sometimes got stranded there, but the puffins that made their nests here every year and laid their eggs and watched their chicks hatch, grow, and then set off into the ocean to try their luck against their many predators. I thought I saw a creature move among the rocks, but no, it was just a clump of grass waving in the wind. The captain went to all the places he knew to find the puffins, and we ignored the rising seas as we scanned the dark face of the rock for signs of life.

After hours of futile searching, we had to admit defeat and recognize that the hour was late, the seas were high, the weather was foul, and the puffins were gone or, perhaps, had never come to roost at all. The captain was baffled and muttered something about it being too late in the season, but a deckhand commented that it was not just that the puffins were not here; it looked as if they had never been here. Whether it was my age, the breakup, the remote location, I am not sure, but the missing puffins were indescribably sad to me and have remained with me ever since as a symbol of something I lost, an opportunity that passed me by, and a time that will never come again. Without the living birds, the stuffed puffs ceased to be a reminder of a living species that populated the region and became instead a melancholic and slightly pathetic marker of a vanishing breed. The wild, I learned too late, is not a place you can go, a site you can visit; it cannot be willed into being, left behind, lost or found. The wild limns our experiences of time and place, past and present, and beckons us to a future we know will never come.

The introduction to this book will not provide a conventional genealogy of wildness; rather, it builds a lexicon within which wildness is the central principle. Appropriately, perhaps, there is not a central argument sweeping all the thoughts along toward a punch line; rather, I offer a vocabulary for wildness that might hold some of the pieces of this book in productive tension. Definitions of *wildness* will jostle with one another for classificatory dominance, and just as quickly as formulations of the wild emerge, they may just as easily recede into babble. We will journey from bewilderment to chaos, from weeds to wandering, from the will to wilderness; we will be in the wild but not imagine ourselves to be of it; we will be guided by unhinged children, poets, animals, and wild thinkers. We will think ourselves wild too and then question the "we," the "wild," and everything in between. Like the stuffed puffs, after all, the human subject of Euro-American philosophy and romance may itself be nothing more than a relic of a time long past, living in the ruins of a world that once beckoned and looking ahead to oblivion: less an angel of history and more a ghost dancing at its own funeral.

ACKNOWLEDGMENTS

Wild Things was written in the long shadow cast by the death of José Esteban Muñoz and is dedicated to his memory. I hope this book can live up to the shared project that he, Tavia Nyong'o, and myself imagined we were all writing. As I was developing some ideas for this project on wildness, I quickly became aware that Nyong'o and Muñoz were also, together and separately, exploring some similar questions about queerness, new materialism, and alternative political imaginaries also under the rubric of *wildness*. Indeed, in 2013, Nyong'o and Muñoz taught and curated a class titled "Wildness." This class, and I quote from its syllabus, proposed to "employ wildness and the wild as critical tropes that potentially open a conversation across queer studies, ecology, aesthetics, animal studies, disability studies, and critical race studies." The syllabus was an inspired mix of readings on new ecology, animal studies, and queer theory, and José and Tavia supplemented the readings with walks around the city accompanied by invited guests.

While I was invited to visit the class, I never did make it to New York City that fall, and the conversation that Muñoz, Nyong'o, and I had wanted to stage about cohabiting the critical terrain of wildness was constantly and fatally deferred. We had hoped to create a small book out of these conversations titled *Three Paths to the Wild*, which would cover some common interests we share on race, anarchy, punk, sexuality, desire, animals/pets/children, music, high and low theory, a new term for queer vitality, queer eco-critical endeavors. In *Three Paths* we wanted, separately and passionately, to do something that would not exactly introduce a project so much as immediately occupy it, inhabit it, and begin to live with and in it. We had wanted to experiment with writing styles, write in and out of each other's chapters, and yet still hold on to those chapters as individually authored but multiply rewritten. All of us had turned to a critique of state politics in the wake of the financial meltdown; we were reading Thoreau, Stefano Harney and Fred Moten, James Scott, Lucy Parsons, Saidiya Hartman, Dean Spade, Jodi Byrd, and others for nonlibertarian models of anarchy and were thinking about *wildness* as a space/name/critical term for what lies beyond current logics of rule. But time, fate, and mortality intervened. José died, tragically young, in December 2013, and our conversation on wildness is now permanently delayed and can only be rudely transferred to this text.

Apart from the conversations between José, Tavia, and myself, this book was written with, for, and alongside the wild theorizings of a large and unwieldy group of thinkers who, I hope, will not mind finding their names listed under the heading of "wild theory." They include Branka Arsić, Jane Bennett, Lauren Berlant, Rizvana Bradley, Jayna Brown, Judith Butler, Jodi Byrd, Mel Chen, Pete Coviello, Harry Dodge, Roderick Ferguson, Stefano Harney, Macarena Gómez-Barris, Gayatri Gopinath, Saidiya Hartman, Zakiyyah Jackson, Kara Keeling, Lisa Lowe, Dana Luciano, Eng-Beng Lim, Fred Moten, Martin Manalansan, Uri McMillan, Maggie Nelson, Tavia Nyong'o, Paul B. Preciado, Chandan Reddy, C. Riley Snorton, Julia Bryan Wilson. Thanks to New York friends Tina Campt, Kandice Chu, Arnaldo Cruz-Malave, Cathy Davidson, Lisa Duggan, David Eng, Licia Fiol-Matta, Keri Kenetsky, Lura Kipnis, Iona Mancheong, Miller Oberman, Jordy Rosenberg, Daniel Da Silva. Much gratitude to my new colleagues at Columbia who have all influenced my thinking profoundly in a very short period of time: Vanessa Agard-Jones, Joseph Albernaz, Branka Arsić, Marcellus Blount (in memorium), George Chauncey, Sarah Cole, Julie Crawford, Denise Cruz, Patricia Dailey, Brent Edwards, Katherine Franke, Farah Jasmine Griffin, Bernard Harcourt, Saidiya Hartman, Marianne Hirsch, Gil Hochberg, Jean Howard, Tey Meadow, Audra Simpson. Friends further flung include Tosh Bascara, Sara Davidmann, Carla Freccero, Dominique Grisard, Silas Howard, Josh Kun, Katrin Pahl, Jens Rydstrom, Julietta Singh, Katherine Bond Stockton, Damon Young. Thank you to the readers of this book who tried hard to wrangle its unruliness into a legible form: Jayna Brown, Kandice Chu, Pete Coviello, Dana Luciano, and, as always, Ken Wissoker. Many missteps surely remain, but the book exists only because of the rigorous readings I received. For research assistance, thank you to Sam Davis and Diana Newby Rose.

The gorgeous image on the cover of *Wild Things*, a sculpture by Candice Lin titled *Petrification*, has been lifted from an installation by Lin at the Los Angeles–based gallery Commonwealth and Council in 2016. I am deeply grateful to Lin for allowing me to use this sculpture, to extract it from the larger installation. I let it stand here as a marker of things, dead and alive, that escape the webs of classification cast by human knowledge and endeavor.

Finally, special thanks to my cherished friends Lisa Lowe, Ira Livingston, Gayatri Gopinath, and Macarena Gómez-Barris, my wild muse.

Part I

Sex in the Wild

Sex before, after, and against Nature

Wild—
Grow or develop
without restraint
or discipline.
—Oxford
English
Dictionary

I n *Where the Wild Things Are,* Maurice Sendak's beloved book for children of all ages, we follow a young and untamed traveler as he learns the difference between the domestic world of the family and the wild world of lost and lonely creatures. This simple story of Max's journey maps the potential and the dangers of wildness. All at once, wildness appears in the book as a mark of exclusion, a place of exile, and it reveals the violence required to maintain radical separations between here and there, home and away, human and wild thing. *Wild Things: The Disorder of Desire* explores the wild not simply as a space beyond the home but also as a challenge to an assumed order of things from, by, and on behalf of things that refuse and resist order itself. Wildness names simultaneously a chaotic force of nature, the outside of categorization, unrestrained forms of embodiment, the refusal to submit to social regulation, loss of control, the unpredictable. This sequence suggests a romantic wild, a space of potential, an undoing that beckons and seduces. But, obviously, the wild has also served to name the orders of being that colonial authority comes to tame: the others to a disastrous discourse of civilization, the racialized orientation to order, the reifying operations of racial discourse (wild "things"). For this reason, to work with the wild is also to risk reengaging these meanings. I take the risk here because wildness offers proximity to the critiques of those regimes of meaning, and it opens up the possibility of unmaking and unbuilding worlds.

For example, *Where the Wild Things Are* opens with Max, a young boy dressed in wolf's clothing, creating disorder in the family home. Max, wielding a large hammer, knocks a large nail into the wall to hang a knotted sheet across the room. His act of building here—over this makeshift rope he has draped a curtain to create a shelter and has hung, from a clothes hanger, a threadbare stuffed toy dog—is also a scene of unmaking. Max himself balances precariously on an uneven stack of books to hammer his nail at the right height, and his imprecise banging has created a large hole in the wall. This tableau of destruction captures the work of this book, the art of wildness and the space of disorder. Max is potentially an anticolonial wanderer who refuses to settle the wild places he visits and who rejects the leadership he is offered. And Sendak presents him here in layered complexity as an image of wild subjectivity. Max is young; he inhabits the family home against his own will; he simultaneously destroys that home and attempts to build another world within it. He uses books practically and not metaphysically, and he drapes himself in the costume of a wild animal signifying the chaos of childhood. The stuffed animal hanging at the other end of the rope poses questions about the relations between child, wild creatures, and beloved toys. The stuffed animal is both Max's alter ego and what he fears becoming in the orbit of his all-too-present mother and his very absent father. Max has a long furry tail, a phallic symbol of authority, but no power to go with it. He is small (hence the stack of books he needs for height and the oversized tool in his hand), he is impotent, and he is angry. In the next panel, on the next page, the trouble continues as Max, in the wolf costume, chases the family dog down the stairs with a fork in his hand. Does he intend to kill the pet or eat it? Is his confusion about the status of the household animal another sign of his immaturity or a refusal to observe the proper distinctions between humans and animals and between different kinds of animality? Max is suspended in this panel just above the ground; he is not flying exactly, but neither is he standing; he occupies a space of suspension, hand still raised, tool/weapon at the ready, anger now turned to glee. The wild, these two panels demonstrate, maps a set of relations between humans and animals, human representations of animals, animals in effigy (the stuffed dog), pets, family, world, performance, costume, nature, space, and temporality. The book asks both *where* the wild things are and *when* the wild things are; it provides few answers but many questions.

Some of the questions posed by Sendak's classic story have been asked before in other mythic tales about young adventurers and wild creatures. And many of these stories—like Burroughs's *Tarzan* or Kipling's *Just So Stories*— have served to confirm an imperial order of things within which the domestic and the wild are not simply markers of the proximity to home but also serve a racial system within which wildness represents a time before, a primitive past, and unrestrained temperament. So conventional is this mapping of the human that it continues to play across contemporary variations on the theme of human-nonhuman relations in such novels as *Life of Pi* (2001) by Yann Martel and, as earlier work of mine has shown, throughout an animated universe of films pitting humans against robots, monsters, fish, and rogue pets. But, as we will see, the wild does not simply name a space of nonhuman animality that must submit to human control; it also questions the hierarchies of being that have been designed to mark and patrol the boundaries between the human and everything else.

Maurice Sendak's conjuring of the wild acknowledges these hierarchies and then tries to undermine them. Sendak creates a visual vortex in the first few pages of the book by setting up a series of receding mirrored surfaces within which confusion about authority, order, hierarchy, and sequence prevails. Thus, we see on the wall behind Max, as he chases a pet dog in his wolf costume, a painting, an image of a wild creature we will soon meet. The artist's signature, "by Max," sits beneath the image, forging a relation between Maurice Sendak, the author, and Max, the protagonist, the child in the wolf's costume and the queer adult artist who draws him, draws him drawing wild things, and draws millions of children into the wild. But the hierarchies that are supposed to separate author from creation are further confused when Max's mother calls him a "wild thing" and sends him to his room without supper. Refusing the authority of his mother, and eschewing an identification with his absent father, Max conjures other worlds. A forest grows that night in Max's room "and the walls became the world all around."[1] Because Max could not go wild, the wild came to him, at night and in his imagination. But rather than being a place of wonder and innocence, the wild in Sendak's genius conjuring is a place of ruination, destitution, anarchy, and despair. The wild, Sendak warns, is neither a place you occupy nor an identity to claim. The wild is an uneven space of aesthetic power ("by Max") and an equivocal and limited source of opposition. We will follow Max to where the wild things are not to know them and to love them or destroy them, but to map the shape of the world that depends on their rejection. And when we come to where the wild things are, we can decide whether to answer the call to stillness or whether, instead, to start the wild rumpus.

Before Nature: Hello from the Other Side

I've forgotten how it felt before the world fell at our feet . . .
—Adele, "Hello"

The wild plays a part in most theories of sexuality, and sexuality plays its role in most theories of wildness. For the past one hundred and fifty-odd years, heterosexuality and homosexuality have sat opposite each other on a seesaw weighted one way or the other by public opinion, legal rulings, medical expertise, religious belief, and political necessity. The natural condition of heterosexuality, doctors, lawyers, priests, and politicians have proposed, can be deduced from the mechanics of reproduction, the morphologies of sexed bodies and the social structures of family and work. And the unnatural condition of both homosexuality and transsexuality, some of the same sources aver, can be confirmed by the Bible, multiple court cases and legal trials, medical investigations, and political animus. But in a world where neither *nature* nor *God* holds the same sway over human understandings of good and evil, normal and perverse, bodies and life, we must consider what sexuality in general, and what specifically queerness, might be *after* nature.

Wild Things makes the case for considering modern sexuality as a discursive force that runs in several directions at once—toward the consolidation of self within the modern period, away from the rituals and prohibitions of religious belief, and toward indeterminate modes of embodiment. In terms of what Michel Foucault called "the history of sexuality," queer bodies reenter the symbolic order through a "reverse discourse" whereby they fashion both classification and rejection into selfhood.[2] The term that medicine used to pathologize nonnormative sexual desire, in other words, *homosexual*, now becomes the route to acceptance. This is an *incorporative* model of sexual definition. Another model of sexuality links sexuality to nature and produces natural and unnatural forms of desire. This *ecological* model looks for connections between environmental ethics and queer politics.[3] This model is often invested in space, terrain, and geography and tethered to oppositions between rural and urban areas that then give rise to concepts of "eco-sexual resistance."[4]

INTRODUCTION TO PART I

But sexuality has also been cast as a *postnatural phenomenon*, and I join with this project by adding the notion of a disordered or wild desire to the postnatural sense of a proliferating set of desires. After nature, desire is profoundly cultural and barely connected at all to nineteenth-century narratives of the natural. We are in need of new lexicons for the forms of desire and the shapes of bodily legibility and illegibility that currently make up our postnatural world. And so, the category of *wildness* in this book will stand for the order of things that we have left behind, the anticipatory mood that accompanies all claims of coming after something, and the unknown future that, for now at least, still beckons from the horizon. Wildness is all at once what we were, what we have become, and what we will be or, even, what we will cease to be in the event of postnatural climate collapse. And, as this book reveals, while those who want to go into the wild almost always operate in bad faith, others spin wildness into an orientation to the void, an ontology "beyond the human," as Eduardo Kohn puts it,[5] and a disorder that reminds us of a time, in Adele's words from her song "Hello" (2015), "before the world fell at our feet." But wildness is not simply the opposite of order, nor the intensification of the natural. Nor is wildness a conventionally defined political project oriented toward disturbance; wildness is the absence of order, the entropic force of a chaos that constantly spins away from biopolitical attempts to manage life and bodies and desires. Wildness has no goal, no point of liberation that beckons off in the distance, no shape that must be assumed, no outcome that must be desired. Wildness, instead, disorders desire and desires disorder. Beyond the human, wildness spins narratives of vegetal growth, viral multiplication, dynamic systems of nonhuman exchange. But in the realm of the human, a colonial realm within which the human functions as a sovereign power, the terminology of the wild has been a disaster.

Wildness, indeed, has simultaneously provided the lexicon for massive systems of violence and the justification for the removal of Native and Black peoples. Wildness, in other words, has historically been weaponized and has provided some of the language for what Sylvia Wynter has called the "coloniality of being."[6] Within this structure of being, Wynter proposes, bourgeois humanism produced an imperial order of *man* dependent on a series of foundational hierarchies all organized around an exaggerated sense of the power of colonial masculinity. This power, furthermore, expressed itself through seemingly neutral formulations of power—order, law, social stability—while actually constituting entire groups of people as irrational, unstable, and violent. As Wynter writes, "it was to be the peoples of the militarily expropriated New

World territories (i.e., Indians), as well as the enslaved peoples of Black Africa (i.e., Negroes), that were made to reoccupy the matrix slot of Otherness—to be made into the physical referent of the idea of the irrational/subrational Human Other, to this first degodded (if still hybridly religio-secular) 'descriptive statement' of the human in history, as the descriptive statement that would be foundational to modernity" (266). Where a coloniality of being invests the colonial explorer with the god-like qualities of creativity, omniscience, and benevolence, so too a system of racialization ascribes everything else to the peoples to be colonized. Wildness takes its place within this new order of being and, in the eighteenth and nineteenth centuries, could be relied on as shorthand for the supposed savagery of Indigenous peoples and specifically their "savage sexualities," as Kanaka Maoli scholar J. Kēhaulani Kauanui puts it. These "savage sexualities" in a Hawaiian context, Kauanui claims, were actually alternative formations of desire and kinship but were cast by missionaries as evidence of "backsliding into 'heathendom.'"[7] Wildness was also part of a set of alienating languages used to justify slavery. For this reason, working with wildness as a concept risks animating long-established discursive connections between Native peoples and wildness, on the one hand, and Black people and wildness, on the other.

In earlier periods, wildness was less of a racial term and more of a description of states of being against which social norms could be established. Wildness, as Hayden White comments in an essay titled "Forms of Wildness," belonged to a class of "self-authenticating devices," like "heresy" and "madness," which, according to him, did not simply describe a state of being so much as "confirm the value of their dialectical antitheses."[8] And so, wildness, White proposed, particularly in premodern thought, lent value to the term *civilization* while defining through opposition a negative terrain and value, a state "hostile to normal humanity" and a way of being defined as "passionate and bewildered" (165) because not constrained and ordered. But how does wildness function in a modern context, and can it be anything but the opposite of a supposedly positive, indeed normative, value to which it lends weight? I argue that wildness can escape its function as a negative condition and can name a form of being that flees from possessive strictures of governance and remain opposed to so-called normal humanity. In what follows, I try to offer another account of wildness within which it functions as a form of disorder that will not submit to rule, a mode of unknowing, a resistant ontology, and a fantasy of life beyond the human.

Modernist literature, we well know, has incorporated some understanding of the wild as part of a colonial sensibility that is both drawn to and repelled by expressions of wildness—hence we get movements like primitivism that direct desire and fear onto a precivilized past represented using the language of racial otherness. And we see art movements like Fauvism (French for wild beasts) within which the artist tries to capture the unruliness of emotional turmoil as a riot of color. All too often, as these movements show, wildness has been associated with racialized forms of precivilized disorder, as a mode of being that, even though it represents something that white Europeans felt they had lost, must nonetheless be tamed and governed. Within England specifically, wildness has functioned disastrously as part of an elaborate spatial sense of national belonging that has supposedly been spoiled in the postcolonial period by unchecked immigration and the collapse of a rigidly maintained class system. However, modernist texts, often canonical works, also show the fault lines that had begun to appear in such binary constructions as domesticity and wildness. This book dips in and out of literary modernism—represented here by T. S. Eliot, W. B. Yeats, Stravinsky, Nijinsky, and others—precisely because the works that depend on a fantasy of wildness also, sometimes unwittingly, become the foundation for a new articulation. And so, to take one example, while Stravinsky's *The Rite of Spring* depended on fantasies of Native and folk cultures for its soundscapes and its mise-en-scène (the sacrifice of a young maiden in a folk fertility rite), the symphony was quoted extensively in jazz works that followed by artists such as Alice Coltrane and Ornette Coleman.[9] *The Rite of Spring* also served as the basis for a queer performance of Indigenous gender variance created by First Nations two-spirit artist Kent Monkman, whose work I explore in chapter 2.

Colonial notions of the wild—savage otherness, immaturity, apocalypse—are all too familiar, but they do not exhaust the meaning of wildness and neither do all fantasies of becoming feral fall under the sway of primitivist notions of unspoiled nature or fetishistic desires for a pure otherness. Furthermore, the materials that modernists drew on to sketch this shaky opposition between modern and primitive, civilized and wild, are not static or immobile—like the rhythms that Stravinsky borrowed from Russian folk music, the phrasings of the wild contaminate the texts into which they are drawn and create the seeds of alternate formulation of origins, influence, order, authority. And so, to return to Kent Monkman, who paints massive canvases in response to nineteenth-century landscape painters like George Catlin, Albert Bierstadt, and Thomas Cole, Monkman reformulates the relations between copy and original in a truly queer mode. In one brilliant painting, *Trappers of Men*, for example, Monkman paints his alter ego, Miss Chief Eagle Testickle, appearing in a vision on a lake to the painters Piet Mondrian and Jackson Pollock. While Mondrian faints before the apparition of Miss Chief, Pollock catches his fall and watches as Mondrian's paintbrush splashes paint onto a buffalo hide. As Monkman comments in a lecture, Pollock was influenced by "Native pictographs and sand paintings."[10] Far from being the author of the new, in Monkman's counter-history of art, Pollack accidently chances on an aesthetic method that may be new to him but has a long history among Indigenous artists. Monkman comments in the same lecture, "My work has been about challenging history and about how history . . . depends upon the teller." In this version of history, modernist aesthetics are deeply dependent on the material they mine, discard, and then represent as primitive. But Monkman does not destroy the modernist frame; he works patiently within it, bringing disorder to scenes of vertical authority, queer sexuality to scenes of reproductive plenitude, and Native cosmologies as the frame for modernist vision. Here, Monkman practices a decolonial disarticulation of the material conditions for modernist aesthetic production.

In Monkman's revisions of the modern, history is a wild site of human unknowing, a space of pleasurable bewilderment, and a relation to disorder that, as I will explain later in this book, gives rise to an epistemology of the wild or, using terminology from a writer drawn to the strange world of falconry, what I will call an epistemology of the ferox (Latin for fierce or wild; see chapter 3). Queer theory has long been a site for rethinking epistemologies, and queerness has been inextricably linked to ways of knowing and not knowing and even forms of knowing that depend on not knowing. Eve Sedgwick's *Epistemology of the Closet* is the obvious reference point when considering domains of bodily forms of knowledge, but the closet has proven to be too narrow and even too domestic as a symbol, and numerous critics have proposed other epistemologies over the years. Whether or not we accept the closet as a dominant mechanism for sexual knowledge, however, Sedgwick's emphasis on epistemologies has been a durable and irreversible contribution to the study of sexuality. Wildness too offers access to other forms of knowledge, but with wildness we leave the strictures, indeed the internal confines, of the home and enter a larger world of vegetation and animals, rocks and landscapes, water, and creatures seen and unseen. The epistemology of the closet, indeed, like other urban and colonial models of knowing, depends on the obliteration of ways of knowing that have been associated with Native cosmologies and ignores what Macarena Gómez-Barris calls queer and decolonial epistemes and "submerged perspectives" or, in her terms, "a fish-eye episteme" that sees from below the usual modes of perception.[11] An epistemology of wildness, or an epistemology of the ferox, both swap out the image of an interior room representing a secret self for a wide-open space across which an unknowable self is dispersed.

INTRODUCTION TO PART I

This book therefore seeks out another history of sexuality, one essentially at odds with the closet and the metaphors of *out* and *in*. But because an epistemology of the ferox is at least in part the other to the epistemology of the closet, certain figures may appear in both archives and then demand a new archive, or a rethinking of the modernist archive altogether, and new ways of reading canonical authors *against* the great tradition into which they have been placed. This scrambled history gives rise, as Monkman's comment on historical perspective implied, not only to different and decolonial inscriptions of authority but also to queer theories of historical temporality itself. Other histories of sexuality, in other words, lie nestled in the category of the wild, sexualities that are, in Pete Coviello's terms "untimely" in the sense that they were not properly scooped up by new classifications of homosexuality in the late nineteenth and early twentieth centuries, but lingered in the unspoken forms of address, gesture, and relation that preceded the sexual ordering of things.

As some new materialist work shows—think here of Jane Bennett in her turn to the vibrancy of the material world, or of Eduardo Kohn in his conjuring of "how forests think," or of Branka Arsić in her analysis of vitalism—wildness often offers a way of being in the world differently, of interacting with rather than separating from vegetal and animal forms of life.[12] In her book on Thoreau, for example, Bennett is able to bring out a rich understanding of wildness as a provocation, a retreat from the conventional, an affront to the normal and the expected, and an environmental condition—Thoreau, she offers, finds wildness in unhuman geographies like the woods but also in fleeting states like moonlight.[13] For Thoreau, we learn from Bennett, the wild nestles up to the good not as a moral investment in the natural, but as a longing, in Bennett's words, for something "extraordinary, unencompassable" (72). And this queer something that exceeds the ordinary and resides in the irrational can be accessed through alternative relations to vegetation, to animals, to beauty, to politics, to life and to death. Bennett connects Thoreau's wild to Nietzsche, but wildness of this kind also makes an appearance in Foucault's *The Order of Things*, wherein Foucault argues that, in a postreligious world, "transferring its most secret essence from the vegetable to the animal kingdom, life has left the tabulated space of order and become wild once more. The same movement that dooms it to death reveals it as murderous. It kills because it lives. Nature can no longer be good."[14]

Nature can no longer be good. In one of those broad sweeps that punctuates *The Order of Things*, Foucault makes an enormous claim, one that no doubt can never be verified or, for that matter, denied, and he makes the modern episteme a framework that takes shape around a core of unknowing and un-being, and that unleashes as much as it frames. In *The Order of Things*, in the chapter where this extraordinary passage occurs, Foucault lays out the history of thought on nature and shows how, as I have also been claiming, a fragment of the antinatural can be found within all natural histories. Making a break between eighteenth-century narratives of "a progressive gradation" and nineteenth-century notions of "radical discontinuity" (300), Foucault proposes that once "historicity" is introduced to the concept of nature, "it constitutes a sort of fundamental mode of being" that is expressed "in the form of animality" (301). The animal, for Foucault, is that form of being that is "the bearer of death," and, as such, he says, "it belongs to nature only at the price of containing within itself a nucleus of anti-nature" (302). This antinatural centerpiece, a version of which Foucault ties to Sade, embraces sexuality as death, as the potential for evil, and as a mode of embodiment and knowing that is oriented ambivalently toward un-being. Foucault gives this ambivalent mode of knowing a name, "the wild," and speculates that within a modern equation, life is forever in danger of "becoming wild once more" (302). While the "once more" indicates that wildness is behind us but could come again, the "becoming" suggests that wildness is always still to come. What is this *wildness* that threatens to engulf life or that accompanies the knowledge of death? And what is the meaning of the "untamed ontology" that bears the body, as he puts it, "towards a precarious form" (303) and threatens to destroy us metaphysically even before we meet our inevitable end?

While Foucault's casting of the wild as after God but also after a moral order guaranteed by God sounds like the opposite of Thoreau's claim that the wild lives next to the good, it in fact repeats Thoreau's sense that life always exceeds our attempt to know and classify and escapes the order we attempt to impose on it. Wildness for Thoreau is a constantly renewed relation to other forms of life; for Foucault it is an experience of finitude lived within what he calls "an untamed ontology." The untamed or wild ontology is a form of being that lies, according to Foucault, "on the other side of all the things that are" and "even beyond those that can be" (303). It is, in fact, *a disorder of things* that emerges and takes its ghastly shape in the shadows cast by the very project that discerns, desires, and demands order in the first place. This sense of a disorderly orientation to time and to life as it is remapped by death is expressed in many modernist art forms, including, perhaps most famously in T. S. Eliot's *Four Quartets*, a poem cycle that offers many of the epigraphs for this book. This series of poems, too often read only as a religious cycle, expresses a version of the "untamed ontology" that Foucault describes and offers numerous succinct formulations of the experience of mortality that opens onto a specifically spiritual wilderness. And yet, the poem expresses a very secular sense of the relation between life and death: "In my beginning is my end."[15] Eliot indeed stages a series of confrontations with absence: "To arrive where you are, to get from where you are not / You must go by a way wherein there is no ecstasy" ("East Coker," 29). He faces head-on the inevitability of loss: "But this thing is sure / That time is not healer: the patient is no longer here" ("Dry Salvages," 41). He conjures a world where there is neither fixity nor order, neither inevitability nor directionality, "Neither plenitude nor vacancy" ("Burnt Norton," 17). Indeed, the poet is haunted in *Four Quartets* by "the passage which we did not take" and "the door we never opened" ("Burnt Norton," 13). Like Thoreau, the poet hears voices in birdsong and follows them toward "the still point of the turning world" ("Burnt Norton," 15). Eliot's song to the eternal time of nature, the abbreviated transit of the human, and the realization that "as we grow older / The world becomes stranger, the pattern more complicated / Of dead and living" ("East Coker," 31) is embedded also in the structures of desire that reach for the feral, the divine, and the unknowable. This form of desire is not simply religious, and neither is it homosexuality or its suppression within heteronormativity; it is, rather, the disordered backdrop to all narratives of the human that seem committed to order, regulation, harmony, and stability.

Wild Things explores what Eliot names the complex pattern "of dead and living" ("East Corker," 31) in relation to modern narratives of sexuality that subscribe neither to the neat binaries of sexual orientation (as psychoanalysis did) nor to more scrambled sets of perverse fixations (as early sexology did). Indeed, Eliot himself is one of the odd figures who, in this book, represent forms of desire not well captured by the medical, social, and even slang terms designed to represent them. Eliot, like other so-called loners in this book, lived a life at the very edge of our definitions of sexuality. "Neither flesh nor fleshless / Neither from nor towards" is how he might have described the orientation of the wild things who live neither in nature nor beyond it within "both a new world / and the old made explicit" ("Burnt Norton," 15, 16). Some biographers have suggested that his homosexuality makes sense of Eliot's poems; other commentators merely place him among the Bloomsbury group of sexual indeterminates and leave it at that.[16] The poetry suggests not one thing or the other, but all things, wild things, and a postnatural "place of disaffection" ("Burnt Norton," 17).

Early queer theory rightly noted the very recent provenance of forms of desire organized according to the homosexual-heterosexual logic.[17] And following Foucault, queer theorists were quick to affirm that the homosexual emerged out of a new logic of the body that saw a "personage" where previously there had been a set of behaviors. But the formal classification of the homosexual did not simply siphon off the vast networks of desire and activity that made up, and continue to make up, modern selves and neatly canter them into the silos of hetero and homo. Rather, the organization of bodies undertaken by modern sexology also resulted in another realm of disorganization, a set of remaindered categories that seem quaint and strange to contemporary scholars.[18] For Foucault, the morass of such perversions—which include "zoophiles," "zooerasts," "auto-monosexualists," among many others, are swept away by the force of specification that descends on the field of "strange baptismal names" never to return.[19] However, these other sexualities are not so easily contained, and their disorganizations of desire continue to impact the project of sexual classification well into the middle of the twentieth century. We need a way to register those bodies that congregate or disperse around the boundaries of a history of sexuality that has named names and made order out of chaos, and in so doing we will not simply be locating subjugated figures or celebrating a naughty and subversive set of nonconformists; rather, we will also be engaging disorderly forms of history, desires that lie beyond the consensus terms of their eras. While the arc of modern queer histories has bent toward legibility, recognition, maturity, and mutuality, wild bodies plot a different course through history and appear only at the very edge of definition, flickering in and out of meaning and sense and tending toward bewilderment. Bewilderment, furthermore, as a form of lostness and unknowing, is not a politically charged statement about being and knowing; it is simply the space rendered by the absence of meaning and direction.

In other words, our now familiar narrative about the history of sexuality, which moves easily from the multiple modalities of desire and bodies to the tidy binary formation of homo/hetero, must ultimately be rethought in terms of the perversions that have been swept under the carpet within twentieth-century projects of sexual classification but which actually speak of much more unstable ecologies of embodiment than those to which we have previously subscribed. This is in part the argument in Pete Coviello's book *Tomorrow's Parties*, where he argues that the modern order of sexuality had the effect of stilling an older and "untimely" language of insinuation and "impassioned ambivalence."[20] Coviello finds a vocabulary (in Thoreau, Whitman, Orne Jewitt, and others) for nineteenth-century sexual expressions that escaped a modern net of classification and appeared instead under the headings of such terms as "extravagant," "unyarded," or "errant" (10). We can stretch this sense of untimely desire, disorderly bodily expression, and untidy identities out of the nineteenth century and into the early twentieth. At stake here is not periodization per se so much as finding vocabulary, narratives, and figurations for the inevitable *disorder* of things, the ways of being that resist expert knowledge, that fail to resolve into identity forms, and that find expression in the practices of runaways, spinsters, eccentrics, and recluses. The unruly lives of the lost, the lonely, and the lunatic call their hellos from what Foucault calls "the other side of all the things that are."[21] The wild, like nature, we could say with Foucault, can no longer be good.

After Nature

The notion of desires contrary to nature has been central to most modern understandings of queer desire, and yet, with the exception of Paul Preciado's *Countersexual Manifesto* from the late 1990s, few accounts grapple with what happens to such understandings when nature is no more.[22] But what *was* nature in the realm of sexuality, and when and why did we leave nature behind? And why, as Preciado proposes, do we continue to study and describe sex "as if it formed part of the natural history of human societies" (7)? In the medieval period in general, the unnatural was often understood to be nested within the natural as a subcategory and as part of nature's overall plan.[23] As Joan Cadden remarks, following an Aristotelian line of thought, the belief was that "nature did everything for a purpose and nothing in vain."[24] Within this model and this understanding of nature, unnatural desires constituted the distortion of nature's purpose within an individual body and, sometimes, indicated that unnatural habits had evolved in the individual over time causing them to become defective but not classifying them as a particular or fixed type of person.

As early as 1533 in England, the buggery act sought to criminalize sodomitical activity between men or between men and beasts and classified such crimes as "against nature."[25] This clustering of crimes against nature to include both anal sex between men and sex between men and animals indicates how differently the concepts of crime, nature, and sexuality were defined in the early modern period. While modern legal action against sodomy eventually uncoupled bestiality from anal sex between men, we will see that within various contemporary accounts of intimacies between humans and animals this connection reappears like a shadow formation. Indeed, the lingering afterimages of early constructions of sex, nature, gender, and crime imply a palimpsestic structure for the history of sexuality within which, as Eve Sedgwick proposed several decades ago, "the historical search for a Great Paradigm Shift may obscure the present conditions of sexuality."[26] In place of the paradigm shift, Sedgwick offered a more finely tuned model of history within which "modern homo/heterosexual definition are structured, not by the supersession of one model and the consequent withering away of another, but instead by the relations enabled by the unrationalized coexistence of different models during the times they do coexist" (47). Sedgwick encourages attention to the relations between multiple readings of nature, the unnatural and the antinatural as they overlap within legislation, social and religious belief systems, and individual bodies. As an example of the payoff of such a method, we might consider precisely the evolution of discourses of bestiality and the classification of this behavior. If sex with animals was once so commonplace as to require legal intervention, and if it once rounded out a set of unnatural activities that included same-sex sexual acts, by the beginning of the twentieth century and within a domestic realm newly marked by the inclusion of animals as pets, the taboo on sex with animals was reinforced even as it was disarticulated from anal sex between men. Nonetheless, as we will see, some twentieth-century writers articulated a love for their pets that exceeds their intimacy with any other human being. Does pet love stand in for what was once a commonplace understanding of sex with animals? Does it substitute acceptable relations to animals over and against carnal relations? By the same token, do we understand the household pet wholly within a discourse of domestication or as part of a constantly shifting relation to wildness?

The transformation of animals from sexual partners to pets, a definition of domestication if ever there was one, indicates other kinds of shifts in the way we have perceived the natural and the perverse, the domestic and the wild, the sexual and the intimate. It also suggests that the template for life we call nature is subject to kaleidoscopic changes in the period in which modern sexuality emerged. If in earlier periods, unnatural desire was considered as a (twisted) part of a natural order or things, by the eighteenth century, as Susan Sontag proposed in her famous "Notes on Camp," nature was no longer a given, it had become a matter of taste and part of an evolving aesthetic split between the desire to fortify the natural and the will to improve on it or violate it. Sontag wrote: "In the 18th century, people of taste either patronized nature (Strawberry Hill) or attempted to remake it into something artificial (Versailles). . . . Today's Camp taste effaces nature, or else contradicts it outright."[27] With Oscar Wilde as her guide, Sontag offers an account of the cleaving of nature from aesthetics and, by implication, of homosexual taste from normal sensibilities (Wilde: "The more we study art, the less we care for nature"[28]). For Sontag, the emergence of a theatrical sensibility at odds with the natural is linked to the emergence of homosexuality. And, of course, Wilde's work makes clear why. To the extent that the newly formed regime of heterosexuality staked its claim

INTRODUCTION TO PART I

to dominance on the bedrock of the natural, the homosexual must invest in all available antinatural terrain.[29]

Homosexuality indeed depends on, requires, and bolsters this split between the natural and the aesthetic, the normal and the aberrant, the domestic and the wild. By the end of the nineteenth century, various writers had taken the "against nature" charge of perversity and turned it from a sin into an indulgence to the point that a dandy like Wilde could quip to a knowing audience: "To be natural is such a very difficult pose to keep up."[30] If by 1895, the year *An Ideal Husband* hit the London stage, Wilde could both entertain the theatergoing public with the poses assumed by husband and wife *and* be put on trial for posing as a natural and indeed ideal husband, then it is reasonable to propose that the natural and the antinatural entered the twentieth century together, tethered at the waist or connected in some more intimate way, and with one forever destined to pull the other behind it within a new regime of truth. As a consequence, by the end of the twentieth century and into the first few decades of the twenty-first century, the idea of a sexuality that is against nature is both an assumption and a constant site of struggle. And of course, this charge of unnaturalness has shaped certain forms of resistance. While aesthetes from Oscar Wilde to RuPaul have presumed that nature is man-made and therefore subject to alternative discursive constructions, scientists from Simon LeVay to Dean Hamer insist that homosexuality is coded into the body and thus part of an eternal and unchanging natural order. The more some insist that nature has nothing to do with modern formulations of desire and embodiment, the more others offer proof of a *natural* blueprint for desire. Ultimately, however, the die was cast in the late nineteenth century for the end of nature altogether, and the gay science community's insistence on gay genes, gay seagulls, lesbian ducks, transgender fish, and so on is a mere afterglow of an argument settled long ago.

The argument was staged and resolved moreover not in terms of a divide between nature and postnature, but in terms of an order of things that was resolutely *against* nature. And so, in addition to the various quips on the subject by Oscar Wilde, we can also look to such gloriously decadent, lush, and louche treatises as *À rebours*, by J.-K. Huysmans, in which nature becomes not the site of hideous transgression, but the object of arch critique.[31] If earlier sexual dissidents had feared to find themselves on the wrong side of nature, now they situated themselves against it. *À rebours* deserves a closer look because it has established, more or less, the terms of an antinatural discourse that is associated with modern homosexuality, on the one hand, and with an emergent model of a prosthetic self, on the other.

Against Nature

À rebours, which has been loosely translated as *Against the Grain* or *Against Nature* but more literally means "in reverse," is probably best known as the little yellow book carried around by Dorian Gray in Wilde's novel *The Picture of Dorian Gray* (1891) and can be read as a kind of anti-Thoreauvian text that nonetheless takes up a similar relation to nature if from an opposite position.[32] In this book, Huysmans smuggles what amounts to an antinaturalist manifesto into a shaggy dog tale about a dissolute young man, Des Esseintes, who tires of "human stupidity" (chapter 1) and withdraws from the metropolitan life of Paris to a house in the country. He lives in his mansion occupying his time by making interior design decisions and offering sermons "on dandyism" (chapter 2) to the tradesmen who come to do his bidding. The style of clothes he wears and the way he furnishes his home are part of the unfolding narrative of a man *against* nature, someone who, moreover, contrary to the developing logic about the urban as the "natural" habitat of the homosexual, reverses out of the city but does not do so to make a return to nature. Instead, he sets out to establish himself against nature *in* nature.

Returning to *À rebours* from the contemporary vantage point of what I am posing as a period "after nature," we can find the hallmarks of late nineteenth-century constructions of the dandy and the gay aesthete in the elevation of form over function, which remain the mainstay of queer critiques of nature. The antihero of *À rebours*, Des Esseintes, offers an homage to artifice, "the distinctive mark of man's genius," and proposes that "Nature had had her day" (48). He continues: "By the disgusting sameness of her landscapes and skies, she had once and for all wearied the considerate patience of æsthetes. Really, what dullness! the dullness of the specialist confined to his narrow work. What manners! the manners of the tradesman offering one particular ware to the exclusion of all others. What a monotonous storehouse of fields and trees! What a banal agency of mountains and seas!" (48). This hilarious and counterintuitive rant against nature's banality and homogeneity, especially if read against romantic odes to the unknowability of nature (think Shelley's *Mont Blanc* and its "everlasting universe of things"[33]) situates the lethargic, bored, unimpressed dandy as the vector for a playful inversion of art and nature. Here art replaces the exhausted and inadequate creations of nature, figured in the text as a driveling old woman, and technology replaces the exalted beauty of human, here figured as a desirable young woman. Huysmans writes of nature: "Closely observe that work of hers which is considered the most exquisite, that creation of hers whose beauty is everywhere conceded the most perfect and original—woman. Has not man made, for his own use, an animated and artificial being which easily equals woman, from the point of view of plastic beauty? Is there a woman, whose form is more dazzling, more splendid than the two locomotives that pass over the Northern Railroad lines?" (49). The passage builds bathetically to the anticlimactic substitution of woman with the railroad and leaves contemporary readers in the dark as to what kind of man prefers a locomotive (or two) to a woman. One answer, of course, is a perverted man, a man for whom nature has been replaced by machinery and reproduction by invention. But another would be the postnatural man, a defiant figure who finds himself outside nature and therefore against its most spectacular displays as exemplified by heterosexual love.

But the locomotive signifies more than just a technological substitute for the woman. Offering the possibility of moving people quickly from place to place, the train became a figure of modernity in the late nineteenth century and has become the centerpiece of recent characterizations of our own postnatural world in terms of the time of the Anthropocene. Tim Morton, in a book also interested in the aftermath of nature ("I capitalize Nature precisely to denature it," he writes), dates the Anthropocene, or the era within which humans began to do irreversible damage to the earth, back to 1784 and to the invention of the steam engine by James Watt.[34] And yet while Morton and others do the important work of offering us ways of understanding the new meaning of the human in a world in which human agency depends on the destruction of all other forms of life, the dating of the Anthropocene to the invention of the steam engine is misguided in that it presumes a division between humans and technology, which is precisely in question at that time. And, of course, as Macarena Gómez-Barris and others have pointed out, this date for the onset of the ruination of the earth ignores the context of colonial capitalism, which, as she argues, was "the main catastrophic event that has gobbled up the planet's resources."[35] In keeping with this more precise dating of the Anthropocene in relation to colonialism rather than to European invention, we can read the train in Huysmans's text not as the beginning of a new phase of human endeavor, but as the beginning of the end of a colonial version of the human. If *Against the Grain*, among other texts we will look at, marks the onset of a form of subjectivity that we might call postnatural, it is hugely significant that postnatural man (and the postnatural subject is clearly gendered here as male, perhaps problematically) in Huysmans's *Against the Grain* is obviously, if not explicitly, queer.

The bored, fatigued, jaded, campy narrator's desire for the railroad, after all, replaces his desire for woman but does not simply replace it with a desire for men. Queer desire here, as in Thoreau oddly enough, is not simply same-sex desire: for Thoreau, queerness situates human desire within a wild world of other desires and pleasures; for Huysmans, queerness attends to a machinic eroticism, an antinatural force of motion, a desire, in other words, not to be *on* a train nor a deep admiration *for* the train, but a desire directed *at* the train. Strange as this may sound, if we glance at avant-garde films like Kenneth Anger's 1964 film *Scorpio Rising*, we can find echoes of this early fixation on the machine in later queer imagery. While the train is the object of Des Esseintes's desire, in *Scorpio Rising*, a queer visual erotics wraps itself around motorcycles, leather jackets, and the paraphernalia of biker worlds. And, more recently, in Preciado's *Countersexual Manifesto*, the discourse of nature disappears altogether with the presumption that the history of sexuality is a history of technology. Preciado uses another symbol to represent new technosexuality, though, and he attaches his theory of prosthetic desire to the silicon dildo. The dildo, like the train and like the motorcycle, represents the postnatural fusing of human with machine and an understanding of the body as always supported and extended by necessary prosthetics. This too is the end of nature.

But the antinatural stance of Des Esseintes is not simply fetishistic nor merely the preference for the made over the born; rather, it serves as a deep critique of the concept of nature around which a moral order was taking shape at the turn of the past century. This concept, which takes legal root within sodomy laws and which guides all kinds of interventions, medical and psychological, into the lives of perverts, sets up the unnatural as a domain of criminality and pathology and invites those who reside there to either agonize over their fate and strive to be recognized as natural or cleave to the attack on nature and make the artificial into a style, a preference, a new orientation to wildness. Like Dorian Gray, Des Esseintes is firmly in the camp camp, and he makes the natural into a deeply gauche and unpleasant set of aesthetic choices. Accordingly, he eschews not women and marriage per se, but the world in which they appear as the right and true, natural, and inevitable match for men. As in the works of Oscar Wilde, for Huysmans, the natural is always presented as a pose, a front, a surface—Wilde proposed: "Being natural is simply a pose, and the most irritating pose I know."[36] But more than this, in *Against the Grain*, nature is an anachronism, part of a past to which the narrator does not wish to return and a hallmark of the morality to which he is indifferent. For Des Esseintes, the world is better experienced in its mechanical and aesthetic forms—why go to the ocean when you can look at mechanical fish in an aquarium, as he does, and why swim in the sea if you can take a salt bath in Paris? Why leave your house to travel abroad when you can read about distant lands? When he finally leaves Paris for seclusion, Des Esseintes remarks: "He hated the new generation with all the energy in him. They were frightful clodhoppers who seemed to find it necessary to talk and laugh boisterously in restaurants and cafés. They jostled you on sidewalks without begging pardon. They pushed the wheels of their perambulators against your legs, without even apologizing" (54). Anticipating the link made by Lee Edelman between queerness and the death drive, Des Esseintes despises not just the "new generation," but generation itself, and here the pram, its contents barely worth mentioning, becomes the very opposite of the train. While the pram holding the baby should represent a glorious future, here it holds only the promise of more of the same. It is the train that represents motion itself, a propulsive force that, unlike the perambulator, is weighed down by neither destination nor origin.

But my purpose here is not to hold up *À rebours* as some kind of proto queer marvel, nor to place it in the pantheon of early queer literature. It is, after all, a text as despicable as it is seductive. Like the spectacle of the bejeweled tortoise Des Esseintes orders for his living room, hoping that the dullness of the animal's color will take the edge off a carpet that strikes him as too loud, the novel both satirizes and invests in an aesthetic for which all must be sacrificed.[37] I linger on *À rebours* not to enshrine it in a new queer postnatural canon, but to notice that we can catch a glimpse of the end of queerness at the moment of its emergence. The ennui of a Dorian Gray and a Des Esseintes, like the angular oddness of Nijinski's dances just a decade later, speak to the emergent discourse of a queerness that we have established as against nature even as it marks, and becomes the maligned figure for, a period that we recognize with alarm as *after* nature.

Before Nature

While Huysmans and Wilde defiantly pose their languid and anti-virile queer characters against nature, occupying the edgy terrain of a literary avant-garde that is ahead of the game by declaring the game to be over, there were other authors in that same decisive period whom we have characterized as "beginning" the modern era of sexuality, who tried to grab the reins of nature before it bolted the stable. Take Radclyffe Hall's work, for example, with its embarrassing treatises on nature and its love affair between the masculine invert and a succession of horses that hold and carry her, protect and love her in a way no human will.[38] Hall's justifications for her hero, Stephen Gordon's, existence is not that she defies nature, but that, like all living things, she has her place within it. While Hall and others desperately tried to jam their masculine but not male protagonists into an extended conception of nature, Wilde and Des Esseintes found nature itself to be the problem. For this reason, perhaps, modern readers prefer the arch dandy to the dowdy and gender-inverted dyke—Wilde's work remains part of a tried and true canon of Western literature, in other words, while *The Well of Loneliness* is and remains a slightly embarrassing, if necessary, literary experiment. The dandy hates the system that hates him and is bored by that which demands meaning, indifferent to that which intends to invoke passion, and poses himself ahead of the modern, disdaining to look back. By contrast, the dyke is hurt by the order that names her as its problem and wears her sense of injustice like a badge, a scar, an open wound. She is not ahead of a curve looking back; she realizes that she is always behind in a world governed by notions of "sequence," which add up, as Annmarie Jagose proposes, only within a system of valuation that ascribes "consequence" linearly and sequentially.[39]

In *The Well of Loneliness*, Hall's antihero, Stephen, longs to be admitted to the fraternity her father represents but instead recognizes herself as monstrous to that community. Only her tutor, Puddle, offers her the explanation for who she desperately desires to be: "You're neither unnatural, nor abominable, nor mad; you're as much a part of what people call nature as anyone else; only you're unexplained as yet—you've not got your niche in creation."[40] It is this notion of existing without explanation, without a niche, outside of an orderly and inevitable scheme of life, and not simply the antinatural poses of the dandies that captures what I am calling *wildness* in this book. While Thoreau found this lack of explanation to be a source of comfort, and while the dandy opposes the system altogether, the dyke, the symbol of negation against which the whole order of nature is levied, cannot shrug off the insult for which she is the primary symbol. The dandy is not wild because he gives the system he opposes meaning. And within that system, he also has meaning, even if it is negative. But the dyke, or the gender-variant subject, then and now, is a wild card, a slice of disorder, a source of bewilderment and an anachronism even in her own time or, rather, because she has no time that is hers. The genderqueer person, however, Stephen Gordon for one, inhabits an odd temporality too—not a future that will never come, but a past that is always already over.

Such a figure, for example, makes an appearance in a recent queer historical novel, *Confessions of the Fox*, by Jordy Rosenberg. Set in eighteenth-century London, *Confessions of the Fox* defines its gender transient hero as a "sexual chimera" but as unclassifiable in the terms of the day. Rosenberg writes of Jack in terms that echo Hall: "And something clarify'd itself to him, as if out of a Fog. He was something—just as his mother had said—that existed only as a

Scrawl on the world's landscape—as if someone had come along and stepped on a beautiful painting of sunflowers with a jackboot full of Shite—and that monstrous blob of shite splatted in the middle of a field—that blob, Jack considered, was he."[41] A blob, a scrawl, a monstrous being that is both natural, as in part of nature, and monstrous, as in exceeding the natural order, Rosenberg's character occupies precisely this space of transit between a *before* and an *after* nature. As I have written about before under the heading of "female masculinity," and, more recently, "trans*," the gender-queer subject represents an unscripted, declassified relation to being—s/he is wild because unnamable, beyond order because unexplained; s/he has no place in creation and as such escapes and defies the regimes of regulation and containment that shape the world for everyone else.[42] You are not unnatural, nor abominable, Puddle assures her masculine but female charge; you are part of nature but *unexplained*. What is this odd corner of nature? Where is it? Who lives there? Who leaves there? Who is made legible to the system of classification by rounding out the category against which classification makes its claim on knowledge? Perversely, however, my archive in *Wild Things* is more often than not made up of people and characters born male, not female, recognizably gay, not lesbian, and disordered according to logics that lie beyond the gender binary. *Wild Things* presumes that the masculine lesbian is always already wild, to use a by now quaint deconstructive syntax, and so we leave her in her spectacular ruination where the wild things are and go in search of the other forms of wildness, lostness, and misshapen hope that linger on the margins of early modern aesthetic and scientific knowledge. The weird white male loners who keep popping up in these chapters in the location I am calling "wild" are not there as a personification of that which escapes knowledge; rather, they are the beginning and the end of definitions that were, at that time, under construction. Like T. S. Eliot, the Roger Casements, T. H. Whites, and Nijinskys who wander in and out of these pages are not the heroes of those "untamed ontologies" that Foucault tried to locate outside an "order of things"; they are, rather, the still center of a storm, the question mark left in the wake of a morality organized around the natural; they are, indeed, like the zombies of my final chapter, not good or bad, not heroes or goats; they are simply the sites of struggle that the canon has retained. They are the wild things who survived precisely because so many others did not.

Modernism indeed offers many of the texts for the archive I have assembled here not because it offers us a group of wild thinkers or wild revolutionary poets and dancers, but because the very classifications that seemed established and right in the nineteenth century begin to wobble and topple over in the modernist period. Accordingly, a novel such as Joseph Conrad's *Heart of Darkness* (1902) can serve both as the master text of a civilizing and colonial order and the narrative of its undoing. A poem such as W. B. Yeats's "The Second Coming" (1919) may offer the iconic images for the unfolding of European fascism as well as provide the language for Chinua Achebe's classic postcolonial novel *Things Fall Apart* (1958). And, as I claimed earlier, *The Rite of Spring* both snatches the rhythms of folk music and becomes a reference point for jazz music built on those same sequences later in the century. The archive of wildness I have assembled here, accordingly, is neither a new canon nor an alternative canon; it is the canon read against canons, the great tradition read against greatness and tradition, the disorder of things read through the marks of their violent submission to order.

But the disorder of things speaks not only of chaos but also of the reduction of bodies to things. In other words, the archive of wildness is also an archive of *things*—wild things, things that fall apart. The thingliness of this archive references the indeterminacy of bodies and beings outside of what has been understood as order (the order of things) but also conjures the life of objects, the racial cleaving of subjects from objects, and what Fanon calls the facticity of racial fetishism. In "The Fact of Blackness" (1952) (chapter 5 of *Black Skin, White Masks* [1967]), Frantz Fanon writes that he entered the world "with the will to find the meaning in things" but then discovers that "I am an object among other objects."[43] This discovery that the meaning in "things" is denied to one who must take his place among them, within that order of things, leads Fanon to claim that Blackness "fixes" him, makes him a casualty of the white need to own life, occupy subjectivity, and make worlds. "The white man," wrote Fanon, "wants the world; he wants it for himself alone" (128), and because the white man must be master, Fanon comments, "he enslaves it." The white man enslaves the world. He renders the world his and his alone and reduces Blackness, in Fanon's words, to "savages, brutes, illiterates" (117). From such a position, the position of the object, the thing, the savage, there are a few possibilities—the racialized other can demand recognition by presenting himself as human in the terms proffered by white society, or they can refuse the category altogether and twist the terminology of otherness into a rebuke, use it to unmake the world of white mastery and make a virtue out of what Fred Moten calls "the resistance of the object."[44]

This is, at least in part, Fanon's strategy, and it is certainly a part of queer critiques of normative ideologies of sexual comportment. While late nineteenth-century science, psychology, and literature found ways to classify new forms of human behavior and interaction, some bodies, many bodies, fell outside of those classifications and remained in the wild, so to speak, beyond the human zoo, inexplicable, discomforting, shocking, exploitable, displayable. This language of wildness, zoos, expertise, scientific observation, and the definitional capture of forms of embodiment, however, describes a larger orbit of exclusion and fetishistic fixing than that of the genteel and aristocratic worlds of Stephen Gordon and Oscar Wilde. Wilde may have been, like Huysmans, against nature, and Hall may have been before nature or, possibly, like Jack Sheppard, in excess of nature, but the language of wildness was used then as now not to type degenerate elites, but to draw attention to the danger of those outside of classification itself. When *wildness* was used by elites as a rhetorical device in the early years of the twentieth century it was often as a disastrous and lawless precursor to fascism. And so, like so many of the terms in our critical vocabulary, we must drag wildness through its masculinist and gloried projects if only to find out what lies on the side.

Beyond Nature

The wild, when not figured as either a glorious unspoiled past or an exciting machinic future, when not a prefascist cleaving to war and masculinity nor a postliberal, postpolitical regime of anything goes, can, under certain circumstances, and on account of its now intuitive set of associations with the nonhuman, the animal, the queer, and the subordinated, be available for the exploration of subaltern and subterranean and particularly racialized forms of queer or perverse desire and embodiment. Certainly, this is how Jordy Rosenberg deploys the wildness of Jack Sheppard in *Confessions of the Fox* where Jack becomes part of a seething underworld of prostitutes, workers, revolutionaries, and even objects. The association of wildness with dynamic forms of life outside the human has also been called "animacy" by Mel Chen and used to indicate racialized hierarchies of liveliness and inertia.[45] But the an/archive of the wildness that lies beyond nature is, above all, a record of stolen life, Black life, Indigenous life, Brown life and death, lives lived well beyond the purview of recognition, respectability, and so on. For this reason, C. Riley Snorton, in *Black on Both Sides: A Racial History of Trans Identity*, describes his book as "principally concerned with the mechanics of invention by which I mean that I am seeking to understand the conditions of emergence of things and beings that may not yet exist."[46] Snorton's comment recognizes the very different temporalities of emergence for Black bodies and situates his work as a search for "a vocabulary for black and trans life" (xiv). This book too assumes that queer of color and trans forms of otherness remain without a vocabulary. The terminologies that have been levied against them have sometimes included the notion of wildness in their lexicons. Here I want to explore that same term as part of its ongoing emergence.

Take, for example, the resurgent interest in the speculative fictions of work of Octavia Butler and Samuel Delany. In such novels as *Wild Seed*, *Parable of the Sower*, and *Parable of the Talents* by Butler and in fantastical stories of desire like *Dhalgren* and *Stars in My Pocket Like Grains of Sand* by Delany, fantasies of immortality, new forms of community, alternative systems, and sexual difference and lingering threats of slavery and incarceration form the backdrop to thorough reimaginings of the relations between bodies and nature. The return to these works now and the resurgent interest in the archives of Afro futurism in work by Kara Keeling and Jayna Brown, among others, coincides with new episodes of anti-Black, state-authorized violence committed by the police and then refashioned by the media into narratives of defense and justifiable homicide. The science-fictional conjuring of life otherwise and elsewhere, of wild life beyond the multiple forms of containment that contemporary life imposes on Black embodiment, operates in the shadow of a seemingly inevitable set of cultural algorithms that make Blackness equivalent to and the very form of wildness.

As Fanon articulated, Blackness, on account of its very specific relation to property, has been situated as a realm of "value," to use Lindon Barrett's terminology, that limns enlightenment principles with their negative reflection.[47] Not simply the slave to a master nor darkness to light, Blackness, within a white imaginary, must be pressed into the service of negation itself. But negation is a wide and deep terrain and has reappeared in Black radical thought as the unknowable, the unthinkable, straying (Saidiya Hartman), flight (Keeling). Being beyond order, Blackness has been written as disorder and as the definition of wildness itself. Having been defined as such, Blackness is structurally positioned, qua Frank Wilderson's reading of Fanon, to desire the "end of the world" through decolonizing violence.[48] The order of things as it emerges through a mania for classification and identification recognizes the wildness proper to racial otherness and is part of the structural machinery designed to render racial antagonism as unthinkable. If nineteenth- and early twentieth-century expert knowledges tried to rationalize a colonial order, the wildness that it ascribed to Black otherness becomes a disordering force of opposition greatly feared and often conjured in order to be foreclosed. It was, for example, the language of wildness and wilding that helped condemn five young men of color to prison terms in 1990 for a crime they did not commit. The case of the Central Park Jogger, and the subsequent conviction of four Black teenagers and one Latino teenager for the crimes committed against her, shows how intuitive the connection between wildness and Black criminality had become by the end of the past century.[49] It also demonstrated how necessary an intuitive connection between Blackness and wildness might be for the legitimation of state violence.

Blackness has been used as a synonym for a colonialist and racist understanding of wildness, but Blackness has also occupied the space of wildness in order to flee the "world" in which it can only function as the not-subject. Along those lines, Saidiya Hartman has defined "waywardness" as a form both of early twentieth-century criminality and of wild mobility outside of liberal structures of rule. In the chapter titled "A Short Entry on the Possible," in her book *Wayward Lives, Beautiful Experiments*, Hartman defines "waywardness" as "the practice of the social otherwise, the insurgent ground that enabled new possibilities and new vocabularies. . . . It is a queer resource of black survival. It is a beautiful experiment in how to live."[50] For Hartman, waywardness is a mode of escape, an activity by which the Black body slips out of the trap of liberal personhood and falls into a wild and extravagant relation to beauty and freedom. Histories of the medicalization and criminalization of desire abound within queer studies, but Hartman's book reminds us that the life of desire is multifaceted. It lives in the joy of assembly, in the longing for beautiful things, in fantasies of surplus, in "moments of tenderness" (156), in experiences of Black girls and women in "open rebellion" (62) to systems of management, control, and incarceration. In the stories that Hartman gathers in *Wayward Lives*, desire spills over the categories designed to manage it and emerges as a kind of wildness within "practices of intimacy and affiliation" (221). The book is full of promiscuous scenes of sexual abandonment, flirtations expressed in song, scenes of erotic assembly. In other words, desire in this book is not the expression of identity, but rather a term for the extravagant acts of wayward Black bodies committed to "experiments in living free" (34). That notion of "extravagance," a term Coviello also uses to explore unsorted terrains of libidinal uncertainty, conjures within it an excess, a form of wanting that reaches beyond the necessary, a relation to being that extends to what Wilderson terms as "freedom from the world, freedom from Humanity, freedom from everyone (including one's Black self)."[51]

Few texts conjure this relation between wildness and Blackness better than Isaac Julien's *Looking for Langston* (1989), where wildness is both a relation to fugitivity and a refusal of the world within which Blackness must take flight. At the end of the film, for example, a mixed group of Black and white gay men are dancing in a warehouse. As the music speeds up and the dancing becomes wild, Julien's camera moves back and forth between the space of the nightclub and scenes of a white male mob gathering outside. Julien's montage sequence brings inside and outside closer and closer together and creates a fearful anticipation of a violent confrontation. The spectator fears for the gay men who have gathered together at a memorial to dance in the face of death and to love in the midst of crisis. But at the climax of this montage, the police and the white thugs enter an empty space and encounter only traces of the dancers. The dancers, who have engaged rituals of joyful mourning that exceed conventional religious practices, have now left the space for an elsewhere that we do not see and on behalf of a practice of evacuation that eludes theory. They are elsewhere and will remain elsewhere. The dancers, as T. S. Eliot puts it, "are all gone under the hill" ("East Coker," 27).

The practitioners of queer and Black leisure, who leave by the back door to avoid confrontation, refuse the oppositions of right and wrong, Black and white, the law and outlaws, straight and gay, in favor of the destitution of the space of encounter. Julien's dancers, an undercommons of sorts, have not simply disappeared. As the police look around for the "deviants" they came to discipline, they see only smoke and mirrors, but the dancers live on in a place we cannot yet see and in a time that Keeling has described in terms of multiple "black futures."[52] Julien's sleight of hand here, a result of rapid crosscutting that puts two incompatible temporalities and ideologies in dialogue, conjures the utopian, the dystopian, queer nightlife, and fugitivity all in one sequence. By the end of the film, we have not located Langston Hughes or his queerness; instead, we have entered into a representational maelstrom within which queerness, along with white normativity, disappears into the night. In its wake are emptiness, wildness, and irreversible disruptions of time and space.

The emptiness Julien offers viewers in place of a scene of confrontation is not a scene of nothing; it is, rather, a void, an empty space wild with meaning. Wildness inheres to the void, as Karen Barad might put it, because, as she writes, "nothingness" is the "scene of wild activities."[53] Just as the vacuum, in her account, seethes with particles that are both there and not there and, in so doing, creates deep indeterminacy, so wildness represents an abundance *and* an absence of meaning. The space that the gay men abandon in *Looking for Langston* is not just empty; it teems with their absence and is not so much vacant as evacuated. The evacuation of space here can be read through Wilderson's articulation of "the impossibility of black ontology" and understood as a gesture of refusal within which Julien sets up a confrontation between whiteness/law/violence/normativity and Blackness/criminality/opposition/aberration only to flag the dependence of the first set of terms on the second set.[54] As such, the cinematic erasure of the scene of Black queer pleasure is also part of a Black cinematic conjuring of wildness where wildness seeks to leave the encounter between white subjects and Black objects behind. The empty ballroom visually captures Wilderson's pithy formulation of a humanism dependent on anti-Blackness: "No slave. No world" (11). Julien looks into the void here, a void created by the illegibility of Langston Hughes's sexuality and the withdrawal of Black gay desire and an evacuation and silence that indicates without revealing other worlds. Rather than seeking out stray bodies within a history of sexuality and wrangling them into legibility, this book recognizes the motion of straying itself as a disorderly relation to history and desire. The dancing bodies that disappear in Julien's film retreat from the oncoming charge of the police—they do not stay to be counted or to be arrested; instead they spin out of the space of history altogether, angels in tow, tuxedos flying, leaving behind a lone disco ball and a space teeming with their absence. Julien's film resists the urge to pull its subject firmly into the category of *gay* and instead joins forces with the illegibility Langston represents, which all kinds of bodies represent, and offers a poetic meditation instead on loss, love, and the disorder of desire.

The Disorder of *Wild Things*

As befits a book about wildness and disorder, chaos and mess, this book locates conversations and narratives about the wild in a sprawling an/archive—where the an/archive becomes a space of the unrecoverable, the lost, and the illegible—of canonical and ephemeral texts, images, and performances. Sexuality is a central component to most definitions of wildness, and so archives of sexual otherness must be central to the effort to enter its orbit. As I have shown, scholarship and writings on sexuality in the twentieth century set up claims about sexuality and desire that were for or against nature. In premodern discourses, nature was God's work, but by the nineteenth century, as Foucault proposes in *The Order of Things*, nature was man's work. Scientists and humanists invented and explored the natural world in order to challenge or validate various man-made systems of morality and to create, by the end of that century, a new system of norms. What grounds our conception of sexuality, desire, and sexual conduct after nature? As much as this book traces a genealogy for wildness, it also offers an alternative history of sexuality within which the so-called natural world is neither the backdrop for human romance nor the guarantor of normativity. Wildness indeed seeks the unmaking of that world and represents its undoing. While I take up the whole project of unbuilding, unmaking, and unbecoming, or the anarchitectures of wildness, in a companion volume, *The*

Wild Beyond, this book traces the unruly passage of wildness through modernism and into and then out of the canon of modernist thought. One could easily write a book on wildness that only trafficked in the speculative fictions of a utopian relation to disorder. And while *The Wild Beyond* registers much of that utopian energy, this book must, to use Donna Haraway's apt phrase, "stay with the trouble" of the terminology in order to hold back from the romance of opposition and in order to register the violence that has expelled wild things from the world in the first place.[55] Accordingly, an array of desires and desiring characters occupy the modernist landscape of wildness. Many, like young Max from *Where the Wild Things Are* but also like Henry David Thoreau, T. H. White, and Helen Macdonald, have withdrawn from human-to-human contact altogether and find themselves inspired and excited by wildness itself. Still others, hoping to find an intimate passage to wildness or, conversely, to erect a boundary against wildness, invest in libidinal relations with animals. Some of the figures in this book are oddly reclusive; others go in search of companionship; all exceed the classifications we have created for a realm of natural and orderly desires. Queerness and wildness in this project are not synonyms, nor does one extend the other; rather, wildness takes the anti-identitarian refusal embedded in queer theory and connects it to other sites of productive confusion, taxonomic limits, and boundary collapse.

In my first chapter, "Wildness, Loss, and Death," I retell the story of Roger Casement by locating it within Michael Taussig's ethnography of wildness and alongside an ethos of bewilderment that emerges out of colonial contact. In the second chapter I extend this theme of precontemporary sexual definition and colonial production but also connect the wildness of pre-homosexual life to aesthetic wildness and to the antilogic of queer Indigenous bewilderment. I begin the chapter by focusing on an infamous but ephemeral performance event from 1913 in which the performance itself was overwhelmed by the material it was supposed to channel. The one and only performance of Stravinsky/Nijinsky's *The Rite of Spring* in Paris that year created a riotous mood in the theater, and critics identified in the ballet a sense of wildness that was new and unforgettable. The chaotic force field generated by *The Rite of Spring* and inhabited by those who created it and those who witnessed it can be linked to other, more recent, forms of queer art that both engage the awkward choreographies of *The Rite of Spring* but also replace the incorporative relation to the Indigenous in the ballet with a queer Indigenous aesthetic of cacophony and bewilderment.

The next chapter of *Wild Things* examines the sexuality of pre-homosexual subjects who fantasize about becoming feral. "The Epistemology of the Ferox: Sex, Death, and Falconry," links Thoreau's writings on wildness to an odd series of twentieth-century queer memoirs about human loneliness as confronted through the authors' attempts to train wild birds. Authors as different as T. H. White, Glenway Wescott, Barry Hinton, Langston Hughes, J. A. Baker, and most recently, Helen Macdonald have written recollections of their experiences of falconry filled with sexual longing and isolation.

In the second part of the book, I take the focus on the wildness of the hawk from chapter 3, along with its epistemology of the ferox, and ask about the relations between humans and animals that ferality implies. Chapter 4 turns to the "wild things" of my book's title and explores relations between animals, children, and wildness in the popular imagination. Sendak's *Where the Wild Things Are* is perhaps the best-known contemporary book on wildness. Sendak identified wildness with childhood enchantment but also, as I proposed earlier, with ruination and despair. I pair this book with Martel's *Life of Pi* to draw out the connections that both authors make between the child and the animal, the beast and the sovereign, wildness and freedom. The relations to animals that humans cultivate in the household turn away from wildness and use techniques of domestication to bond with animals, to tame animals, and to turn them into pets. Chapter 5 looks into the process of domestication and asks whether, in blurring the boundaries between human and animal, pet and child, we might, unwittingly, blur the boundaries between life and death—the figure of the zombie representing this confusion.

Like many explanatory systems that we use to justify our particular modes of classifying bodies and types of persons, wildness contains histories that are at once discriminatory and liberating, revelatory and incriminating, surprising and all too pedestrian. Wildness does not promise freedom, nor does it name a new mode of identification; rather it offers a rubric for passions, affects, movements, and ways of thinking that exceed conventional oppositions between animal, vegetable, and mineral. Wildness also lays waste to oppositions that structure modern life.

If we return to the space opened up in *Where the Wild Things Are* for reverie and dreams, night journeys and escape, and we return to Max on the stairs of the family home, suspended between the world and freedom, the order of things and extravagant desires, beauty and the inexpressible, heaven and hell, we enter the space of the wild: "and the walls became the world all around." But we cannot stay there. Bewilderment, the process of becoming wild by shedding knowledge (as opposed to becoming civilized by acquiring it), offers both escape and madness, desire and disorder. In the panels toward the end of Sendak's book, the wild creatures hang with Max from the trees, repeating the image from the beginning of the book when Max's stuffed toy hung from the makeshift clothesline and Max held the line suspended. Now he takes his place among the wild things—creatures, children, stuffed toys, prosthetics— and hangs with them from trees, a crown on his head and his feet kicking the ground away. There are no words in this section of the book, only gorgeous images of revelry and chaos. When the words return, it is to articulate Max's new authority, " 'Now stop!' Max said and sent the wild things off to bed without their supper" (28). Max has become the parent he once opposed. He has wielded the authority he once rejected. He has wrangled the wild into a state of stillness. He is now ready to enter the world created for him and to leave the wild things to their ruination. Can we, unlike Max, enter the wild rumpus, the disorder of desire, not to tame it nor to perform wildness with it, but to eschew the order of things with its private property, its cooked meals, and its family homes? Can we instead live with the bewilderment that accompanies the desire to end that world without knowing what comes next?

ONE

Wildness, Loss, and Death

Wild—(of a place or region) Uncultivated or uninhabited; hence, waste, desert, desolate.
—*Oxford English Dictionary*

Wildness also raises the specter of death of the symbolic function itself. It is the spirit of the unknown and the disorderly, loose in the forest encircling the city and the sown land, disrupting the conventions upon which meaning and the shaping function of images rests. Wildness challenges the unity of the symbol, the transcendent totalization binding the image to that which it represents. Wildness pries open this unity and its place creates slippage and a grinding articulation between signifier and signified. Wildness makes of these connections spaces of darkness and light in which objects stare out in their mottled nakedness while signifiers float by. Wildness is the death space of signification.
—Michael Taussig

What we call the beginning is often the end.
—T. S. Eliot

Let us start at the end. The end of an era, the end of a rope, the end of history, origins, futurity, sex, gender, order, meaning, the end of everything. Let us begin in 1916, when an Irish man was hung in England for treason and abandoned by supporters on account of homosexual activities he recorded in what came to be called the *Black Diaries*. Let us start in the murky, illegible, confounding, bewildering terrain that Joseph Conrad called "darkness," in the time-space that T. S. Eliot called "here, now, always," and in the baffling diary entries of Roger Casement, a queer Irishman.[1]

And we start here not because the wild is the production of modernist sensibilities, but because within modernism it is impossible to discern where the domestic, the civilized, and the orderly end and where the foreign, the barbaric, and the wild begin. "In my beginning is my end," wrote Eliot in *The Four Quartets*, a poetry cycle that confronts not the meaningless of existence, but the beginning of an environmental unraveling.[2] "We live in the flicker," wrote Conrad; "may it last as long as the old earth keeps on rolling."[3] Turns out that may not be much longer, and the flicker in Conrad, like the mortality that Eliot glimpses, presses against life itself. In this chapter, wildness is the name for the force unleashed by colonial brutality and the domain of life that exceeds a colonial will to power and a form of desire that subjugates and submits in the same gesture.

Roger Casement (1864–1916), in brief, was an Irish diplomat who worked for the British foreign office in the Congo and the Putumayo region of South America. After witnessing horrific scenes of colonial brutality, Casement attempted to craft an international law to which colonizers would be subject. For this work he was celebrated as a humanitarian. However, when in 1914 Casement decided to take up the cause of Irish nationalism and planned to encourage Ireland to go to war with England in alliance with the Germans, he was arrested and condemned to die by an English court. Opposition mounted from Irish nationalists, but after the English government found and circulated Casement's diaries of his homosexual activities in the Congo and Peru, he was abandoned and eventually hung for treason.

Casement, also author of early human rights legislation, is only the first of a parade of odd figures in this book who will articulate desire not *as* wild but *for* the wild. Like others, Casement appears here not because he was before his time, nor because he was a heroic character whom we want to pluck from the past and to whom we would build a textual monument; Casement appears here as a disruption within the histories of sexuality to which we have subscribed. He is not an ancestor, a forerunner, a precursor. Rather, he expresses in all of its glorious complexity the contradictory set of desires for wildness that we cannot call homosexuality or heterosexuality, that defy classification, for better or for worse, and that stand outside of the conventional terrain we have reserved for more orderly narratives of sexuality. The writers and artists who desire wildness itself are not a group of revolutionaries, nor are they unified in how they desire the wild or how they express that desire. Some court wildness in those bodies they have classified as wild (a colonial relation to the wild); others seek it in animals, birds, or any feral creature (a bestial relation to the body); some seek it through technology (a prosthetic relation to flesh);

and still others seek wildness in death (a necropolitical relation to ecological exhaustion). In later chapters we will meet people who love dogs better than humans and others who watch birds not to know them, but to become them; we meet wild things and others who journey to where the wild things are; we explore desires for disorder, chaos, and death.

Casement himself entered the wilderness at first to save Brown people from white power (to twist a famous phrase by Gayatri Chakravorty Spivak[4]), but like other colonial white men ("rice queens" in the parlance of Eng-Beng Lim[5]), along the way he falls in love with the very idea of a wildness that can be touched and embraced, that is far from Europe and the domestic household, and that takes the form of youthful Black and Brown bodies which become a kind of recompense for the bodily trials of exploration. Casement, accordingly, was all at once a colonial figure, an anticolonial activist, a sexual tourist, and one in a long line of mostly male-bodied people attracted to what we are describing here as, using a very different context from that of Jack London, the call of the wild.

Born and raised in northeast Ireland, Casement combined a healthy sense of social justice with a desire for travel and adventure. His early work alerted him to the extreme and untrammeled violence directed by colonial authorities at the Native populations forced to work for exploitative and brutal rubber companies. Casement, used to making legal arguments to defend the rights and interests of British subjects abroad, after seeing and hearing about the enslavement of Native populations by the Belgians in the Congo and by British companies in the Putumayo district of the Amazon, wrote a series of reports on the rapacious activities of the colonial elite that led to early formulations of universal human rights discourse. He was knighted by the British government in 1911 for his efforts. But after his experiences abroad, after his immersion in the bloody colonial transactions of British and Belgian companies in pursuit of rubber and other lucrative resources, Casement felt sickened not only by what was happening in the colonies but also by what was happening in Ireland, and he came to see the two as related. Casement, tutored in colonial methods of extraction, subjugation, and justification, began to see Ireland's relation to British rule in a new light. By the beginning of World War I, Casement had come to see the Irish as the colonized peoples of Europe; he had joined Sinn Fein and had approached the German government on a mission to persuade them to join forces with Ireland in an attack on England. This turned out to be a fool's errand, and the German government sold Casement out to the British government, turning him over to the British and, in the process, making him into a hero for the cause of Irish independence.[6]

Casement's remarkable transformation, from agent of the state to foreign agent accused of conspiring with Germany and participating in the Easter Rising in Ireland, provides a gateway to the multiple confusing narratives about wildness, politics, sex, and disorder that populate the early years of the twentieth century. Strange as the twists of fate may have been that turned Casement from an upright worker for the British government to a traitor confabulating with the German army on the cusp of World War I, no twist was more strange than the emergence of a batch of diaries associated with Casement and circulated by British officials to offset the growing support for his cause in Ireland. Banking on an irresolvable tension between Irish Catholicism and homosexual activity, the British government made public sections of those diaries in which Casement had recorded his homosexual exploits in the Congo and in the Peruvian Amazon with young Black and Brown men. The exploits took place while he was there to investigate violations of the Native populations, and notes on his sexual encounters dotted otherwise banal recordings of officials he had met, distances he had traveled, and reports he was writing.

As predicted, the public exposure of the diaries dissipated the support for Casement that had come from Ireland and the United States and created a complex legacy for future historians of human rights, sexuality, Irish nationalism, and colonialism. Was Casement a persecuted gay man? Was he a sexual tourist? Did his reports on the abuses perpetrated by Belgian colonial officials in the Congo and the Peruvian Amazon Co. in South America offer the beginnings of an anticolonial discourse or the extension of colonial violence by another means? Was Casement a hero or a goat, a revolutionary or a banal pervert? Was he drawn to what his acquaintance Joseph Conrad called the "wild vitality" of the African men from whom he bought sexual favors?[7] Or, like Conrad and his antihero Kurtz, did he lose himself in what he felt to be a "god-forsaken wilderness" (17)? Just as early literary modernism teems with texts like *Heart of Darkness* (first serialized, 1899) and *Passage to India* (1924), stories of oddly sexed and gendered men who hear the siren call of darkness and the void, so the first few decades of what David Halperin called the "One Hundred Years of Homosexuality" turns up unknowable figures with indecipherable desires.[8] While sexologists, medical doctors, lawyers, and psychoanalysts were busy providing a language for desire in general, all kinds of bodies, with all kinds of desires, were pushed, by a kind of centrifugal force, out from the center of this activity to its margins. Once there, they formed an edge of legibility, the outskirts of more readable expressions of bodily form and content, a wild terrain of the unsorted, the unspeakable, and the unassimilable, another heart of darkness, this one not far off but, in Eliot's words, "now and in England." Echoing Marlow in *Heart of Darkness*, Eliot writes: "There are other places / Which also are the world's end, some at the sea jaws, / Or over a dark lake, in a desert or a city— / But this is the nearest, in place and time, / Now and in England."[9]

Wildness Also Raises the Specter of Death

Roger Casement was not the first and certainly not the last person to seek meaning in darkness only to find the wild. Or is that the other way around? Casement was not the first to seek meaning in wildness and find only death? Half a century later, an anthropologist went looking in the same terrain, the Putumayo region of the Amazon, for wildness and death. What anthropologist Michael Taussig found in his search for healers and shamans became the basis for a widely influential and deeply confounding account of the history of the civilizing mission as it encounters wildness, and the anticolonial mission as it smacks into the hard face of rationalized, quantified violence.[10] In the context of a confrontation with the brute force of the rational, Taussig proposes that wildness can be a "healing power" (219), can offer an alternative episteme, and can shatter the orderly shape of the real in favor of a magical realm of visions.

Death, Taussig offers, is a wild space of unmeaning and un/being where darkness and light, self and other, order and chaos slip out of their orderly opposition, and the symbolic order of signification itself falters and collapses. And "wildness," he suggests, is simultaneously the name for this systemic distress, the ever-present threat of unmeaning, and the impact of death on the system as a whole. In his monumental magical realist anthropology of colonial orders of terror in Colombia, *Shamanism, Colonialism, and the Wild Man* (1987), Taussig pulls us into the dark and distressing struggle over the symbolic that was waged, on the one hand, against Indian bodies by mercenary colonial explorers in the late nineteenth and early twentieth centuries and, on the other, through a war of words in the metropole. Colonialism, Taussig proposed, projects a wildness, a violence, and a savagery onto the other and then seeks to counter the senseless brutality that it imagines inheres to this other order of being with a senseless brutality of its own. Studying the disassembled representational order of empire through the mirrored shards that lay scattered across the occupied terrain, Taussig contests the binary of civilization and wildness and proposes to unleash the wild within knowledge production itself.

As much as wildness speaks of life, liveliness, dynamism, vitality, and excess, it also raises the specter of death. The tidy spaces of life, after all, are limned by the unregulated spaces of what Joseph Roach terms "cities of the dead."[11] At a funeral, Roach reminds us, "the deceased performs the limits of the community called into being by the need to mark its passing" (14). Paradoxically perhaps, the spaces opened by death, as Taussig proposed, offer a first and a last encounter with the unregulated space that limns life and the body and underpins all received wisdom about order and being.

It is within the epistemologies established by colonial encounters, by colonial brutality, and by a colonial will to know that the wild is established as a space of otherness, of primitive anteriority, and as Indigenous knowledge ripe for the taking. In its encounter with imaginary *wild* people, the colonial project confronts very different understandings of body, life, magic, science, value, and resources and attempts to eliminate them wielding the tools of ethnography (writing indigeneity into the past), law (legislating possessive investments in land and resources), and guns (eradicating what could not be fixed). Taussig's wild exploration of the unraveling of reality, representation, and rule under colonialism recognizes the role that ethnography plays in this conjuring and eliminating of wildness, and so he attempts to break with conventional anthropology, failing, for example, to preserve the opposition between a *them* and an *us*. Taussig even contributes to the dissolution of conventional barriers between the scholar and his arena of study by taking drugs with shamans and writing a history of the Putumayo in Colombia as it appears to him in visions as well as in colonial records, in hallucinations as much as in rational explanation. Indeed, Taussig proposes, rational explanation is a centerpiece of colonial terror and so has no place in the dismantling of a colonial epistemology. He writes: "If terror thrives on the production of epistemic murk and metamorphosis, it nevertheless requires the hermeneutic violence that creates feeble fictions in the guise of realism, objectivity, and the like, flattening contradiction and systematizing chaos."[12]

Macarena Gómez-Barris has written clearly and cogently about the function of wildness in relation to "colonial fantasies about taming native peoples while also extracting healing power from them."[13] She cites Taussig as saying: "Going to the Indians for their healing power and killing them for their wildness is not so far apart" and links this insight to the spiritual legacies of shamanism and the spiritual tourism engaged by Europeans and North Americans who are both fascinated by the wildness they glimpse in the Andes and elsewhere and eager to extract value from it.[14] Certainly, as she implies, this extractive logic is at work in Taussig's text, where wildness cannot be simply kept at bay. Operating as both that which cannot be tamed and that which creeps into those who come to tame it, wildness works entropically and within a logic of contamination. And so, Taussig's book itself cannot escape the binary it challenges, and too often Taussig himself, like so many other writers who attempt to immerse themselves in the idiom of an imaginary otherness (Conrad, just to give the most obvious example), actually reproduces the colonial terms of encounter within which a wild other embodies the unknown, the magical, and the antidote to the ills of Euro-American cultural values. But, even as Taussig disappears down the rabbit hole of colonial magical thinking, his experiment is instructive in that it reveals the structures in contemporary epistemologies that prevent us from thinking in new and interesting ways about alternative worlds and realities. Taussig himself cannot resist the call of the wild, but even as he pulls the wild into focus, it eludes clarity and fogs up his text and leaves us unsure as to whether we are back in the heart of darkness with another colonial madman or on the edge of another reality where the wild obliterates sense.

Wildness, Taussig proposes, is "the death space of signification" (219). It cannot mean because it has been cast as that which exceeds meaning. Wildness cannot tell because it frames telling as another tool of colonial rule. Wildness cannot speak without producing both the colonial order that gives it meaning and the disruption of that order through temporal and spatial and bodily excess and eccentricity. Any queer theory of wildness runs the risk of reproducing the stable binary of civilization and barbarity that, as Walter Benjamin proposed, nests one inside the other: "There is no document of civilization that is not at the same time a document of barbarity."[15] But any queer theory that avoids the category of wildness runs the risk of reproducing the norms it critiques and stabilizing the system it seeks to unsettle. Queerness without wildness is just white homosexual desire out of the closet and in sync with a new normal.

The closet itself marks distinctions between the domestic and the wild even as those distinctions exceed its geography and map a wilder terrain. As C. Riley Snorton's book *Nobody Is Supposed to Know*, on Black sexuality, in/visibility, secrecy, and exposure, shows, the closet continues to mark Black bodies as duplicitous and tricky even as it marks white bodies as mysterious or heroic.[16] The Black gay man on "the down low," accordingly, is in a "glass closet" (29)—he is hypervisible and sneakily invisible all at once. The glass closet, according to Snorton, fixes, frames, and exposes Black sexuality; it also holds in place a set of racialized logics that, as Snorton puts it, place "darkness and enlightenment and concealment and freedom in opposition to one another. These logics are put in crisis in the case of blackness, where darkness does not reflect a place from which to escape but a condition of existence. In other words, there can be no elsewhere when darkness is everywhere. In the context of blackness, the closet is not a space of concealment; it is a site for observation, surveillance, and display" (29). The mechanics of knowledge production in the vicinity of Black and Brown bodies always partakes in the discourse of wildness: whether the wild enters as a kind of reiteration of sexual excess or inheres to a darkness that is always the byproduct of and the antithesis of enlightenment discourse, it necessarily produces racialized bodies as unknowable, as spectacles, as specimens, and as an undercommons who nonetheless escape colonial figurations and use signification for their own purposes. As Stefano Harney and Fred Moten put it in *The Undercommons: Fugitive Planning and Black Study*, in a succinct formulation: "We are disruption and consent to disruption. We preserve upheaval."[17]

While for Taussig the wild occupies very specifically the spaces between representation and terror that a colonial order opens and administers, for Stefano Harney and Fred Moten, as well as for such queer theorists as Mel Chen, Tavia Nyong'o, and José Muñoz, wildness surely also inhabits all kinds of other regimes of knowing and being that form part of the making and unmaking of modern, racialized subjectivity. A queer inquisition into wildness—where we might understand wildness as the space that colonialism constructs, marks, and disavows, as well as a space of vibrancy that limns all attempts to demarcate subject from object and as a space of normativity that holds the deviant and the monstrous decisively at bay—was precisely part of José Muñoz's last work on what he called "a sense of brownness."[18] In the writing Muñoz was doing on a "brown undercommons," on feelings of Brownness and on queer new materialisms, he focused on what he thought of as "lives organized and disorganized by world forces of hope and harm."[19] Muñoz also wanted to find spaces of encounter for the Brown commons, spaces that were wild precisely because they were not prescribed by a colonial order of being that designated them as nonsensical or inconsequential. Gesturing to a haptic order of things where touch and randomness as much as analogy and determination gave meaning to bodies in space and time, Muñoz, with his characteristic ability to pull from seemingly incompatible theoretical sources, understood wildness as a staging of encounters between the many who remain many and become a new entity in their multiplicity, and the Brown who remain held within the warm embrace of a commitment to being together even when they are cast as the wild who must be tamed.

Wildness Makes of These Connections Spaces of Darkness and Light

"In the dark and in the shifts between the dark and the light," Taussig narrates from within a yage-induced haze, "objects stare out in their mottled nakedness, while signifiers float by."[20] Recognizing the ways in which the wild has been ascribed to evil, to some colonial notion of primitive personhood, and to a form of chaos that civilization comes to tame, Taussig offers a new relation to wildness that "tears through the tired dichotomies of good and evil, order and chaos, the sanctity of order, and so forth" (220). Like Snorton's sense of darkness that encapsulates a Black relation to negative knowledge, or Moten's understanding of Black aesthetics as the noise that European and American high culture both violently produces in the other and designates as ugly all at once, Taussig offers wildness as a form of connection between spaces of darkness and light.[21] And once these dichotomies have been shredded, what remains "comes down on the side of chaos and its healing creativity is inseparable from that of taking sides."[22] Queer theory after nature necessarily comes down on the side of chaos and remains in productive tension with "the grotesque and the destructive" (220), and in this way, it stays monstrous. If queer theory refuses the monstrous and the dark, it threatens to reproduce orders of knowledge that, like the closet, mark freedom as an accessible space beyond secrecy and simultaneously mark certain racialized bodies as figures for that secrecy. Snorton again: "The closet as it appears in (progress) narratives about gay subject-making serves to draw on an implicit colonialist sensibility that figures the 'dark secrecy' of the closet with the pre-modern and primitive and the subsequent open consciousness of an 'outside' of the closet with modernity and Civilization."[23]

Wildness Challenges the Unity of the Symbol

Failure attends all attempts to make wildness signify as either the opposite of modernity or simply its underbelly. Taussig therefore uses wildness to challenge the unity of the symbol and to fracture meanings that have coalesced around marked bodies. Taussig delves into the colonial archive—as constituted by colonial records as well as by administrative briefs and imperial literature—in order to find a method for the madness and a madness with which to oppose the method. He loops around again and again, as so much colonial and postcolonial material must, to Joseph Conrad's *Heart of Darkness*. But he offsets Conrad's document of barbarity with attention to the briefs of Roger Casement.[24] Casement and Conrad offer weird place markers for the role of sexuality and madness in colonial savagery. Conrad, as Maya Jasanoff shows elegantly in *The Dawn Watch: Joseph Conrad in a Global World*, embodied what we now call "globalization," and his work continues to exert considerable influence precisely because, as Jasanoff puts it, "Conrad's world shimmers beneath the surface of our own."[25] And Roger Casement, who, as I proposed earlier, is sometimes cast as the author of contemporary human rights and at other times as a queer Irish nationalist martyr, represents the world beneath that one. His understanding of desire and his relation to nature, otherness, and sexuality no longer shimmers beneath ours but has been covered over by the epistemologies that fell into place along the lines of a dualistic division of homo and hetero.

The twinning of Conrad's novel with Casement's diaries of his homo/sexual exploits in the Congo and the Amazon within the trope of darkness forces us to see the odd alignments that colonialism constructed within the sexualized trope of *wildness*.[26] When Marlow descended into the heart of darkness, he found the savagery he went to confront in the form of Kurtz, the colonial administrator who has not simply "gone native" or wild but who has, in his managerial madness, transacted the precise terms of what Taussig calls "the colonial mirror of production."[27] Taussig's analysis of the extreme violence meted out by colonists and rubber company employees in the Putumayo against Native peoples they encounter there leads him to conclude: "The terror and the tortures they devised mirrored the horror of the savagery they both feared and fictionalized" (133). And time and again in *Shamanism, Colonialism, and the Wild Man*, Taussig returns to Conrad to provide him with the narrative framework for this vexing and disorienting mirror effect by which colonizers carry out violence against those whom they have dreamed onto this landscape. While Marlow in *Heart of Darkness* recognizes of London that "this too has been one of the dark places of the earth,"[28] still darkness comes to define not empire, but the murky realms it seeks to redeem. Taussig identified in Conrad's novel a methodology for encountering myth within which the author uses "political artistry" to carry out "the mythic subversion of myth" and the imaginative penetration of "the political unconscious of the epoch."[29] Kurtz, accordingly, represents the failure of signification under the intense pressure of a colonial order that sought to divide the dark from the light, the savage from the civilized, the good from and evil. "Wildness," Taussig remarks, "challenges the unity of the symbol, the transcendent totalization binding the image to that which it represents" (219). Wildness introduces the bureaucratic to other murky epistemologies that cannot be subjected to the rule of the pen and that will not submit to the moral clarity that seeks to cleanse it of contradiction.

Like many other writers, including W. G. Sebald, for example, Taussig's interest is piqued by the image we get from Conrad, on his way out of the Congo, of Roger Casement on his way in. Conrad described Casement in a letter in 1890 to a friend thus:

> I can assure you that he is a limpid personality. There is a touch of the Conquistador in him too; for I've seen him start off into an unspeakable wilderness swinging a crook-handled stick for all weapons, with two bull-dogs, Paddy (white) and Biddy (brindle) at his heels, and a Loanda boy carrying a bundle for all company. A few months afterwards it so happened, that I saw him come out again, a little leaner, a little browner, with his stick, dogs and Loanda boy, and quietly serene as though he had been for a stroll in a park.[30]

Many contemporary readers of colonial history might have passed over the appearance of Roger Casement in Taussig's reckoning with colonial orders of terror in Colombia. And in truth, like so many contemporary commentators on Casement, including W. G. Sebald, Taussig has no idea what to do with Casement having summoned him into his text. Casement appears alongside Conrad for both Taussig and Sebald as a well-intentioned wanderer looking for justice in the jungle. But, of course, Casement's legacy is much more troubling and much more significant than this implies, and while Taussig casts Casement as almost a foil for Conrad, in fact Casement represents the deeply contradictory force of European racial and economic thinking on the topic of wildness, indigeneity, sexuality, and power. He also represents a version of the "untimely sexuality" that is the subject of the next two chapters, namely, a homosexuality before homosexuality, a queerness after nature but before queer culture. Casement represents an earlier understanding of same-sex desire that he recorded deliriously in a diary and that ran counter to his well-intentioned reports on colonial violence that were sent back to Britain in the hopes of curbing genocidal murder in the Congo and slave labor in the Amazon.

Capsule histories of Roger Casement are to be found in any number of sources—in Maya Jasanoff's *The Dawn Watch*, where Casement appears as an early reader of *The Heart of Darkness* and one of the first to, as Jasanoff puts it, misread the book and its author as critics of the Congo. Accordingly, when Casement asked Conrad to sign on to his report of the violent practices of Europeans in the Congo, Conrad refused. Jasanoff, perhaps generously, reads Conrad's refusal not simply as hypocrisy, but as a rejection of the "European notion of civilization as a good in itself."[31] Casement also appears in Adam Hochschild's *King Leopold's Ghost*, this time as a British consul in Africa who traveled widely, documenting the travesties he witnessed, shunning the railroad, and often walking hundreds of miles accompanied by his dogs.[32] Hochschild situates Casement's unconventional desires, his homosexuality, as a liability that must inevitably spell his ruination as he went up against the powers that be. Hochschild compares the diaries that Casement kept of his sexual exploits with young African boys to "a time bomb, with a fuse of unknown length" (200).

Taussig, in a way, introduces Casement as part of the wildness he is summoning. But, like Taussig, Casement is an ambivalent figure who, on the one hand, battles against the rigid and contradictory morality of a colonial order of being but, on the other hand, dips his hand in the honey pot of colonial fetishism. How was Roger Casement able to reconcile his role as a major critic of both the English occupation of Ireland and the violent treatment of Indigenous peoples by the rubber merchants in the Amazon while also busily recording his sexual exploits with Native men in his diaries? Casement paid for many of these sexual favors and often recorded his encounters by noting the size and shape of the genitals of the young boys with whom he had sex. Thus, we have to read the legacy of Casement as both an activist against British rule and the violence of colonial missions *and* as a colonial subject who saw Black and Brown bodies as erotic commodities. His notes on his sexual contacts, in the *Black Diaries*, appeared opposite his diary entries on his travels in the Congo and the Amazon, which could be called the white diaries. One page might note atrocities he has witnessed, and on another he offers cryptic details of an encounter:

> August 8: Should arrive in Para and get on shore by 6PM. Will to Valda Peso and cafe's first, then on to cafe in Independencia and back to theatre about 10.30 and Valda Peso at 11. Camrino's first. Arr. Para at 2PM, alongside 3.30PM. Tea and at 5PM with Pogson to Paz cafe. Lovely moco. Then after dinner to Valda Peso, two types, also to gardens of Pracao Republica, two types, Baptista Campos one type. Then Senate Square and Caboclo (boy 16–17) seized hard. Young, stiff, thin, others offered later, on board at 12 midnight.[33]

In one of the best contemporary essays on Casement, Colm Tóibín succinctly describes Casement's legacy as "complex" and "enigmatic."[34] Tóibín recognizes the double bind into which Irish history has placed Casement. Given that the *Black Diaries* were quickly cast as forgeries by Irish nationalists who suspected the British of trying to sully the name of a heroic freedom fighter, contemporary commentators are torn between arguing for the diaries' authenticity and having to make sense of the sexual fetishism they contain or agreeing that the diaries may have been forged and then distancing themselves from accounts of gay sex. When one writer argues that just because Casement wrote about certain forms of sex does not mean he participated in them, Toíbín weighs in, this time not as an Irish writer but as a gay man; he does so to argue that various readers bring their own desires to the text and find there whatever they need to find:

> When, as a gay reader, you study the hastily written diaries, full of short-hand, full of the strangeness of the night on the edge of a park in an old city, you know, as a non-gay reader might not, that most of the time these ring true and are probably what Casement actually did on the day, unlikely as this may be to those of another sexual persuasion. This, in turn, may in the future become another Casement heresy, much reviled for its crudeness. It may also be worth pointing out that there is no evidence to disprove this view.[35]

Casement offers a weird place marker for the role of sexuality and madness in colonial savagery. As previously stated, when he had finished his tour of duty in the Amazon in 1914, he set out to destroy England in a fantasized collaboration with the German government. After Casement was imprisoned for treason, there was an enormous outpouring of sympathy for Casement from Irish nationalists, including Yeats, who penned "The Ghost of Roger Casement" in April 1916, a few months before his execution. But when news broke about the *Black Diaries*, Casement became an embarrassing blot on the Irish struggle for independence. Are these diaries, like Conrad's *Heart of Darkness*, a witness account of colonial brutality, or are they complicit with that violent order, enforcing in aesthetic terms what the political system left undone? Do Casement's sexual exploits represent an attempt to reach across the cultural barriers between Black and white bodies, or are they the intensification of the markers that ascribe humanity to whiteness and wild animality to Blackness?

In August 1916, Casement was hung for treason, and while his supporters abandoned him once his homosexuality became public knowledge, in later years, Irish nationalists have tried to revive his status as a national hero by claiming that only homophobia stood between him and a glorious place in Irish history. These same supporters cast the diaries as plagiarism and accused the British government of manufacturing them to besmirch Casement's reputation. In 1965 his body was exhumed and given a hero's welcome in Ireland. But by 2002, the diaries were forensically confirmed to be authentic and Casement's legacy became even more complex. The illegibility of Casement's legacy, his fluctuation between the poles of exploiter and activist, objectifying fetishist and lover, freedom fighter and predator, is now the legacy of queer studies. Within the framework of wildness, a disorder of things that resists the sorting mechanisms applied by contemporary morality, figures like Casement can finally be reckoned with.

It Is the Spirit of the Unknown and the Disorderly

Wildness remains vital in its stubborn persistence, queerly vital. Can we use this queer vitality to navigate contemporary terrains of contradiction, confrontation, and complicity? These terrains are not the same as the spaces where Taussig confronted his demons, nor are they completely free of the contradictions that Taussig chased through the colonial archive; rather the spaces of contradiction that fascinate us now within the economic, the cultural, and the social are studded with the shards of the colonial order that has been smashed but that lives on as small pieces of discourse embedded in the choices we make, the ways we relate or cannot, and the way we encounter otherness, success, and failure.

Queer wildness, accordingly, inherits this ambivalence that inheres to the mirror of colonial production—it always runs the risk of reproducing the terms that it seeks to displace. Going wild might well propel us into another realm of thought, action, being, and knowing, but it could just as easily result in the reinstatement of an order of rationality that depends completely on the queer, the Brown, and the marginal to play their role as mad, bad, and unruly. In Muñoz's late/early work on wildness (late in his life, early in his thinking on this topic), the wild or wildness functioned as a launching pad for a consideration of the "brown undercommons," and it was in this form of collectivity that Muñoz seemed to lodge his faith in a wildness that was not simply the underside of white colonial fetishism and in a Brownness that exceeded its function as racial foil.

Engaging wildness is always risky. We have located within its spaces of encounter, fantasy, and imagination not simply colonial geographies of madness and mayhem but also devious landscapes of desire. Roger Casement's desire ran haphazardly through the colonial mission and was directed toward a social justice project that intervened on behalf of the tortured and abused Native peoples of the Putumayo and the Congo and toward some of those same young and male people themselves. The legacy of Casement for Irish independence, for human rights discourse, and for gay rights is immensely complicated, and as Toíbín puts it in an article on Casement's legacy, "we all bring our own concerns to Casement's story."[36] In other words, while one critic may want Casement to represent the instability of the text, and another may want to run the machinery of empire through his complicated narrative, the gay reader thinks he finds a hero but then must explain the crude racism that punctuates even parts of the text where he is deeply sympathetic to the victims of colonial brutality. Replete with commentary about the "African savage," the very same African savage whom he paid for sex, in fact, Casement's *Black Diaries* offer us a peek at the contours of wild desire and desire for wildness—it both escapes and participates in the colonial mission.

So much for empire. And so much for the homosexual victim of empire served up a few years earlier in the form of Oscar Wilde, a dandy on a martyr's mission. Wilde and Casement, like the "rice queens" about whom Eng-Beng Lim has written so eloquently, never did stand outside of history. They plopped down right in the middle of the civilizing mission and helped themselves to boys and young men and cried foul when things did not go their way. Wilde's snappy commentary on the dullness of heterosexual culture ("men marry because they are tired, women because they are curious, both are disappointed"[37]), and Casement's brief and fetishistic entries into his diaries were indeed a version of the notations of canonical Western literature taking the measure, literally, of the other, desiring him and wanting him dead at the same time. And while some gay men flirted with wildness in the form of the Native other they came to save, others embraced wildness via aesthetic appropriation and folded the sound of chaos into more orderly music until a "new kind of wildness" emerged.[38]

Art, even today, provides us with witnesses to the wildness of queer lives and the queerness of the wild. It does so by offering us utopic visions but also by joining those visions to madness, failure, the temporality of the belated, darkness, and negativity. Take the work of Nick Cave, a contemporary Black gay artist who builds what he calls "sound suits" from materials others had cast off—buttons, cans, feathers, lost objects, fetishes, and trinkets that he finds and "rescues" from thrift shops and antique sales. Cave actually builds the suits to be worn, whimsical and wild and impractical as they may be, and once the body has been encased in the wondrous suit, Cave thinks of it as a kind of armor. Cave made his first suit in 1992 after the Rodney King beating and created the suits to encase, protect, transform the wearer, imagined here as a Black male who requires a suit of armor in order to make it through the violent landscape of surveillance and profiling. Cave also classifies the suits, which make sound as they move, as a form of speech. He told the *Washington Post*: "I build this sort of suit of armor and by putting it on, I realized that I could make a sound from moving in it. It made me think of ideas around protest and how we should be a voice and speak louder."[39]

Figure 1.1   Nick Cave, *Soundsuit*, 2008. Mixed media including embroidery, fabric,
vintage toys, and mannequin, 94 × 35 × 35 inches. © Nick Cave. Courtesy of the artist
and Jack Shainman Gallery, New York. Photo by James Prinz Photography.

Cave does not say we should *have* a voice; he says we should *be* a voice. This notion of speech as a mode of being, and sound as a form of protest, leavens the hypervisibility that marks the Black male body out for violence and marks it as violent all at once. Cave here deploys a wild and queer logic in that he covers over one form of vulnerable visibility with another form of spectacle—the suits are loud, literally, colorful, full of joy and chaos. They amplify the Black (gay) male body even as they encase it. Far from a closet marking off freedom from confinement, the suits represent a wild remaking of the surface that both hides the body and remakes it as part of a different universe, a utopian space of play and pleasure.

How is it possible for the wild or the space of utopia to appear through the resignification of the primitive and the animalistic in relation to the Black body as it does in Nick Cave's work? How is Cave able to deploy the tropes that have limited the meaning of Blackness and Black queerness to other ends? José Muñoz's work has explained in many different ways exactly how, through such mechanics as "disidentification," queer subjects are always involved in the process of "recycling and rethinking encoded meaning."[40] Muñoz continues: "The process of disidentification scrambles and reconstructs the encoded message of a cultural text in a fashion that both exposes the encoded message's universalizing and exclusionary machinations and recruits its workings to account for, include and empower minority identities and identifications" (31). There is of course a risk in these reconstructions of the encoded messages—the risk is that the replaying of racialized tropes of wildness and primitivism, of disorderliness and belatedness, will simply flow right back into the discursive machinery that produces bodies of color as perpetually out of line, out of time, out of whack, and out of work. But, as Muñoz's work carefully shows, the risk is always worth taking even if and when it leads to failure.

For Muñoz, wildness is this "spirit of the unknown and the disorderly" (219) and is not a spirit that "belongs" to Indigenous contexts and gets stolen by others for other purposes; rather, it describes the space and the modes of knowing and unknowing that emerge in the encounter between capital and chaos, privilege and struggle, myth and countermyth. Queerness, Muñoz's legacy instructs us, is what keeps the horizon at bay and what runs to greet it. And wildness manages the space between here and now, then and there, and names what comes after nature, after queerness and before the world they have dreamed. Let *wildness* stand here as part of the critical vocabulary that Muñoz's work leaves behind, as a name for the faltering efforts of incorporation, as a name for all that quietly and in insignificant acts picks away at the fabric of hegemony. And let wildness speak not in the language of order and explanation, but in beautiful, countermythologizing grammars of madness. Wildness is not the lack of inscription; it is inscription that seeks not to read or be read, but to leave a mark as evidence of absence, loss, and death. Wildness must take us into its mottled embrace and press us to stare into those places of slippage between language and experience and life and death; wildness can give us access to the unknown and the disorderly, and we will enter there at our own risk.

TWO

"A New Kind of Wildness"

The Rite of Spring and an Indigenous Aesthetics of Bewilderment

> *Wild*—(of persons) Resisting control or restraint,
> unruly, restive; flighty, thoughtless; reckless, careless;
> *fig.* not according to rule, irregular; erratic; unsteady.
>
> —*Oxford English Dictionary*

At the still point of the turning world. Neither flesh nor fleshless;
Neither from nor towards; at the still point, there the dance is,
But neither arrest nor movement. And do not call it fixity,
Where past and future are gathered. Neither movement from nor towards,
Neither ascent nor decline. Except for the point, the still point,
There would be no dance, and there is only the dance.

> —T. S. Eliot, "Burnt Norton"

> It is a piece of wreckage from the past, teeming, eaten through by a familiar and monstrous life.
>
> —Jacques Rivière

Un-art: *The Rite of Spring*, 1913

On May 29, 1913, manic man about town, aristocratic flaneur, and diarist extraordinaire Count Harry Kessler went to see the premiere of *The Rite of Spring*. In his diary entry for the day before, he had predicted, after watching a rehearsal, that the premiere would be "a scandal."[1] And, indeed, it was. The audience, according to Kessler, was, from the beginning, "restless, laughing, whistling, making jokes" (619). The cause of all this restless energy and confusion was, according to

Kessler, the newness of both Vaslav Nijinsky's choreography and Stravinsky's score. The dancers, Kessler tells us, continued their performance despite the "crazy din," and as a consequence they produced "a thoroughly new vision, something never before seen, enthralling, persuasive, . . . a new kind of wildness, both un-art and art at the same time. All forms laid waste and new ones emerging suddenly from the chaos" (619).

What was this "new kind of wildness"? How was it "un-art and art at the same time"? Should one read this as simply another starting point of modernism and then proceed in an orderly fashion to situate the ballet and the music within a clear genealogy? Or can this wildness instruct us in new ways of listening, different forms of knowing, and alternative logics of embodiment, aesthetic expression, desire, history, and beauty? Can one tell the story of un-art as part and parcel of what is being called new materialism—art not as an expression of a human consciousness, but as the expression of matter itself? Furthermore, what else constituted the wildness of this unprecedented performance? What connections did the ballet forge and display between modern European worlds and so-called traditional folk cultures? What fantasy of pagan wildness were the European audiences responding to?

Kessler was not the only witness to the sheer originality of *The Rite of Spring* that night. French critic Jacques Rivière described the ballet as "biological," by which he meant that the whole movement of the dancers was expended in order to convey the activity of Spring itself.[2] The ballet, for him, was not a human representation of the return of spring; rather, it was the drama of seasonal change played out through human actors who stand in, according to Rivière, for "great swirling accumulations of protoplasm; germinating masses; zones; circles; placentas" (145). This is, announced Rivière, "the horrible work of the cells" and, he adds, it is as if we were watching the drama "under the microscope" (145). The chaotic force field of un-art generated by *The Rite of Spring* and inhabited by those who created it and those who witnessed it, might be understood in a few different ways: as the expression of wild forces that escape human knowledge; as the ephemeral trace of a queer world of utopian collaboration, queer dance, and ambient sexuality; as kinetic and musical fantasy of a so-called primitive past; and as a reversal of temporalities that reaches back in time in order to, in José Muñoz's words, "enact a pre-appearance in the world of another mode of being that is not yet here."[3] This last meaning, the "forward-dawning futurity" (1) that animates Muñoz's work and can be glimpsed in *The Rite of Spring*, echoes through Frank Bidart's long poem on Nijinsky's mad creativity (1919), which begins by describing the dancer as "still gripped by the illusion of a horizon"![4] This illusion, one

Nijinsky shared with Sergei Diaghilev and Stravinsky, implied a bewildering relation to past, present, and future and to space and terrain as well. In this chapter, *The Rite of Spring* represents an early text in queer dance that shows the entanglement of queerness both in colonial definitions of wildness and in queer versions of wildness that jump genres, break loose from history, and reach for new arrangements of bodies, desire, and temporality.

The Rite of Spring is now a well-established symphony and ballet, firmly a part of the Western canon and not an obvious choice for a meditation on wildness, but what has now been tamed was once a runaway performance of madness, queerness, the feral, and exhaustion. The original performances of *The Rite of Spring* in Paris in 1913 drew such ire, indeed, that the performances were halted after only a few nights and only ever revisited as imperfect re-creations of the original choreography. What made audiences respond negatively to Nijinsky's choreography then, and what still strikes some contemporary audiences as shocking now, must be some combination of the awkwardness of the stance (pigeon toed), the performance of broken embodiment rather than a body in flight, and the way the dance exhausts its dancers to the point of near collapse. In terms of the ballet's deliberate failure, we can think of thomas f. defrantz's definition of queer dance as "a hyper-particularity of doing" that produces what he calls "queer failure in dance."[5] Failure here is part of a collapsed inscription of masculine and feminine bodily norms onto the bodies of dancers and the refusal of the divisions between the principals and the chorus. *The Rite of Spring* broke many of the established repertoires of ballet, and in so doing, it unleashed an aesthetic of bewilderment and, as we will see later, marked the necessary failure of modernity.

After watching the mad ballet, Harry Kessler went out into the Parisian night with Diaghilev, Nijinsky, Bakst, and Cocteau, and according to his diary, the men "did a wild tour through the city at night."[6] The wildness of the ballet and the music then extended offstage and into the night, and when the "wild, merry party" (620) concluded their partying at dawn, another "new kind of wildness" took shape around the coordinates of performance, sound, night worlds, queer friendship, ritual, and revelry. The shared, ecstatic, violent communion that the ballet enacts, creates, and conveys and that then plays out in the nocturnal wanderings of Kessler and friends can be understood as the obliteration of the boundaries between on- and offstage within queer dance. And it gives rise to a form of knowledge that does not elucidate but mystifies, does not enlighten but instead bewilders. This aesthetic of bewilderment, an effect of the appropriation of gestures, movements, and rituals believed to descend from a pagan past, emerges here, in the ballet of broken forms, as the bewildering force of the decolonial when it refuses to be stilled by colonial incorporation.

In the twentieth century, as Greil Marcus demonstrates in his punk genealogies in *Lipstick Traces*, certain arrangements of music, motion, art, and meaning capture and participate in moments of cultural upheaval within which a sound, a scream, an image, a performance remakes the cultural landscape entirely or, in this case, channels a temporal shift as organic and aesthetic all at once.[7] These forces of change are not singular, not well explained by the logic of individual genius or singular rebel—instead, the jangly force of change and disruption emerges out of fierce and contentious collaborations. In *Rite of Spring*, Nijinsky and Stravinsky brought dissonant music together with a ballet that challenged the very grammar of the genre. In this chapter we follow instances of visual, sonic, and kinetic rupture that form a part of what Marcus calls "the secret history of the twentieth century," a queer history of mad coincidences, wild dreaming, and a palpable sense of possibility and change. This is the history of un-art—the cultural productions that are not intended to convey beauty, not organized around the notion of singular genius expression, not designed to sooth audiences and to confirm the order of things. Un-art comes to unmake worlds.

The Still Point: *Rite of Spring*

The Rite of Spring, Nijinsky's ballet to Stravinsky's score, as is well known, was performed only a handful of times; its choreography has been lost, and people have relied on hearsay and imagination to even create a sense of what it may have looked like. All performances of the ballet fall into the category of what Joseph Roach calls "surrogation"—or the process by which culture carries out an unending search for origins through a series of restaged performances or, as he puts it, "the doomed search for originals by continuously auditioning stand-ins."[8] While Roach is discussing performance in the context of seventeenth- and eighteenth-century circum-Atlantic worlds, his words describe perfectly the quest to restore *The Rite of Spring* to its original form. "Surrogation" speaks here to the impossibility of ever actually returning to the original and the queerness of all subsequent transmissions. But in the case of *The Rite of Spring*, the desire to re-create became the rather straight quest of Millicent Hodson and Kenneth Archer—who have spoken of *The Rite* as "their first child" and whose relationship developed around its reconstruction. Hodson, in particular, is widely credited with reconstructing the original choreography of *The Rite of Spring*, with help from her assistant and then-husband

Archer, and it is her version of Nijinsky's ballet that has been performed since 1987 by the Joffrey Ballet using the same set designs that Nicholas Roerich contributed to the original performance.[9]

If we disregard such reproductive quests for perfect restoration we are left with a wild text, a text that must remain unknown, unperformable, illegitimate, beyond classification—it exists instead as a legend, a phantasm, a performance that, like so many queer ephemeral acts and performances, can never be repeated. Using Marcus's secret history not as a guide but as a methodology, a project on wildness has to keep telling this incomplete story of silence, dead-ends, and recapitulations without ever finishing it, making it knowable, or taming it. As Isadora Duncan once said, "You were once wild here. Don't let them tame you."[10] And as Frank Bidart writes, in his own very queer re-creation of "The War of Vaslav Nijinsky":

In Suffering, and Nightmare,
I woke at last
to my own nature.[11]

For Bidart, *The Rite of Spring* is the choreography of an insanity that is proper to the world and not simply to the man who dreams it up. Using Nijinsky's diaries and his wife's account of her husband's struggle, Bidart maps a different history for *The Rite* from that of Hodson. Not restoration or even re-creation, Bidart captures the desire to destroy worlds and lives that the impossible dance inhabits. As Bidart writes of the Chosen One's sacrifice, her dance of death, "SHE LEAPS / BECAUSE SHE HATES THE GROUND."[12] She leaps because she hates the ground? Ballet here is not a launching of the body into the air, a defiance of gravity, a glorious martyrdom; it is rather, a refusal of the foundation, a negative aesthetic whereby the script calls for the dancers' collapse.[13]

In 1961, Igor Stravinsky told the *Observer* that his music is "best understood by children and animals."[14] Flirting dangerously with potential characterizations of his work as either childish or crude, Stravinsky made a connection to two audiences generally ignored by composers of classical music. Stravinsky in fact, later in life, embraced the notion that his work might require a nonbourgeois, nonhuman, nonadult listener. He also, perhaps implicitly, proposed that animals and children listen differently, listen for different kinds of sounds, and "understand" music according to principles and standards that are markedly different from those of adult human audiences. If we explore the violated boundaries that Stravinsky's music traverses and argue for its queerness and its wildness, we can embrace rather than reject its "infantile" and "savage" appeal.

While children and animals are often classified together as liminal beings situated on the endlessly shifting border between nature and culture, they are also extra-social, pre- *and* posthuman, and they represent a kind of otherness to the adult human subjectivities against which they are always deemed to be lacking. We will return later to the shared wildness of the animal and the child, but for now, Stravinsky's casual remark also marks the difference between adult human subjects and animals and children in terms of differing degrees of tolerance for chaos, violence, and disorder—perhaps child or animal ears are more attuned to the clashing sounds of an eternal present, more capable of improvising, more tolerant of dissonance.

And, perhaps, in children and animals, Stravinsky sought and imagined an audience willing to listen to the chaos of the world unfiltered, raucous, intermittently melodic but otherwise dispersed into waves of violent and ragged sound. Stravinsky's music, while it annoyed the ears of the Parisian elite, may have corresponded more exactly to the confusing sensorium of the child/animal who seeks to be in and be with the world rather than to master and manage it. Let's take the implied child/animal listener as an access point to a wild musical text, a text, moreover, that offers a soundscape within which a set of distinctions associated with modernity—animal/human, child/adult, nature/culture, traditional/modern—become impossible to uphold. As Bruno Latour says in *We Were Never Modern*: "All of culture and all of nature get churned up again every day."[15] And, he implies, every day we try to separate out what cannot be held apart. Stravinsky's *Rite of Spring* was assaultive precisely because it "churned up" the very categories of child/adult, animal/human, science/philosophy that his world was trying to separate—he joined what was seen as separate, he separated what was understood to be whole. Stravinsky made music out of the mess of living.

Stravinsky also, in his music, turned to face the noise of modernity, its unregulated spaces full of fear and pleasure, and he confronted the new chaos of a new era. This gesture can also be found in the work of Walter Benjamin, who proposes that we turn toward rather than away from "the storm blowing from paradise."[16] This turning toward the storm, the wind, the noise, the blitz is also akin to recommendations we find in Fred Moten's poetic meditations on "the problem of the alternative."[17] Moten proposes that we become the problem we seek to solve: "Jazz," he writes, "does not disappear the problem; it is the problem, and will not disappear" (xii). Moten argues for becoming the problem that refuses to be resolved and for facing the storm that seeks to blow one away and for standing within the force of its fury. By this means we consent to disruption; we are the wild rumpus.

Wildness understood as a form of unchecked growth, and as the movement toward the storm, is a crucial part of un-art work. Indeed, we could say that *The Rite of Spring* is the rhythm of this unchecked growth as expressed across different bodies. Stravinsky himself told Robert Craft that there was no system to his composition; instead he said: "I am the vessel through which Le Sacre passed."[18] Nijinsky used similar language to describe his choreography, telling a reporter in February 1913 of his ballet, "It is the life of the stones and the trees. There are no human beings in it. It is a thing of concrete masses, not individual effects."[19] While we could easily fold this sentiment into a Romantic recognition of the cruelty of nature ("nature red in tooth and claw"), this is something altogether different. The Romantic notion of cruel nature sets this cold indifference in perspective by investing in the warmth and breadth of humanity. Nijinsky's choreography and Stravinsky's music have no such connection to the ordinary binarism of warm and cold, human and animal. Instead, the ballet as un-art stages and unleashes what Jane Bennett has called a "vibrant materialism" through which we can glimpse a seething nonhuman world of wild activity.[20] Can un-art, like nature, offer a portal to the wild? In what forms does un-art arrive, and what is its relation to queerness? *The Rite of Spring*, like other un-art texts, seeks to replace art and genius, genres and training, order and symmetry, reproduction and generation with a regimen of the wild that might arrive as violence, or self-destruction, or in the form of the ugly, the broken, the asymmetrical, the unnatural, and the awkward. It was this version of violence—the violence of broken form—that for Rivière held the secret to Nijinsky's ballet: "Grace is not synonymous with the curve; grace is not incompatible with an angular design. There is grace here."[21] And at the level of music, the wildness inheres to the dissonance, but not only that: music critics also write about the absorption of Lithuanian folk melodies into the orchestration of the piece, the use of heavy repetition of certain phrases, the layering of notes that are played all at once instead of in sequence, and the innovative use of rhythm.

We will return momentarily to what might be queer about the music. But to describe the collaborations that inspired *Rite of Spring* as queer is hardly controversial at this point. Plenty has been written on the sexual relationship between Diaghilev and Nijinsky, and recently speculation has also been proffered about Stravinsky's possible erotic entanglements with Maurice Ravel and Diaghilev, among others. An essay by Robert Craft places Igor Stravinsky in a group of "largely gay artists and intellectuals" in Paris at the turn of the last century, a group ironically called Les Apaches (ironic given the incorporation of Indigenous folk music into *The Rite of Spring*) and including composers, poets, and publishers, Ravel and Stravinsky among them.[22] The queerness of the piece, its anarchic elements, should be considered then alongside the emergent "gay" communities out of which both the ballet and the music emerged, communities of men and women who may well have been engaged in same-sex relations but who would not have thought of themselves as gay in any straightforward way.

Diaghilev, even before his collaboration on the ballet with Stravinsky and Nijinsky, was a major player in the emergence of twentieth-century notions of gay life—a bon vivant and a major tastemaker in Russia as well as France, Diaghilev had early on tried his hand at writing music and was, by some accounts, a pretty good composer, but as Diaghilev's biographer Sjeng Scheijen puts it, "his failure as a composer helped him realize that his genius lay not in artistic creation, but in perceiving the genius of others."[23] Failure here is a portal to creativity. Diaghilev's homosexuality was apparently tolerated in Russia in the late nineteenth and early twentieth centuries, and even after he left Russia he "lived an openly homosexual lifestyle at a time when 'sexual deviancy' was considered an illness" (4). This is not to say that Diaghilev escaped the language of deviance when trying to explain his own desires, and, indeed, he wrote letters about visiting the clinic of Richard von Krafft-Ebing in 1902. At the time, Krafft-Ebing was, as Scheijen puts it, "a celebrated Austro-German psychiatrist and sexologist best known for his studies of sexual aberrations" (121). While on holiday with his much younger lover (and cousin!), Dmitry "Dima" Filosofov, Diaghilev wrote a letter home to say: "We spent one and a half months in Venice and now we're in Graz, in the sanatorium of the famous Krafft-Ebing. I don't think I have gone mad, but my accursed nerves need some looking after. But we can talk about ourselves when we meet—I don't yet know how soon that will be. Dima will return in three weeks but perhaps I'll hang around here for a bit longer, for they think I'm ill."[24] Using the language of "nerves" and "illness," Diaghilev turned to the new terminology of psychological instability rather than sexual aberration for what ails him here. Krafft-Ebing's work had been translated into Russian in 1887, and no doubt this is how Diaghilev knew about his work, but however much he may have suffered from nerves in relation to his sexual "illness," one thing is sure and that is that Diaghilev was open and even flamboyant about his sexuality. He walked around in Paris with Oscar Wilde in 1898, he visited Krafft-Ebing in 1902, and he eventually vigorously pursued a young, wild dancer, Nijinsky, who welcomed the attentions of the older man. The two began a creative, sexual, and aesthetic collaboration in 1908 that lasted five years and culminated in the scandal of *The Rite of Spring*.

In his book on nineteenth-century desire before the onset of the taxonomical divisions of the modern period, Peter Coviello charts territories of illegible intimacies and "inarticulate longings" or what he calls "the extravagances that flourish in the space of a not-yet-congealed sexual specificity."[25] His book *Tomorrow's Parties*, moreover, does not treat pre-articulate sexualities as forms of desire that lack a language and then spring into being when one emerges. Rather, and here Coviello echoes Muñoz, he represents his archive as brimming with what Muñoz called "the outlines of any number of broken-off, uncreated futures, futures that would not come to be" (20). At least one such "uncreated future" can be found in *The Rite of Spring* when it emerges in 1913 on the very cusp of the articulation of this new and orderly language of desire. The identities of Stravinsky, Diaghilev, and Nijinsky are all part of the untimely sexualities described by Coviello, and the out-of-time quality of their desires is reflected in the wild temporalities of *Rite of Spring* in terms of both musical tempos and the odd time/space of the ballet, which is set in a fantasy of the past but conjures a future never to come. The wild aesthetic, which we can glimpse only through accounts of the performances by the astounded witnesses who were there, like Kessler and Rivière, can be characterized as *queer*, using Muñoz's articulation of queerness as a kind of excess, or *wild*, using Bennett's sense of the wild fugitivity of life that the human mind can only chase, and *disorderly*, in relation to Coviello's conjuring of a world of unsorted desires. This excess can be located in the odd relations between the three men who created *The Rite of Spring*, in the audience that witnessed it, in the breathless responses it generated, and in the illegible dance moves and inverted musical score that represent it. As I have said, the ballet itself is elusive and comes to us only as hearsay, as a story of aesthetic upheaval in the received conventions of movement. The music itself, Stravinsky's symphony, becomes wild and queer through the use of the inversion of sound, the emphasis on percussive noise over soothing strings, and what we might call a queer sense of timing.

While many critics have drawn attention to the way that instruments are used oddly in *The Rite of Spring*, few if any remark upon what kind of inversion of sound is performed here. The bassoon, most notably in the opening movement, is often discussed in terms of an inversion effect—the register for the opening bars of the symphony are at the very upper range of the instrument. So, literally, an instrument usually played in the masculine/low range is played high. Critics repeatedly discuss, in addition, the "inversion of chords," and the Augurs chord itself, notoriously hard to define, is discussed as an inversion of a chord. Daniel Chua writes: "In other words, the chord is 'upside down,' requiring some kind of topsy-turvy tonal theory. This is not as bizarre as it may sound. From the perspective of harmonic dualism, for example, such 'topsy-turvy' thinking is quite possible; thus David Lewin can analyse the 'E minor triad' in the opening bassoon melody of the Rite as an inverted structure."[26]

The strings and the percussion switch places so that the strings back up the percussive sound of *The Rite*; that the conflict, the rhythm, the clashing noise of cymbals and drums make up the foreground; and that the repetitive "motto chord" (63) eludes definition and becomes polytonal and was heard as a mess of "wrong notes" (75). Chua again: "Tonal noise is a modernist critique of official culture; instead of employing unpitched instruments to signify the pagan world, Stravinsky has turned the agent of musical civility into a barbaric thud, reducing tonality to its very opposite; and to underline the point, the strings, which Stravinsky regarded as 'representative of the human voice,' are transformed from their expressive role within the nineteenth-century orchestra into a battery of percussion instruments" (77). Finally, the piece as a whole, musically and in terms of its choreography, proceeds according to a queer temporality—it "evolves creatively," to use a Bergsonian term, and its chords do not so much progress and then resolve so much as pile on top of each other and overlap. The only way for the melodies to resolve is for them to end, to cease abruptly, as they do at the end of the whole work.

The queerness of *The Rite*, then, is better located in its inverted sounds, its ugly dance steps, and its orientation to wild disorder and death.[27] This queer reading of *The Rite* works well with Lee Edelman's connection between queerness and the death drive and Leo Bersani's understanding of queerness as an investment not in community and togetherness, but in self-shattering and unraveling. These psychoanalytic readings of the anti-reproductive force of queerness certainly find expression in the narrative, the music, and the choreography of *The Rite of Spring*, but what we want to identify as wild also exceeds a psychoanalytic reading given that it seems to eschew the human body and express a set of desires that surround the body rather than flow through it.

Adorno, famously, read Stravinsky's music against Schoenberg's (whose he favored), and he commented of Stravinsky: "His music knows nothing of memory and thus nothing of any temporal continuity of duration."[28] What looped and repeated was heard as simplistic and stuck in the eternal present of childhood; what refused to progress was heard as regressive; what shocked was heard as devoid of modern "anxiety." For Adorno, Stravinsky catered to the popular, sacrificed complexity to rhythm and beat, lacked authenticity, and masqueraded as rebellious but ultimately sounded the call of blind conformism. In fact, Stravinsky's music shocked precisely because it refused progression altogether and definitely refuted the fantasy of progression that fuels our notions of childish repetition and supports our fantasies of adulthood as achievement. This resistance to a colonial order of advancement over and against a primitive set of practices, peoples, and terrains certainly makes up what we recognize as the primitivism of *The Rite of Spring*, but it also codes into the whole piece an anticolonial disorder that resisted the representation of the modern as that which follows some primitive state of being, and it locates horror, violence, sacrifice, and wildness at the very heart of modernity.

What is the modern savagery that *The Rite* depicts and describes? What contemporary forms of violence and sacrifice does it conjure and even predict, and in what ways does *The Rite* associate new forms of violence with capitalism, heteronormativity, and a colonial willingness to sacrifice the other for the sake of the self. Together, Stravinsky and Nijinsky sonically and physically conjure the barbarity of their moment—a time when the weak must be sacrificed to the strong, the ancient gives way to the modern, the animal to the human, and social complexity itself must be rendered plain by the withering forces of science, conquest, philosophy, and aesthetics. The music, the choreography, and the reference to a lost world of pagan rituals all point to the frenzied pace of change in the early twentieth century, the sense of loss and sacrifice that such a pace inspires, and the desire to find markers of hope in relation to the new and figures of blame in relation to the old.

This said, *The Rite of Spring* does not exist. The attempts to re-create it are all exercises in surrogation, and their failures emphasize the lostness of the ballet, the irretrievability of the past, the unknowability of the future. The lostness of the ballet is captured by the phenomenal essay that Jacques Rivière penned after witnessing the performance. He summarized the dancers in *The Rite of Spring* and the movement that courses through them as follows: "Like animals tirelessly pacing in their cages and coming up to touch the bars with their foreheads, they carry it around with themselves, without understanding it. These beings have no other organ but their entire organism. With it they seek; they move, here, there, stop; they hurl themselves like a wave and wait . . . there is nothing that has preceded their existence, nothing that must overtake; no ideal to recover. If we stay with them, we have already gone the whole way."[29] *The Rite of Spring* is not a ballet, not a symphony; it is a wild movement of sound and limbs, the queerness of jangling nerves, the cacophony of colonial encounters; wildness is dance as a broken and awkward stance, a jump into oblivion, an animal in its pen—it is the wild and the tame and all the creatures in between. We stay with them, we fall to earth, we must always go all the way.

Exhaustion

The Rite of Spring has entered history as more than a score, a symphony, or a ballet. It has gone down in history as an event.[30] The specific event, of course, was the Parisian performance at which everyone, even those like Gertrude Stein who missed it, claimed to have been present and which, retrospectively, has been written into the history of modernism as a "riot." If it was a riot, in any case, it was a bourgeois riot of sensibility and not a riot of the masses against the elites. The outrage provoked by the Parisian performance of *The Rite of Spring* in 1913 has been attributed to many factors, some of which we have considered here, but others include a sense of violated form in the choreography, the awkwardness of the stances of the maidens with their turned-in toes, and the constant jumping of the young men who often bounced in place rather than leaping gracefully across the stage. Millicent Hodson, indeed, notes that the jumping in the ballet was incredibly difficult for the dancers, and some reported that the physicality required along with the mathematical precision made some parts of the choreography almost undanceable. And, of course, Nijinsky references this impossibility in the final solo performance of the Chosen One, in which the young virgin who is to be ritually sacrificed literally dances herself to death. The physical rigor of Nijinsky's choreography was brought to the fore by Pina Bausch's version of it, and in a production of Bausch's *Rite* at BAM in Brooklyn in 2017, the performers highlighted the exhaustion that the performance demands as they sweated and grunted, panted, and fell apart violently and exquisitely.

The exhaustion that the ballet inflicts upon its dancers echoes the theme of exhaustion that the fertility rite itself implies. Indeed, by the beginning of the twentieth century, one of the problems that blew in on a storm of modern anxiety was that of a fear of degeneration and, its twinned concern, extinction. By 1940, that connection was cemented in the Disney animated film *Fantasia*, when Walt Disney used *The Rite of Spring* as a soundtrack for the sequence on the extinction of the dinosaurs. This section of the animated film captured the horror at the heart of the music in terms of the obliteration of worlds. The film invested in a survival of the fittest cycle within which dinosaurs do battle and only the strong survive within an evolutionary and then degenerating cycle. Disney, in the late 1930s, was still considered a visionary and had not yet been pegged as a Nazi sympathizer or as anti-Semitic, but *Fantasia*'s dinosaur chapter certainly hinted at a world view within which a primitive past dies making way for new life. Disney's musical collaborator on *Fantasia*, the famous conductor Leopold Stokowski, compared Disney to Diaghilev in terms of his ability to bring artists together to produce new work,[31] and he praised Disney for seeing the potential in Stravinsky's score. And while Disney was able to capture one interpretation of *The Rite of Spring*'s orientation toward death and extinction, it is also possible to read another narrative of disappearance into this ballet, for Stravinsky claimed early on in his career (and later denied) that he had been inspired in writing *The Rite of Spring* by folk music of Russia. The dark episode of *Fantasia*, where dinosaurs fight to the death to the score of what should be a fertility ritual, links the violence of the modern to the extinction enacted against traditional societies and tribal cultures within a colonial context. The dance of the dinosaurs in *Fantasia*, indeed, positions the dinosaurs as a stand-in for the Native peoples represented in the ballet, and it naturalizes their decline by making it seem as if Native peoples, like the dinosaurs, are destroyed by a natural disaster rather than by colonial violence. Here Disney merges scientific notions of primitive life with more modernist narratives about Indigenous peoples and collapses these very different discourses about extinction.

The animation set to *The Rite of Spring* in *Fantasia* is noticeably different from that of other pieces in the film—unlike the clear and Technicolor of such sequences as "The Sorcerer's Apprentice," the images in the dinosaur sequence are jagged and blurry but also deeply atmospheric. The menacing atmosphere of the piece as a whole is captured both by the primordial terror inspired by the *Tyrannosaurus rex*—clearly representing both colonial terror and fantasized primeval savagery—but also by the sense of a dance of death within which all of nature participates. The dinosaurs, because they are extinct, represent the end of the world or the end of *a* world, an ending that in 1940 seemed highly probable in relation to Indigenous peoples and that now looks weirdly prescient given the genocidal missions to come. Indeed, we could say that *The Rite of Spring* provides a soundtrack for modern expressions of colonial violence, for the responses to wildness expressed by Conrad in *Heart of Darkness* and by Roger Casement in his *Black Diaries*. The colonial violence enacted in the Americas, South Africa, the Congo, and elsewhere that eradicated Native peoples through genocidal settlement missions, the violence enacted against peasants across Russia, and the violence to come in the form of fascist racial cleansing projects meet in this strange dance of death. This then is the cacophony that enchants, estranges, seduces, and repels its Parisian audiences in 1913 in *The Rite of Spring*. *Fantasia* brings to the surface what lurks in the background in the ballet—the death not just of the maiden, but of the Indian, the Native other, and in the death of the Native the ballet projects a fear of the inevitable death of the European.

Stravinsky, casting the rural Russian peasant as a surrogate for many other Native peoples whose worlds were being decimated by the march of the modern, brought his modern Parisian audience to its feet by confronting them with the noise of colonial violence, a violence at work in the casting of the other as childish, deviant, animal-like, and backward. While the rationality of bureaucratic rule, of governance, and of the harsh imposition of so-called order on peoples around the world sought to represent itself as right and good and true, the deviants, the natives, the rural peoples against whom this cultural war was waged raised a cacophonous noise in response. Whether the Parisian audience who tried to drown the wailing noise of the high bassoon, the percussion-heavy symphony, and the screeching violins wanted to obliterate the noise of its own murderous impulses or whether it could not stand to witness the broken gestures, the crooked stances, and the wild leaps of the target of its violence is anyone's guess, but what is beyond doubt is that *The Rite of Spring* captures the cacophony of that clash and draws out its wildness.

The jarring quality of the musical score itself, its foregrounding of percussion and rhythm, may have been off-putting to the original Parisian audience, but of course it did not prevent Stravinsky's symphony from becoming one of the most popular pieces of music of the twentieth century. It has influenced many different kinds of music, including, most notably, jazz, and strains of Stravinsky's score can be found in a range of jazz pieces, including Alice Coltrane's "Eternity" (1976) and Ornette Coleman's "Sleep Talking" (2005).

And while the music for *The Rite of Spring* lives on through many different genres of contemporary music, Nijinsky's choreography has all but disappeared, like the dinosaurs. So, what did the audiences in 1913 see in Nijinsky's ballet that created such outrage that the music was drowned out by boos and catcalls? In a perceptive essay, "Racism at *The Rite*," an account of that first performance which is quite different from many other breathless accounts of the newness of the piece, Tamara Levitz makes it quite clear why she believes the ballet provoked a riot. She comments: "A detailed analysis of the soundscape at the premiere reveals that the ballet did not incite an angry riot because of its newness, as Gergiev and the musical establishment have come to believe, but rather provoked a xenophobic response from critics who associated the ballet with cultural practices of colonized people of color they considered racially inferior to themselves, and who reproduced everyday racist discourse about those peoples in their reviews."[32] Levitz pored over the eyewitness accounts of what happened in the Théâtre des Champs-Élysées that night and accounts for the different groups in the audience from different parts of Paris, for the critics, for the foreigners present, and notes that the reviews focus on movements that gave rise to disgusted responses. Those movements include, as she writes: "the stamping . . . frenzy . . . puppet-like movements . . . automaticity, trembling, jerky gestures, vibrating, and shuddering" (149). All of these movements, of course, have made their way into subsequent productions of *The Rite* and make up a dissonant choreography that breaks with the graceful flow of traditional ballet and is received by the critics as 'primitive' forms of movement. Levitz proposes as much and writes that "the dancers' noisy movements unsettled their notion of Western ballet, causing them to perceive *The Rite* as unbeautiful, uncivilized, and consequently—from their racially informed perspective— as created by non-Europeans lesser than themselves" (152). The audience, one is tempted to propose, found the ballet to be wild and attributed its wildness to the intrusion of primitive dance forms that lurked in the folk rhythms selected by Stravinsky and to the narrative of an ancient ritual of sacrifice that the ballet repurposed. Diaghilev made clear this pagan origin of the story, and in publicity for the *Rite*, Levitz reminds us, he described the ballet as evocative of "the first gestures of Pagan Russia" (153). And the critics, Levitz continues, understood the ballet to have erred in privileging the primitive and in foregrounding colonial spectacles that many associated with, in her words, "the Aissawas in Algiers and Tangiers, and Native Americans elsewhere" (154). One critic, Pierre Lalo, identified source material for *The Rite* with "the spectacle of choreographic exercises" associated with "various Eskimo, Fuegian and Maori peoples," which, according to him, reappeared in *The Rite* but in a more "barbaric" and "more shapeless form."[33] Stravinsky's music, meanwhile, was often compared to animalistic noise and connected to African American jazz as a way of diminishing its artfulness.

Levitz's reading of *The Rite* is an important reminder that the so-called riot it provoked was born of bourgeois sensibilities that, when confronted with the sounds of implicitly Black (jazz) and Native aesthetics, responded with shock and outrage. Like Adorno, the audience at the ballet felt insulted by the combination of dissonance and supposedly immature noisemaking and responded accordingly. Of course, since then, the ballet and the symphony have become comfortably situated at the heart of Western culture, and this moment of ragged and wild aesthetic disruption has been safely incorporated into European nostalgia for high cultural opposition to a burgeoning culture industry. And so we cannot find the disruptive element of *The Rite of Spring* any longer in performances of either the music or the ballet; rather, it is the legacy of aesthetic wildness that *The Rite* leaves in its wake that remains interesting—a legacy that is both queer, given the collaborative activity that gave birth to it, and decolonial, given the conditions of its rejection in 1913. The legacy, indeed, can be traced by moving away from the iconic text that sounded the alarm on other forms of aesthetic rupture and toward a cacophony that Chickasaw scholar Jodi Byrd argues is both part of certain Native epistemologies and that constitutes the babble of colonial discourse on Native others.[34] What I want to call bewilderment in what follows is an aesthetic operation in which the colonial absorption of so-called primitive texts, as we saw in the case of *The Rite*, fails to quiet the unruly productions of decolonial noise. Instead, as happened in Paris in 1913, the text becomes bewildering to its intended viewers and useful to its decolonizing heirs. It becomes, in other words, part of the failure of modernity.

Bewilderment

Thus far I have proposed that wildness is easily recognizable as part of a colonial epistemology within which colonizers cast nonmetropolitan spaces and people as savage, wild, and in need of cultivation. Wildness, as Michael Taussig offers, is both the glow of a projected vision of the other used by colonizers and an actual description of other ways of situating bodies in relation to drugs, spirituality, and quests for knowledge. And, as a text like *The Rite* makes all too clear, Western modernisms have incorporated the echoes of Indigenous forms of the life that they have destroyed or eliminated, often as a chorus to their own master texts. The impact of this mode of incorporation, when it fails, as we saw in relation to both Conrad and Casement, is one of bewilderment.

Bewilderment holds the wild within it; emerges out of precolonial notions of space, orientation, and navigation; and refers to an immersive sense of being lost or of standing outside of a system of knowing or of merging with other systems of space and time that linger in the background to those we have selected as meaningful in the contemporary world. Bewilderment probably shares in the kind of magical/delightful/scary forms of unknowing that we also associate with enchantment/bafflement/confusion and that emerge in work by authors like Taussig and Bennett as an alternative set of relations to magic, healing, and knowing. Indeed, bewilderment suggests a becoming that moves in an opposite direction to colonial knowing. And while the definition of bewilderment that tethers it to geography is useful, it cannot explain the bewildering impact of a text like *The Rite*.

In its early uses, *bewilderment* was indeed a term connected to navigation. Samuel Johnson is credited with the following eighteenth-century definition of the word: "to lose in pathless places, to confound for want of a plain road."[35] The first uses of the word, according to the *Oxford English Dictionary*, can be traced back to 1613. The *OED* defines "bewilderment" in connection to the verb "wilder": "to lead one astray, (reflexive) to stray, to wander."[36] As with Johnson's definition, also listed in the *OED*, the word combines a disorientation to space with a wandering movement free of any destination and a form of unknowing created when no "plain road" exists. Given the colonial preoccupation with roads, mapping, navigation, and so on, and given the history of colonial notions of freedom that connect to mobility,[37] the concept of bewilderment, which can also join to synonyms like amazement (originally meaning lost in a maze) and astonishment (originally meaning knocked out by a stone), clearly leads in the opposite direction, into the woods rather than out of them. It also reminds us that three or four hundred years ago travelers regularly experienced being lost (in mazes, no less; and, apparently, they were regularly hit in the head by stones). States of bewilderment therefore might have been cultivated and inhabited more easily. Nowadays we understand bewilderment as an impediment to knowledge and power. From a decolonial perspective, however, and with an anti-Enlightenment intent, we might find artists and thinkers who want to re-wild life, re-think nature, and reintroduce bewilderment. But these geographical descriptions of the term remain neutral in relation to the positionalities of those who are bewildered by certain terrains and texts and others who are not. Bewilderment, as an aesthetic strategy, indicates the presence of much larger aesthetic frames.

Poet Fanny Howe, in a beautiful essay titled "Bewilderment," describes the term as naming both a "poetics and an ethics."[38] For her, bewilderment ensues when characters in her novels confront impossibly contradictory situations that alert them to the complexity of life. These situations cannot be resolved, narratively or poetically, and so lead to a state of bewilderment. Howe writes: "In the Dictionary, to bewilder is 'to cause to lose one's sense of where one is.'" And she continues: "The wilderness as metaphor is in this case not evocative enough because causing a complete failure in the magnet, the compass, the scale, the stars and the movement of the rivers is more than getting lost in the woods. Bewilderment is an enchantment that follows a complete collapse of reference and reconcilability."[39] Making bewilderment into a state of being that exceeds the simple fact of disorientation in relation to space, Howe locates bewilderment, much as Taussig did and as Conrad did before him, as a relation to language itself. Within a magical or "enchanted" process, language and experience simply fail to connect, creating a "complete collapse of reference." This collapse, as Taussig's experiences in the Amazon attest, opens up new epistemological frames—the magical, the spiritual, the vegetal—even as it continues to frame the land in settler colonial terms.

Howe, finally, locates bewilderment as an altered relation to the ordinary, which she terms "an explosion of parts, the quotidian smeared."[40] This smudging of the ordinary is evocative of both an epistemology within which the settled becomes disturbing and terrain remains wild. Bewilderment is most often associated with woods and getting lost, but, of course, the woods are not a neutral space, equally welcoming or scary to all. While the woods have been conventionally a place where women should not go alone, they are also replete with racial terror. Poet Fred Moten, in *The Feel Trio* (2014), describes multiple scenes of racial terror that play out in unforgiving landscapes and counters them with images of fugitivity. Moten writes: "I ran from it and was still in it."[41] This construction whereby escape cannot deliver the racialized subject to freedom, however ("I . . . was still in it"), does not imply the totality of capture. Running is important in Moten's poetic universe, arrival less so. And as for Howe, the relationship to freedom, fugitivity, and capture are all also relations to language and naming.

We understand from Moten's haunting scenes of fugitivity that, for some, the woods may be dark and deep, but they are not always lovely. In the racialized landscape of North America, the woods have harbored the dark secrets of lynching and therefore still cannot represent refuge for many African Americans. In a haunting essay titled "Ecomelancholia: Slavery, War, and Black Ecological Imaginings" (2011), scholar Jennifer James argues that slavery and racial terror have, as she puts it, "attenuated African Americans' connection to nature."[42] Recognizing that the relation to wilderness is fraught for Native Americans and African Americans, who have both been identified with the wild and punished there, James offers an understanding of racism that is terrain-based, geographic—racial zoning, in her terms. Describing the African American relation to the natural world as "dangerously broken" (174), James lists the multiple sources of trouble that lurk outside of urban areas, including the KKK, the memory of slavery, plantations, and so on. "Ecomelancholia," accordingly, names an irresolvable relation to the so-called natural world that cannot be repressed or resolved.

As we can hear in this discussion of bewilderment, the figures of Blackness and of indigeneity haunt all discussions of wildness and wilderness. In Conrad's *Heart of Darkness*, for example, he turns the wilderness into a character that is, by turns, "patient,"[43] "mysterious" (7), "God-forsaken" (19), and "silent" (36) and then locates its embodiment in the spectacle of the "wild and gorgeous" (101) woman. This woman, he writes, "was "savage and superb, wild-eyed and magnificent" and is identified with "the wilderness itself" (101). This startling and telling figure of wilderness in the center of one of European modernism's most iconic texts demands an answer to a haunting question asked by Byrd, namely, "What is the wild to the American Indian?"[44] The Native fuses with wildness, and in this case wilderness, in a way that forces us to ask whether those who represent or stand in for the wild can also claim it.

One answer to this question lies in relation to what Byrd calls an "indigenous critique of colonialism."[45] Like Taussig, Byrd describes a mirroring relation between settler colonial discourses and the epistemologies they come to destroy. And, so, Byrd uses the notion of "cacophonies of colonialism" (xxvii) to describe the contradictory materials levied by colonial masters against other civilizations in the form of the Native peoples they are about to conquer. Colonialism, for Byrd, is a violent clash of cultures, systems, and peoples that "creates shockwaves that ripple outward from the collision in time, space and popular culture" (xxvii). While some of these shockwaves result in the babble of anthropological and orientalist literatures that summon Native peoples as barbaric, primitive, and culturally backward, others emerge in the form of an "indigenous critical theory" (xxx) that "helps to identify the processes that have kept indigenous peoples as a necessary pre-conditional presence within theories of colonialism" (xxxiv). Noting that the Indian inevitably appears in colonial productions as dead, past, inert, and savage—or, we might add in reference to *The Rite*, as a clumsy and disjunctive fragment of a world gone by—Byrd uses the metaphor of cacophony—an apt metaphor for various forms of wildness summoned in *The Rite of Spring*—and the Choctaw word *haksuba* (xxvii) to summon the swirling noise and chaos of the colonial encounter. While the colonial narrative wants to smooth out the dissonance of cacophonous encounters by vertically projecting violence, noise, and savagery onto the other and claiming a rational certitude for itself, Byrd makes cacophony into a horizontal landscape of cultural collision. And so, what the colonizer cannot understand, what he is bewildered by, becomes the source of chaos and noise and represents a chaotic world of ungovernable peoples—exactly the mise-en-scène of *The Rite*. But by the same token, peoples who fear conquest, and who seek to be and to become ungovernable, might anchor the noise that represents them or the silence or the brutality to their own aesthetic projects.

Failure of Modernity

In 2008, Kent Monkman, a queer Canadian, Swampy Kree, two-spirit artist, offered a response to a George Catlin painting titled *Dance to the Berdashe-Saukie* (1891). It is unnecessary to go into the many levels at which this painting misinterpreted two-spirit bodies in Native cultures; what is much more interesting is Monkman's re-creation of the dance in his own installation titled *Dance to the Berdashe* and installed as a five-channel video at the Montreal Museum of Fine Art. On his website, the dance is described as a "Monkmanian version of this scene, displayed on five screens in the shape of buffalo hides." With the hides as screens, the viewer would see Monkman's performance alter ego, Miss Chief Eagle Testickle, dancing the role of the berdashe in a sly re-creation of Catlin's painting. "The choreography," we are told, was "created by Canadian Cree actor, choreographer and dancer Michael Greyeyes" and "is based on both the traditional powwow and contemporary dance." Finally, the description of the piece on the website informs the reader that "The music, written by Toronto composer Phil Strong, is a free syncopated version of Stravinsky's *Rite of Spring*, a modern masterpiece also inspired by ancient tribal rituals."[46]

In taking back this dance from Catlin's colonialist interpretation and setting the dance of the berdashe to *The Rite of Spring*, Monkman deploys a decolonial strategy of fighting fire with fire, noise with noise, cacophony with cacophony, riot with upheaval. He also places himself squarely within the ballet as its principal dancer—Monkman occupies the role, most obviously, of the Chosen One, the maiden who must be sacrificed in the ballet and the berdashe figure, who in Catlin's racist painting, stands in the place of an anticivilizational ethos. Monkman cites Catlin's diaries in justifying his re-creation of the painting, noting that Catlin viewed the dance with the gender-ambiguous figure as "one of the most unaccountable and disgusting customs that I have ever met in Indian country."[47] He continued: "I should wish that it might be extinguished before it be more fully recorded." In this gesture, Catlin unwittingly records the very dance he hoped to extinguish, he expresses disgust at the spectacle he sits down to paint, he moves toward the source of his own repulsion. Monkman counters this colonial sequence of parry and thrust with his own dance, a dance that rhymes with Moten's formulation—"I ran from it and was still in it." Monkman takes the source of colonial bewilderment, joins it to the ambiguous and ambivalent text of *The Rite of Spring* and renders the queer decolonial as "the quotidian smeared."

In his enormous archive of work—encompassing massive paintings, performances, installations, and lectures—Monkman takes significant moments in Western art history and repaints or re-performs them with reference to the obliteration of Native peoples. In an interview with Lucy Lippard for the catalog that accompanied his 2016 show *Failure of Modernity*, Monkman equates modernity with "a culture of deliberate or willful amnesia" and tells Lippard that he incorporates pieces of modernist culture into his work because that period of cultural production ran concurrently with "the most aggressive and most devastating period of time for First Nations people."[48] And while this has the effect of making modernist art secondary to the primary texts of Native cultural production, his use of *The Rite of Spring* in the critique of Catlin is a little different. Rather than subsuming *The Rite of Spring* or just making it continuous with anti-Indigenous representational practices, Monkman uses the music for his own performance of bewilderment, gender-ambiguous anti-colonial choreography, and more.

Monkman, when not performing in drag as Miss Chief Eagle Testickle, paints massive oil canvases of the "wild west" where "Indians" chase cowboys across the landscape on a quest for homoerotic encounters rather than violent battle and where the terms of conquest are often reversed. His paintings, cheeky send-ups of "wild west" landscape paintings by Charles M. Russell (1864–1926), George Catlin (1796–1872), Albert Bierstadt (1830–1902), and others from the turn of the last century, combine camp and cacophony to produce a counternarrative of conquest. Monkman's paintings, like some of the music and choreographies discussed here, represent a wild aesthetic, cacophonous and straining the boundaries of genre and history. In one painting titled *The Scream* (2017), for example, a work that appeared in the show titled *Shame and Prejudice: A Story of Resilience*, Monkman paints a tableau in which red-coated Canadian soldiers and priests and nuns in black smocks tear infants from their mothers' arms. The scene is modern rather than historic, with all figures in modern dress, and the implication is that the devastation of Native families continues in the present rather than being an "unfortunate" episode from the past. At the same time, a variety of birds swoop down upon the soldiers and priests and protest with the Indigenous mothers against the outrages committed here. In the center of the canvas, two soldiers restrain a mother as a priest carries away her child. The mother's mouth is open, and her scream, we understand, *is* the painting. Any painting that titles itself *The Scream* obviously references Edvard Munch's classic image from 1893. Munch's painting has, much like *The Rite*, become central to understandings of modernist encounters with "the horror" of contemporary life. The ambiguously gendered figure in Munch's *The Scream*, has his hands on his ears and conveys flesh as a conduit for total confusion and devastation. The background of the painting echoes the figure's confusion, and a swirl of abstract color conveys noise and liquid pain. By contrast, Monkman refuses the abstraction of screaming and depicts the mothers' screams as outraged response to colonial theft. The paint-

Figure 2.1   Kent Monkman, *The Scream*, 2017. Acrylic on canvas, 84 × 126 inches. Image courtesy of the artist.

ing constitutes a decolonial, musical rejoinder to the destruction of Indigenous futures that the painting implies as much as it answers visually to Munch's screaming homunculus.

Monkman's scream can be read through modernist painting, on the one hand, and through jazz, on the other. Abbey Lincoln's long-drawn-out scream in the middle section of her collaboration with Max Roach on the triptych "Prayer/Protest/Peace," from the album *We Insist* (1960), registers for Fred Moten as the sound of Black pain and protest and as Black music itself. "Where speech turns shriek turns song," he writes, we hear a history all at once of Black radicalism, Black pain, refusal, outrage, an aesthetics made up of all that has been pushed to the margins of white modernism; we hear jazz, improvised noise; we hear wildness.[49]

The verticality of Munch's *The Scream* is countered in Monkman's painting by a horizontal field of action. And while Munch offers one figure as iconic of the experience of modern havoc, Monkman offers multiple mothers, many soldiers, several religious figures, and many children. The far horizon of the painting features three children running out of the frame, their backs turned

CHAPTER TWO

to this scene of brutality, their destination unclear, but the horizon beckons. The chaotic spectacle of struggle that the painting as a whole depicts is precisely bewildering in its busyness and in the multiple locations of encounter. Bewilderment as a decolonial strategy in this painting, and in all of Monkman's work, resonates with Byrd's spatialized understanding of the colonial encounter within a horizontal landscape. Her point is that all forms of chaos and cacophony are not alike, and while colonial chaos, which Ann Laura Stoler describes in *Along the Archival Grain* as part anxiety and part "disabled histories," is disbursed through violent acts and massive bureaucracies alike, Indigenous cacophony might be the noise of multiplicity, the sound of contesting histories and traditions, and the visions of other worlds that some believe exist alongside the one in which we are currently stranded.[50] This horizontality is an important aspect of wildness and of the Indigenous confrontation with colonial rule. Horizontality eschews the hierarchies installed by vertical models, and it puts everything on the same plane to compete for dominance or access. The impact of horizontality becomes clear visually in Monkman's canvases.

Bewilderment, we will recall, in its archaic usage meant being led into the woods and left there—be-wild-erment—both a transformation from tamed to free, from found to lost, from belonging to abandonment, and from knowing to confused. But for Monkman, bewilderment resides within the mastering of and restaging of Western art. In many of Monkman's paintings we see key scenes from Canadian colonial encounters painted along a horizontal axis in oil and with mimetic precision. A work from 2016, for example, titled humorously *The Daddies* and based on Robert Harris's 1883 commissioned portrait of twenty-three of the so-called Fathers of the Confederation, perfectly renders the lineup of the original painting, but in the foreground where, in the original, there was only an empty stool, Monkman adds his alter ego, Miss Chief Eagle Testickle. With all eyes on her naked figure, the trans* feminine, two-spirit Indigenous subject holds court, mouth open to address (scream at?) the room, hand raised for emphasis, and hir muscular body seated on a stool covered in a Hudson trading blanket. The original painting was lost a hundred years earlier when it burned in a fire, and so this work, coming exactly one hundred years later and situated in relation to the festivities for Canada's 150-year birthday, was actually a copy of a copy. The copy of a copy recalls perfectly Judith Butler's foundational definition of modern gender and applies the concept of performativity precisely to those subjects considered to be irrefutably original (Native peoples) and irretrievably lost (part of an earlier more primitive world). In Monkman's mirrors held up to nature, nature itself recedes from view and is replaced by a trickster aesthetic that both introduces chaos into the orderly images of rule and imagines new forms of rule in the disorderly figures of Indigenous rebellion and knowledge.

In another painting (which I have written about elsewhere), *Seeing Red* (2014), Monkman, again using a horizontal axis, and again incorporating iconic images from Western art, captures the aftermath of a riot.[51] Using a horizontal grid, imagery jostles for attention, and contemporary quotidian signs, like shoes hanging on an overhead wire, sit alongside ornamentation from eras past—like an angel but also a totem pole. And at ground level, a colonial figure lies prone on the ground, potentially dead. This is no ordinary figure, however; it is Edouard Manet's "dead toreador" from his 1864 painting of the same name. So thorough is Monkman's knowledge of modernist Western art, moreover, that he does not simply take the toreador and repaint him on his own canvas; he also refers to the original form of the painting. Manet's toreador, in fact, originally appeared in a larger work titled *Incident in the Bull Ring* that also featured the bull. Dissatisfied with the painting, Manet cut the piece in two and named one *The Bullfight* and the other *Dead Toreador*. The *Dead Toreador* comprised the lower half of a painting arranged vertically with the other bullfighters at the top of the frame and the bull in the center between the living and the dead toreador. By taking this painting and its historical context and placing it now within a horizontal frame where the bull reappears, wounded but alive, and a Native toreador, Miss Chief Eagle Testickle herself, positions herself "on top," as June Scudeler puts it in an essay on Monkman's "sovereign erotics,"[52] and controls the entire scene, Monkman reimagines the hierarchical ordering of animal, human, primitive, cultured, heavenly, earthly, life, and death. In *Seeing Red* a cacophony of symbols—fire, helicopter, healer, death dealer, Picasso, Monkman, police, warriors, feathers, blankets, spears, bulls, heels, nonbinary bodies, graffiti—compete with one another with no single regime of truth unifying the scene. To see red, Monkman implies, is to see above and below and around the world and history as painted, narrated, and imagined by Western art; it is to offer bewilderment in place of knowing and true riot in place of the fake riot that greeted *The Rite of Spring* and other avant-garde texts brimming with cultural appropriation.

Quite obviously, Monkman is not, in any simple way, directly responding to a text like *The Rite of Spring*. But then again, he is not *not* responding to the incomplete incorporation of Indigenous texts that this text represents and that stands in for all kinds of appropriative gestures in modern art. The version of representation that swirls beneath the surface of *The Rite*, that screams from music and that emerges through the open mouths of Monkman's mothers and the fires in *Seeing Red* is what Macarena Gómez-Barris calls "sub-

Figure 2.2   Kent Monkman, *Seeing Red*, 2014. Acrylic on canvas, 84 × 126 inches. Image courtesy of the artist.

merged perspectives," those modes of seeing and knowing that emerge in "the extractive zone" and through which something we recognize as "the environment" speaks.[53] Monkman's paintings, in other words, respond to the world created by and incompletely critiqued within *The Rite*, and his visual universe offers another world, a competing world, seething with the imagery that settler representations must repress. His painting *Cain and Abel* (2017), for example, features two nude transmasculine bodies engaged in epic combat as a female figure, reminiscent of John Gast's allegorical figure of *American Progress*, halfheartedly strives to intercede. In the background, scenes of despair, rape, and plunder both reference and upend gender and racial conventions of conquest and white settlement. The story of Cain and Abel, of course, represents more than sibling rivalry. The brothers represented not only dynamics of family drama but also contrasting relationships to the land: Abel, in the biblical myth, was a shepherd, while Cain was a farmer. In Monkman's hands, the brothers are locked in a mortal conflict that continues to haunt modernity and that marks its failure: that of settlers versus nomads, owners versus temporary residents, people who stay put and seek to extract value from the land versus

Figure 2.3 Kent Monkman, *Cain and Abel*, 2017. Acrylic on canvas, 48 × 72 inches. Image courtesy of the artist.

people who move around and see the land as a resource, not capital. Abel, the nomadic sheep herder falls at the hands of his brother and becomes the first martyr for wildness, the first victim of civilization. The fact that the bodies of Cain and Abel in the painting are transgender or two-spirited, with male torsos and female genitalia, suggests that different relations to the body, to gender, and to reproduction also are at stake in the conflict. Their "inversion" echoes some of the inverted cords that create disharmony in *The Rite*. As the bodies of cowboys are tossed aside by Indians in the backdrop, the painting offers to reverse the terms of civilization and wildness, turning the former into a lost cause and the latter into the future whose time has come. Monkman's work here and in hundreds of massive, bright canvases does nothing short of repainting the world, the wild, and everything in it.

CHAPTER TWO

The Epistemology
of the Ferox

Sex, Death, and Falconry

Wild—(of an animal or plant) Living or growing in the
natural environment; not domesticated or cultivated.
> —*Oxford English Dictionary*

Go, said the bird, for the leaves were full of children,
Hidden excitedly, containing laughter.
Go, go, go, said the bird: human kind
Cannot bear very much reality.
Time past and time future
What might have been and what has been
Point to one end, which is always present.
> —T. S. Eliot, "Burnt Norton"

Fĕrox, fĕrōcis adj.—
Highspirited, dashing,
fiery, impetuous,
warlike, bold, wild
[Latin; cf. *fĕrus* wild,
untamed . . .].
> —*Oxford English Dictionary*

Wildness beckons and seduces, it promises extremes, and as we saw in the last chapter, it weaves a spell of bewilderment. It is an invitation to step outside of the ordinary and into a world shared with animals, oriented to predation and networked with nonhuman codes of interaction, flight, and resistance. So intensely alluring is this world of wild things, which limns our own, that some humans have longed to enter it not as visitors, but as part of it. The into-the-wild narratives I trace here, however, depart from the white male romance of masculine self-sufficiency and rugged individualism that was rendered hegemonic by Jack London and others.[1] Such narratives were always a part of masculinist colonial fantasies of conquest. The experience of becoming feral that I investigate in this chapter concerns intimate relations between queer humans and the wild birds that they try and fail to train and that embody a feral orientation to being that stubbornly resists domestication. Wildness, in the texts examined here, is an immersive experience mostly written about by lonely, unusual figures who hover on the edge of various definitions of perversity and who dream of a sexual world beyond the hetero-domestic. This world, populated by raptors bristling with sharp talons, razor-like beaks, and extraordinary range of vision, is a world where desire is an urgent hunger that must be appeased and sex constitutes a range of activities and sensitivities not well described by such terms as *sexual orientation*. The desire for wildness that we hear about in this chapter cannot be found in the catalogs of sexual identity produced by Freud or by Kraft-Ebing and Havelock Ellis before him, and it stands apart from the tidy homo/hetero binary we have used to explain and understand the organization of bodies at the turn of the last century. The desires here gathered under the heading of the *ferox* merge with other partial and contradictory formations (a desire for flogging and cuddling, rapacious greed and care, pedophilic fantasies, predatory practices, and deep, often erotic, regard for the child). These desires are not nice or right, good or true; they are feral and unbound; they long to fly.

Becoming Hawk

"A peregrine, fears nothing he can see clearly and far off. Approach him across open ground with a steady unfaltering movement."[2] So cautions J. A. Baker in his 1967 classic, *The Peregrine*. Baker offers this advice to all those who would track, follow, and seek out wild birds. He continues: "Let your shape grow in size but do not alter its outline. Never hide yourself unless concealment is complete. Be alone. Shun the furtive oddity of man, cringe from the hostile eyes of farms. Learn to fear" (13). Be alone, do not hide, hold your shape, slip out of the role of fearless predator, attune yourself to the world without cover of other humans. With these injunctions, Baker offers wisdom not on how to train your falcon, but on how to become one. And through this longing for the life of the bird, and this instruction manual on what it is like to be a falcon, Baker enters the wild and slips into another understanding of self, one that "shuns the furtive oddity of man" (13) that never hides unless completely, that lives with fear. Baker goes in search of falcons (a female hawk) and tiercels (a male hawk) in order to lose himself in a form of life that is totally alien. He wants, in the process, to become strange to himself; he longs to denature his own sense of the human and at the same time shove human forms deep into the brutality of a natural world that exists without them. His quest is to recognize the alterity of the bird in every move it makes, to lose himself in the odd sensibilities that make up the being of the bird, and to pursue the question of what it might mean to become feral. Like the other loners and bird fanciers tracked in this chapter, Baker's obsession with wild and winged predators forces him to see the world differently and to recalibrate the meanings of sleep, hunger, need, death, and flight. These desires, as all-consuming as they become for the bird fanciers who indulge them, must be understood not as the displaced desires of closeted men, melancholic spinsters, and odd bachelors, but as part of an eccentric epistemology, a mode of embodiment in which subjects orient away from social training and toward the wild. This is an epistemology of the feral, or as I will term it here for reasons that will be revealed, an epistemology of the ferox.

The ferox or feral names an eccentric relation to desire, to becoming and unbecoming; it frames an orientation that turns away from the human and toward the animal; it offers approximate language for a wildness that exceeds human classification; the feral, indeed, is situated beyond human language and can be approximated only by using the grammars available for expressions of love, desire, and sex. Dianne Chisholm, in an essay on "biophilia" in the work of Ellen Meloy, tracks a similarly eco-erotic domain beyond the human and finds an ethnography of this domain in Meloy's work.[3] Engaging Meloy's accounts of her pursuit of bighorn sheep through "their seasonal cataclysms of rutting, lambing and survival canyoneering" (361), Chisholm notes the ways that Meloy is "stirred by the movements of the pack to a threshold of becoming other-than-human" (362), and she continues: "She desires to sense what the bighorn senses, to know the bighorn's world" (361). This desire for knowledge beyond the human is simultaneously sexual and ecological, tethered to a project of wanting to know how animals want to be in the world and thrumming erotically to the experiences, sexual and nonsexual, of other creatures in the wild. Chisholm meticulously records the emergence of other erotic orientations in Meloy's work and notes how often, in scientific writing, the erotic falls out of biological taxonomies or else becomes domesticated in relation to languages of wives and husbands. Not so in Meloy's work, where wildness, erotics, and knowing nestle against each other on behalf of a deeper relation to ecologically responsible practices. But not all relations to the wild use this alibi of ecological awareness. For some humans, wild animals, specifically wild birds and, more precisely, hawks, represent the bristling potential of a set of desires that have little to do with the homosexual/heterosexual binary that emerged as the twentieth century's most dominant classificatory axis for sexuality or ecological consciousness that spurs on contemporary forms of knowledge. And these desires for wildness hold within them a range of other similarly expunged topographies of sexual longing, bodily practices, and intensified sites of fantasy.

Eve Sedgwick refers, in *Epistemology of the Closet*, to the fertile and abandoned terrains that fall away in the wake of the homosexual/heterosexual binary and expresses amazement that "of the very many dimensions along which the genital activity of one person can be differentiated from that of another"—and here she includes preferences for certain acts, or physical types and sexological types, such as zoophiles, zooerasts, gynecomasts, and for child-love and autoeroticism—"precisely one, the gender of object choice, emerged from the turn of the century, and has remained as *the* dimension denoted by the now ubiquitous category of 'sexual orientation.'"[4] Given the centrifugal force generated on at least white bodies by the beginning of the twentieth century by a new and powerful epistemological system, one tethered furthermore to the new biopolitical regimes described by Foucault, it is understandable that multiple sexual practices and modes of identification would be streamlined into a singular model, but it is also highly plausible that not all bodies would be immediately pulled into compliance.

The desire to become feral, for a particular, and even peculiar, set of queerish writers in the early to the mid twentieth century was expressed in relation to hawks, both in terms of training them and in relation to *becoming hawk*. The sense that a form of wildness could be contracted through the bird and experienced vicariously or through a literal contact high is conveyed in the writings examined here, sometimes in terms of a lyrical excess, sometimes as a sadomasochistic relation between human and bird, often as a tethering to a nonhuman other who engages in a nonmutual, nonreciprocal, impermanent, and fleeting mode of communication. The kind of intimacy that the human-bird relation spawns—indeed, in all its violence, its discontinuity, and its lack of progress or internal coherence—is redolent of what Tim Morton has termed a "queer ecology," by which he means a broad network of relations and dependencies, a "mesh" in his terms, that links animals to humans and both to the landscape in nonessential ways.[5] But Morton also links queer ecology to what he calls "unfathomable intimacies" (280), a term that resonates with Sedgwick's sense of a multiverse of sexual desires that the homo/hetero binary replaces and, eventually, renders illegible. Morton describes these intimacies in terms of "pleasures that are not heteronormative, not genital, not geared to ideologies about where the body stops and starts" (280). Morton here dialogues with Catriona Mortimer-Sandilands and Bruce Erickson's formulation of queer ecologies, which they define in terms of the need "to probe the intersections of sex and nature with an eye to developing a sexual politics that more clearly includes considerations of the natural world and its biosocial constitution, and an environmental politics that demonstrates an understanding of the ways in which sexual relations organize and influence both the material world of nature and our perceptions, experiences, and constitutions of that world."[6] As in the work of Dianne Chisholm, clearly, Mortimer-Sandilands and Erickson lay out a clearly ethical project. But as is the way with so much in the orbit of the erotic, the ethical is not always of paramount concern. Wildness, we recall, after Foucault's formulation of nature, eschews the good for other metrics of value.

While the queer ecological concept of nonheteronormative and nongenital desires is fairly easy to grasp and imagine, ideologies about "where the body stops and starts" are more elusive, and morality, when it comes to wild birds, is pretty much off the table. Unlike Ellen Meloy's communion with animals in the desert—according to Chisholm, Meloy "desires to know what desert bighorn desire and to relay to her own species what might be done to aid its survival" (372)—the bird fanciers tracked herein just want proximity to the bird and harbor few illusions about saving it. J. A. Baker certainly experiences the world of hawks queerly and through the kind of porousness that Morton's term implies, his descriptions of the peregrine falcons he tracks betray a susceptibility to the nonhuman other that winnows down the barriers between his world and theirs and that requires extraordinary leaps of lyricism to capture. Baker does worry that the peregrines he tracks are endangered, but he articulates little in the way of a program for survival, and his attraction to the wild is born of other material.

If Sedgwick's epistemology emerged as a consequence of the increasingly open secret of homosexuality at the beginning of the twentieth century, the epistemology of the ferox recognizes a wider material purview within which knowing and, more importantly, unknowing take place. The closet, Sedgwick claims, provides a mechanism in the twentieth century by which homosexuality can be known precisely by remaining silent or inarticulate. Hence, the now-ubiquitous phrase coined in relation to Oscar Wilde with reference to a silenced homosexuality, namely, "the love that dare not speak its name," registers an epistemology within which something can be known simply on account of its status as unspeakable. The axis of speakable/unspeakable, like that of knowable/unknowable is, for Sedgwick, part of a structure of knowing determined in large part by ignorance and by that which cannot and indeed must not speak. So, what structures of knowing and unknowing attend differently to the sexual body in an epistemology of the ferox? In reading of deep and "unfathomable" intimacies between men, women, and birds of prey, we will discern structures that are less about discerning what you should and should not know and more about knowing that there are entire systems of knowing, signifying, and desiring that simply exceed the human. The desire of a bird for meat, for example, or the desires experienced by falconers within hunting, are just two instances of a set of desires and a form of knowledge that can be shared between human and bird but that rightly belong to the bird. As we proceed, we will have to decide whether the desires of the bird remain completely inaccessible or whether, in the companionship between human and bird, and in the currents of need that arc back and forth between falcon and falconer, an alien shape of desire otherwise can be discerned.

In *The Peregrine*, Baker does not simply share in the desires of the birds he follows; he experiences a kind of love for the birds and an identification with them that causes him to deeply desire to become hawk. His passion for wildness spills onto the page as a song to the birds he tracks, and the text is not just any song, but a veritable love song. Baker conveys his passion for the hawks through a poetic narrative of such intensity that often it fails to even locate the author in time and space and becomes a song without a singer, a call without a caller, a sensibility without a subject. Indeed, this love song, like all good love songs, sublimates the author to the beloved and brings *him* to the point of extinction: "Wherever he goes, this winter," Baker promises, "I will follow him. I will share the fear, and the exaltation, and the boredom, of the hunting life. I will follow him until my predatory human shape no longer darkens in terror the shaken kaleidoscope of colour that stains the deep fovea of his brilliant eye. My pagan head shall sink into the winter land and there be purified."[7] Baker here is the wife who pledges to follow the lover into darkness and through bleak periods of waiting as well as across the hard terrain of "a winter land." He is the beloved who is lost in the otherness of his object of desire; he is desiring in a mode that places him in a passive and not an active role.[8] But he is also the keen observer who looks back at the bird and sees, in this memorable phrase, "the shaken kaleidoscope of colour" in his eye. The breathless pledges to the bird, followed by this astonishing image, amount to love and locate that love in the restless motion of the hawk's gaze, the intensity of watching that precedes the strike or kill and that is part of single-minded pursuit of prey. Baker describes his hunt with and for the birds as a desire to dwell at the edge of things: "I have always longed to be part of the outward life, to be out there at the edge of things, to let the human taint wash away in emptiness and silence as the fox sloughs his smell into the cold unworldliness of water; to return to town a stranger. Wandering flushes a glory that fades with arrival."⁹ In passages such as this, infused with melancholy and oriented toward an unbecoming, the proximity to wildness makes the writer long to remove the "human taint" in order to live among the wild things. With phrases like "the cold unworldliness of water," Baker seeks to make a language for the experience of becoming animal and unbecoming human—the "unworldliness of water," after all, indicates an element, water, within which the human world cannot prevail. Baker's travels across Essex in search of the hawks place him in closer and closer proximity to the birds, and as he becomes part of their orbit, he loosens his hold on the world of humans, even as it loosens its hold on him.

Baker, a little-read naturalist in his time and not originally a bird watcher at all, according to one introduction to *The Peregrine* by Mark Cocker, lived all of his sixty-one years in Essex and was part of no artistic community. He was not a librarian or hunter, and yet he conveys an encyclopedic knowledge of the birds he tracks and a hunter's instinct about how to find them. Baker was, however, deeply concerned in the early 1960s about a precipitous decline in the number of peregrines in England due to the use of certain toxic chemicals in farming. Believing that the bird was about to die out (it has since recovered in numbers), Baker set out to observe, record, and capture the habits of peregrines—sometimes he tracked mating pairs, at other times he followed a single falcon or tiercel, at all times he trained his whole intellectual being, his powers of observation, his instinct for the bird's movement on this one species. The sadness that hangs over the whole book emerges from Baker's assessment of the approaching extinction of the birds he tracks, and his commentary is all at once a primer on hawk habits, a lament for the impending extinction of the bird or at least of the natural habitats in which such birds thrived, and an elegy for the human and beyond the human, for nature itself.

The Peregrine is a postnature, queer love letter to an era coming to an abrupt and catastrophic close. The book is also, however—and this is where it perhaps departs from a queer ecological orientation—a deep critique of the human: "Like the hawk, I heard and hated the sound of man, that faceless horror of the stony places. I stifled in the same filthy sack of fear. I shared the same hunter's longing for the wild home none can know, alone with the sight and smell of the quarry, under the indifferent sky" (144–45). Baker places himself alongside the hawk, both in opposition to "man" and in search of "the wild home none can know." He lives now closer to death and attempts to empty out the "I" or "faceless horror" and comes close to or approximates the I/eye of the hawk. "The peregrine," he offers, "lives in a pouring away world of no attachment, a world of wakes and tilting, of sinking planes of land and water" (35). Baker's ability to render the world of the falcon depends on this kind of syntax—"a pouring away world of no attachment"—within which the rules of grammar are shuffled to give access to the experience of flight, the feral refusal of attachment, and a dipping and flowing sense of perception. This flow of perception indeed brings Baker into the temporality of the hawk, a sharp temporality that is all present tense and that moves very fast even as he himself is stilled and must move very slowly in order not to startle the birds. Baker is immersed in the hawk, in the hawks' needs and desires, in their struggle for survival, in their hovering and all-consuming presence. His absorption by and with the hawks indeed orients him to new and different forms of desire and need.

By the end of the book, the reader has learned much about the choreography of predation and flight, about blood lust, about fear, but all we know of the author is that he desires the wildness he associates with this bird and that, unlike a falconer, he has no desire to capture and train the wild bird. He instead situates himself as a witness to wildness, as a solitary watcher, an animal among animals, a body longing to be relieved of the "human taint" and to find the very "edge of things," which will, inevitably, also represent the edge of something human. Baker's writing captures a sense of the wild that not only merges human with animal but also mimics the rhythms of desire and disappointment that haunt the pursuit of the bird and that characterize the rise and fall of the bird's own predatory flights. In the process of learning about the bird, Baker unlearns the human and produces a language of an otherworldly desire, a song of wildness.

The Peregrine by Baker, says Helen Macdonald, the author of *H Is for Hawk* (2014)[10] and now one of the best-known contemporary commentators on predatory birds, is frightening for its lack of hope, its dark predictions of the end. "His hawks," Macdonald writes, "were made of death" (200). They are death dealing and on an inexorable trajectory toward extinction. Her hawk, Macdonald hopes, represents "life" and therefore futurity and potentiality. While this is a nice way of thinking about the epistemology of the ferox, as an orientation toward possibility and potentiality, Macdonald's story of training her hawk, and the story within the story that she tells about T. H. White trying to train his goshawk in the 1930s, suggests more of a kinship between Baker and Macdonald than she might like to imagine, and it certainly forges a link between White and Baker as loners obsessing over their birds and losing themselves within the bird's ferocious indifference.

Helen Macdonald's meditations on training a hawk in the wake of losing her father may articulate a difference between herself and Baker, but she shares with him a sense of becoming hawk. In *H Is for Hawk*, Macdonald repeats some of Baker's refrains: she too cautions that in training a hawk you must learn to become invisible; she too claims that, in training the bird and living alongside it, "I was turning into a hawk" (84), that "I have gone half bird myself" (161), and that, then, "as the hawk became tamer I was growing wilder" (108); like Baker, Macdonald feels that hunting with the hawk "took me to the very edge of being a human": another hawk book, another turn of the epistemology of the ferox at the very edge of the human. In communion with the bird that can never be thoroughly tamed, the human, it seems, turns wild and begins to share in the bird's orientation to death and predation. The desire of the hawk, after all, is always for death. It hunts, it stalks, it kills, it eats. Macdonald tells us, "I'd already discovered that all sorts of predatory taxonomies are buried in the baby goshawk's brain" (137), but along with predation in the goshawk she discovers a thrill buried deep within her own being in relation to hunting. "I was astounded by the radical change in subjectivity it had installed: how the world dissolved to nothing, yet was so real and tangible it almost hurt" (176). While Baker dissolves into the predation he witnesses and tracks, Macdonald experiences a kind of flickering relation to life and death in the shadow of the hawk—the bird delivers death but is also "brilliance and fury" (53); it connects its human to a "world of things" (275) and to desires that eschew the imposed order of domestic calm, and in so doing, the bird offers the human a "little splinter of wildness" (222).

Perhaps, these memoirs propose, a "little splinter" of wildness is about all a human can reasonably manage. "Human kind," wrote Eliot around the same time that T. H. was trying to train his hawk, "cannot bear very much reality."[11] Humans cannot bear reality but cannot bear the wildness that limns it either, and so in running away from reality while only skirting the wild, the human sets itself up in a fairly small patch of what we call life. Reality, for both Baker and Macdonald, is bound up in death. Macdonald trains her hawk in an effort to get over her father's sudden death, and Baker follows his birds to try to make sense of the brutality of an environmental crisis that has intensified to the point of threatening extinction.

The wild is overwhelming after all in its immensity, its elusiveness, its refusal of the human and in its systems of signification that pointedly ignore human presence. An account of such systems occurs within Eduardo Kohn's stunning ethnography of Ecuadoran forests, where he insists there are "representational forms that go beyond language" and sign systems that are deployed by nonhuman actors.[12] Paying attention to "ecological webs" (13) that connect landscape to animals, dreams to thought, Kohn reconceives of symbolic systems that do not crush all material into one message. His ethnography further-more allows him to draw closer to what we discovered in Baker and Macdon-ald to be an epistemology of wildness and what Kohn calls an "anthropology beyond the human." While the sexual aspect of these alternative ecologies does not interest Kohn, seduction is a deep part of the power of hawks, and the re-lation to the predatory bird gives rise to a sense of not only signifying systems beyond the human but also sexual desires, wild desires that exceed the forms allocated to domestic life. As Macdonald notes, those wild desires are as ter-rifying as they are alluring and can lead both toward the joys of communing with the nonhuman and into authoritarian hierarchies. After all, she reminds us, the imagery of falconry was ubiquitous within the Third Reich, and Her-mann Göring himself was an avid falconer. For Macdonald, however—and in this we can hear echoes of Branca Arsić's reading of Thoreau—the bird is not and must not be a symbol; it cannot function as an icon of this and a represen-tation of that. The hawk is wildness itself in motion and not at all tied to the symbolic functions that humans mete out. And yet, the human mind longs to tether the predatory bird to one representational system or another despite its feral refusal of human contact. The hawk may be an object onto to which we project longing, fear, hope, and fatality, but it offers only a hard, indifferent stare in response.

Turning, Turning in the Widening . . .

Turning and turning in the widening gyre
The falcon cannot hear the falconer;
Things fall apart; the centre cannot hold;
Mere anarchy is loosed upon the world,
—W. B. Yeats, "The Second Coming"

But even as we insist that the hawk or falcon escapes the noose of representa-tion, we remember another mediation on falcons that has supplied modernism with its most iconic image of impending doom—the falconer losing control of his bird and, by implication, the world. Way too much ink has been spilled on W. B. Yeats's poem "The Second Coming" (1920), and I do not intend to add too much to the flood of commentaries here. I only want to say that rather than attending to the looming menace on the poem's horizon, the second coming that is not salvation but ruination, we might instead turn to the poem's central image of a trainer and his bird, a master losing control of the facet of nature over which he thought he held dominion, a human standing in the middle of a force field that is not of his making and will not succumb to his power. The falcon cannot hear the falconer, or does not want to; the call to the bird is lost in the wild, swirling noise of a modern chaos that is not nature, not manageable, not subject to the systems of order and classification that represent the human mark upon the "vibrant matter" of life.[13] The "mere anarchy" that the unmatched pair of the bird and the human trainer loose upon the world, is, then, a spectacle of un-mastered desires. And so, one of the quintessential images of European modernism, a falcon, whose flight represents an anarchistic refusal to obey the call of the master, symbolizes the collapsing of old forms in the shadow of the terrifying shape of the new.

Falconry over the centuries has not only represented the practice of mastery and an extension of animal husbandry, it also bears within it a class system, an order of things that, in Yeats's poem, seems to be coming to an end. As the *Boke of Saint Albans* explained in the medieval period, falconry exists within and names a hierarchical order: "An Eagle for an Emperor, a Gryfalcon for a King, a Peregrine for a Prince, a Saker for a Knight, a Merlin for a Lady, a Goshawk for a Yeoman, a Sparrowhawk for a Priest, a Musket for a Holy water Clerk, a Kestrel for a Knave."[14] Indeed, this hallowed list is the basis for the term *pecking order*, and the concept of having someone "wrapped around your little finger" is similarly drawn from the expansive vocabulary of falconry that ran alongside class systems and, as I am arguing, gave rise to complex erotic systems at the same time.

The last rung of the ladder of social standing in falconry, the kestrel for a knave, lent its name to a book about the falcon used to allegorize a narrative about class and advancement. British children coming of age in the 1970s would not have been reading *Catcher in the Rye* like their US counterparts, but *A Kestrel for a Knave* by Barry Hines, written in 1968. The book, made into a film titled *Kes* (1969) by the great filmmaker of working-class British life Ken Loach, tells the story of Billy Casper, a working-class lad who lives in public housing, slips through the cracks at school, and is abandoned at home. Destined for the mines like his older brother, Billy searches in his environment for a chance for some other kind of life and finds solace in the wild animals of the ridings. He spies a kestrel nesting in an old monastery and scales the wall late one night to get a closer look at the wondrous bird. Reaching into the nest, he draws out the kestrel chicks and then puts one in his pocket and returns home with it. Billy then steals a book on the ancient art of falconry from a local shop and begins to train his bird. The kestrel and Billy share a bond that is not the love of a boy and his pet but that emerges from the sense of wildness that tethers the untrained sensibility of the boy to the untamable nature of the bird. When asked about his new pet by one of his teachers, Billy responds: "It's not a pet, Sir, hawks are not pets.... It's trained that's all. It's fierce, an it's wild, an it's not bothered about anybody."[15]

In *A Kestrel for a Knave*, wildness characterizes working-class defiance in the face of postwar English respectability. The story of Billy Casper packaged wildness, working-class rebellion, and postwar English fortitude and resilience into a masculinist narrative of brutality (the bird dies), survival, and discipline. And while some of us may still thrill at the narrative of liminality that the kestrel-boy relationship captured so well, we must also ask about the colonial and classed order of being that is so neatly packaged into this fable. By training the bird, the novel proposes, Billy Casper learns his proper place in a rigid social order. He learns that you train what is externally wild, and in this way, you discipline the wildness you bear within. We can also look further into the indifferent fierceness of the bird ("it's fierce and it's wild and it's not bothered about anybody") and the passionate investment in its training that conjures the sexual instinct itself. The training of falcons, an ancient art, is, furthermore, a fraternal order, an activity mostly carried out by men, alone or with other men, and it has its own vocabulary, a subcultural structure, and it contains, at various times, an investment in order and mastery, a commitment to nature and wildness, a bloodlust, a fetishistic attachment to the paraphernalia of the art of falconry (jesses, lures, chaps, straps, hoods, etc.) and a deep desire for the feral. While *A Kestrel for a Knave* was surely not referring, in any deliberate way, to a sexual wildness, it nonetheless made a seemingly intuitive connection between the adolescent male outsider or rebel and the wild thing he seeks to know. But more than this, the falcon flying free represents the trajectory of desires that cannot be corralled by the new languages of psychoanalysis, medicine, and sexology.

In both *The Peregrine* and *A Kestrel for a Knave* we can locate wild erotics and an erotic of the wild linked to schemas of mobility, human pathos, the desire to become feral, and cross-species intimacies. But sexuality as such is less obviously foregrounded, even though it inheres to the fetishistic equipment that Billy Casper uses to train his bird and to the lyrical ecstasies expressed by Baker as he follows the hawks and begins to mimic their actions. Other writers, specifically T. H. White, Glenway Wescott, and Helen Macdonald, express specifically sexual investments in bird life. And all the writers studied here find an alternative epistemology within the life of the predatory bird—for Billy Casper, in *A Kestrel for a Knave*, his relation to the bird both demonstrates his ability for mastery, an ability that gives him access to class mobility, and offers him an exit route from the rigid hierarchies of the English system and, more importantly, an alternative to work in the coal mines. The bird that is wild and fierce represents a freedom for the working-class boy, and it is the bird's capacity for flight and domination that he envies and tries to access. Baker, on the other hand, eschews the domination that would be associated with training the peregrine falcons he tracks. Instead he discerns within the habits of the birds a different route to freedom and flight—here it is the total indifference to the human that represents the alien nature of the bird, and this too is the origin of its odd and magnetic power.

A Kestrel for a Knave, as noted earlier, took its title from a quote from the *Boke of Saint Albans* and from a chart that represents the hierarchical order of falconry from emperor to knave. Thus, falconry metes out different levels of sovereignty over the wild that descend from the emperor to the male servant. According to the *Boke of Saint Albans* chart, the kestrel fell low on the scale of privilege. But the *Boke of Saint Albans* seemed unaware of another signifying system within which the term *chicken hawk* refers to older men (hawks) who express a preference for younger men (chickens). In the modern period, eccentric sexuality haunts all relations between human and bird. If the relation between falcon and falconer represented permeability for Baker, class mobility for Barry Hines, anarchy for Yeats, in a few other falcon stories the bird emerges from behind the veil of symbolization and becomes the target of a plethora of human desires and aspirations even as it operates as a prosthetic supplement to the inadequacy of embodiment.

Helen Macdonald plainly acknowledges the sexual allure of falconry and recognizes that she first identified this sexual allure through her reading of T. H. White's *The Goshawk*. Indeed, she describes White's book as follows: "It is comic; it is tragic; it is all absorbing. It is strangely like some of the eighteenth-century stories of seduction."[16] Macdonald herself develops a deeply erotic bond with her hawk, Mabel, and she identifies strongly with the bird: "The hawk," she writes, "was everything I wanted to be: solitary, self-possessed, free from grief, and numb to the hurts of human life" (85). For Macdonald, the hawk is a site of identification, and it fills the massive hole left by her father. When he dies, his sudden death leaves Macdonald stunned and confused: "It happens to everyone," she reminds herself, "but you feel it alone. Shocking loss isn't to be shared, no matter how hard you try" (13). Loss is an avenue to wildness—the irreconcilable knowledge that the loved one is gone and will never return shakes the foundation of human stability and opens the body to its own potential disappearance even as it strums a new chord of sexual longing. Macdonald is broken by her loss as Baker was ruined by his sense of the impending extinction of the birds he loved. But, as Macdonald writes: "When you are broken, you run. But you don't always run away. Sometimes, helplessly, you run towards" (46). The action of running toward the site of brokenness is a remarkable image here, one tied inimitably to the relation to the feral bird but that also resonates with alternative epistemologies, contrary sexual orientations, and a different relation to the body marked by its mortality, splintered by grief and tethered now to a temperamental and nonreciprocating bird. How can we understand this epistemology in which the broken self runs toward the site of injury and, in confronting loss, finds a new constellation of desire and identification?

One answer to this question can be found in the study of mourning and bird life in the works of Thoreau written by Branka Arsić. One of Thoreau's most original readers, Arsić turns specifically, in her book *Bird Relics: Grief and Vitalism in Thoreau*, to the topic of birds and loss.[17] From Thoreau's writing on birds, Arsić retrieves a confrontation with loss, a refusal of ordinary modes of thought that fashion the unbearable into the thinkable, and an abandonment of the rational that allows for a more bodily experience of life and death. By reading Thoreau's writings on crows, for example, Arsić finds examples of other modes of thinking about embodiment in his work. She studies his writings for a larger narrative about loss and mourning and discerns within them a bodily "bearing with" loss and pain rather than a mindful distancing from it (257). In a remarkable act of translation (translating Thoreau's work on birds into a new formulation of the real and the wild and the human), Arsić identifies within Thoreau's writings about birds a structure she calls a "crow epistemology" (257). Thoreau has observed that crows are the only large birds he knows of that "hover and circle about in an irregular and straggling manner." They do so, says Arsić, not because they are too stupid to fly with the wind rather than against it, but because they choose to fly into the very force that opposes them—cruel optimism we might call it, citing Lauren Berlant, or, as Arsić puts it, a way of thinking that "faces, in order to know, what blows it away" (257). This form of knowing, which rises to meet the force of what opposes it and indeed rises up because of the tension between the blowing wind and the weight of the bird, is another description of wildness and resonates with Macdonald's urge to run into the thick of her grief. The large birds straggling around in gusts of wind represent the self-canceling knowledge that Arsić identifies as part of Thoreau's theory of transformation available through grief and suggestive of encounters with bewilderment found in the wild.

Arsić finds another example of this transformative understanding of embodiment in a chapter of Thoreau's *A Week on the Concord and Merrimack*

Rivers (1869), wherein he wrote about watching two hawks playing in the sky. Thoreau, Arsić offers, sees the hawks not as two individual creatures, but as one "feathered body" (38), and through them he provides an empirical example of the connection between beings that makes them dependent, compossible, and part of what Jane Bennett calls his sense of a *heteroverse*.[18] The sense of wildness that thinkers like Bennett and Arsić locate in Thoreau echoes through Macdonald's own experiences of loss, wildness, and brokenness and forms a counterintuitive meditation on loss. Quoting Marianne Moore on loneliness, Macdonald notes that "the cure for loneliness is solitude."[19] We might adapt this insight to say—the cure for grief is discomfort. And, when you are broken, misquoting Fred Moten, you run into the break.

Arsić's crow epistemology—like Sedgwick's epistemology of the closet, like Chisholm's queer biophilia—spins away from neatly organized systems of explanation in favor of enigmatic approaches ("nonce taxonomies," in Sedgwick's terms) to an alternate reality.[20] Arsić terms this "literalism" and comments that Thoreau is attempting to bring language as close to the real as possible (something we saw in Baker too). She writes:

> His wager is that he will start experiencing differently thanks precisely to his (even if always only wished for) emancipation from abstractions embedded in our categories and tropes. He hopes that once his senses are entrusted to an unknown—conceptually unmediated—reality, they will allow him finally to experience how entities, whether corporeal or mental, are not fixed, as our traditional epistemologies would have it, but rather change, and so cancel the generic divides not only among beings (such as when Thoreau becomes a pine tree or a muskrat) but also, as I suggest in what follows, among the living and the dead.[21]

Thoreau's attempt to approach, inhabit, and even participate in a nonhuman natural world, one that has been stripped of the idealizations and abstractions that sit thickly over its essence like coats of paint on wood, inaugurates a mode of nature writing that departs from both the romantic project invested in sublimity and the scientific project invested in the normal. Thoreau gives us, indeed, a queer language and method for approaching the weirdness of nature—the crow epistemology—without explaining it or translating it into human terms. As Bennett reminds us, Thoreau's nature is something that is in excess of the human, and it is a place where religious awe is territorialized—in the absence of God, we have the wonder of natural beauty, the surprise of the unknown and the unfathomable, the contemplative practices of solitariness. Bennett uses Thoreau to give us an example of life as method, a way of being that places the human in relation to the heteroverse or the version of nature that never takes the form of the whole. For Thoreau, he must sojourn with nonhuman entities and environments in order to escape some of the business of human life and to put himself in the way of the excess and the unpredictability of variety. "My Thoreau," writes Bennett, is a "sculptor" (xxx), a craftsman, a sojourner looking to be surprised and to be in relation to that which he cannot master—other languages, wild animals, the weather. Our Thoreau, moving forward, is a watcher of birds, an observer who is pulled into the widening gyre of a nature spinning away from the human and into the wild.

The Bad Falconer

Macdonald filters her story of training a bird in the wake of the loss of her father through the lens offered by T. H. White on his experience of training a goshawk.[22] His book was written in the 1930s but not published until 1951, and even after he published it, White added a postscript because he was mortified by the way his account of trying to train his goshawk revealed what a bad falconer he was at that time. But for Macdonald, White's inability to manage and train his bird represents other failures in his life, most obviously, his inability to manage and train his own wayward desires. Reading White's narrative after her father's death, Macdonald situates the writer as another father figure, a bad father in this case, and she sets up her relation to her bird, her relation to writing, to domesticity, to love, and to desire in opposition to the model he has set up. She is mourning to his melancholia, love to his hate, kindness to his sadism, and life to his death. Macdonald situates herself, in other words, as a good falconer to a bad one, a well-loved daughter training her bird to recover from loss, opposing a man who had been abandoned as a child and seems lonely and queer as an adult. But these two writers, sitting each with a bird in one hand and a pen in the other, have more in common than Macdonald lets on: both writers obtain a wild bird in the wake of a sudden change. Macdonald loses her father, unexpectedly, and White quits his job as a schoolmaster at a nearby school in order to try to make his living as a writer. Both writers fall in love with their birds, both eschew human company for the obsessive need to be with their voracious hawks, and both play out an elaborate and sometimes vicious game of fort/da with the bird in an attempt to train it and demonstrate a kind of mastery over nature. Both fail. Both speak of becoming hawk.

In *The Goshawk*, White, whom Sylvia Townsend Warner in her biography of him described variously as "homosexual," "sadistic," and basically afraid of people, describes what can only be called a romantic attachment to a bird, Gos, that he tries and fails to train.[23] White's attachment to Gos was undoubtedly a deep attachment to wildness and an elaborate fantasy of becoming feral, which he played out at various times in his life. Of course, prior to Helen Macdonald's close reading of *The Goshawk*, White was mostly known as the author of the Arthurian tales *The Sword in the Stone* and *The Once and Future King*. However, as Macdonald narrates, in the 1930s, after retiring from a position as a teacher at Stowe school, White moved to a cottage nearby with his dog and took up falconry. Reading all the books he could find on the subject, White tried to train his goshawk using not modern methods, but the ancient arts of falconry, and he failed spectacularly as his memoir/training diary shows. If for Macdonald falconry "is about revelling in flight"[24] and for Baker it was about catching a glimpse of fugitive birds living on the edge of extinction ("it is a dying world, like Mars, but glowing still"[25]), for White falconry provides an opening to wildness and an opportunity to sit alongside the feral. His attraction to falconry, in other words, was less about the process of training and more about a proximity to wildness. This proximity, which also manifested as a retreat from humanity, allowed for the expression of a series of unclassifiable and unspeakable desires, desires which even his biographer, the very queer Warner, worried about exposing to the world.

Warner struggled mightily with the biography she had been commissioned to write a few years after White's death. Shocked by the books on flagellation she found in his cottage and by an expressed desire for young boys in his diaries, Warner found herself torn between the biographer's desire to paint an accurate and colorful picture of White and a contrary instinct to withhold from a reading public anything that would damn queer people in their eyes. She wrestled with her warring instincts over whether to judge or protect her subject. So overwhelmed was she that, at one point, she wrote to William Maxwell and described White as an octopus! "White has fastened on me. . . . It is like trying to write the biography of a large and animated octopus. . . . I am getting involved in the queerest of correspondences."[26]

The "queerest of correspondences" could well describe White's relations to the animals with which he surrounded himself. In *The Goshawk*, a memoir and a love story as much as anything, White seeks for a language for his love for the untamable bird and finds it in a description he reads of the tendency of goshawks in training to revert quickly and decisively, in the words of one author, "to a feral state." For White, this is a thrilling concept, a reminder of the wildness that cannot be drained out of the bird and that is the source of its appeal. White immediately identifies with the bird even as he seeks to master it. He proposes that he too would like to return to a feral state and writes: "The word feral had a kind of magical potency which allied itself with two other words, 'ferocious' and 'free.' 'Fairy,' 'fey,' 'aeriel' and other discreditable alliances ranged themselves behind the great chord of 'ferox.'"[27] Macdonald, reading between the lines of White's narrative and reading it along with his unpublished papers (where this longer quote appears), proposes that White's love for the hawk allowed him to express the inexpressible—his homosexuality, his sadism, his desire for mastery, and his queer relation to temporality itself.

For Macdonald, then, homosexuality sits in some implicit relationship to wildness, to the love that not only dare not speak its name but that refuses a conventional relation to time and space. While the name for this unruly relation to time and space is given as *homosexual*, in fact it is not entirely clear that this term describes White at all, who had no known male lovers during his adulthood and professed an (unrequited) interest in younger boys. While of course the work of the homo/hetero binary had, by the 1930s, begun neatly to cleave all desires into specific bodies, White nonetheless seemed to know, perhaps better than Macdonald, that the neat lines of division, like so much else in the world of human endeavor, are made to be muddied. In his own writings White did refer to homosexuality, but more often he used the terms "norms" and "abnorms" and asked, in notes he took on the character of Lancelot for his popular narrative of King Arthur, whether people could be "ambisexual."[28] He also once told a pupil that people should sleep together as often as possible because it was "natural and delightful to do so" and then added "not only women, but men, boys, animals, even inanimate objects (he mentioned lamp posts)."[29] Clearly, White's sense of the scope of sexual expression was not limited to the homo/hetero binary, and in fact, he often spoke about his relationship to his dog as being more important to him than any human relation. In fact, when his beloved dog, Brownie, died, he wrote to a friend: "You must try to understand that I am and will remain entirely without wife or brother or sister or child and that Brownie supplied more than the place of these to me. We loved each other more and more every year."[30]

But, Macdonald, who is so brilliant on the topic of the human-animal bond—"wild things are made from human histories"—throughout her reading of *The Goshawk* keeps shoving White into the closet and then reading his every stumbling foray into relationality as failed, lost, misguided, cruel, shameful, and born of an essential loneliness.[31] Because he cannot accept his own desires, she offers, White also cannot train his hawk, cannot keep her, cannot let her go. In Macdonald's compendium, White's myriad desires—for solitude, for collecting things, for home improvement, for falconry, for boys, for spanking, for capture, and for release—are fragments of a homosexuality that never coheres and therefore gets expressed through his broken need to break others: "White had thought he could tame the hawk without breaking its natural spirit. But all he has done is try to break it, over and over again" (162). And she goes further. It occurs to her that "many of our classic books on animals were by gay writers who wrote of their relationships with animals in lieu of human loves of which they could not speak" (41).

And there is it, the love that dare not speak its name that finds a route to expression through a surrogate animal that represents not a human in animal form so much as the wildness of desire itself outside of the lines of, in this instance, class-bound domesticity. And while Macdonald is of course right that White's desire for the bird *is* redirected gay desire, it is also more than this and less than this. It is a desire for the wild and a wild desire. White may well have lacked a language for his desire, and indeed the relation to the hawk may indeed have afforded him an object for it, but if his love could speak, I am not sure that it would have spoken in the language of homosexuality.

Indeed, while some of the biographical notes on White mention his homosexuality, almost all mention his loneliness. Most of the narratives about White refer to him as sad, pathetic, lost. Warner repeatedly describes White as afflicted by loneliness.[32] Macdonald calls him "one of the loneliest men alive."[33] But White's own words are not in reference to either homosexuality or loneliness. He speaks of himself as feral, fairy, and "fey."[34] Macdonald, citing an unpublished manuscript by White, writes: "He wanted to be fey, a fairy, ferox. All those elements of himself he'd pushed away, his sexuality, his desire for cruelty, for mastery: all these were suddenly there in the figure of the hawk" (45).

While the epistemology of the closet has given us an explanation of men like White, namely, that they are in hiding, the category of the *ferox*, a word White used a lot (Latin for ferocious), offers us access to another explanation, a different episteme, one that lies closer to Foucault's "untamed ontology" in *The Order of Things*.[35] The "discreditable alliances" that White intuits behind the state of becoming feral access another language of sexuality for the early twentieth century, for figures who pass in and out of the definitional structures of their time.

So, what if we stuck with the "great chord of ferox"? Like Pete Coviello's terms for premedicalized sexual otherness—extravagant, unyarded, errant— the words gathered under the sign of ferox tell of alternate histories, wild and unsorted lives that have been papered over with moral judgment, medical diagnostics, and normative expectations.[36] The point here is not to find another maligned homosexual and restore his good name; rather, in finding White through Macdonald, and in his feral state, we leave the epistemology of the closet with its obsessive need to know and to decide between two sides of a binary, and we find a constellation of odd singles, fairies, and freaks.

The Gay Falconer

White was not the only writer in the twentieth century to express a deep desire for the freedom that falcons and hawks represented. For a more explicitly gay fictional account of the seductive powers exerted by the hawk we can read *The Pilgrim Hawk* (1940) by Glenway Westcott. Westcott was an openly gay writer and part of the American expatriot literary scene in Paris in the 1920s. This odd novella by him is widely read as a queer tale of exclusion and loss.[37] Called a "neglected masterpiece" by Edmund White, and introduced by Michael Cunningham as "a work of brilliance,"[38] *Pilgrim Hawk* tells the story of a broken marriage with three witnesses—a young American heiress, Alexandra Henry, living in France; her house guest, an American bachelor named Alwyn Tower; and a hawk! The story unfolds over the course of one day in the late 1920s and involves a visit by the troubled couple, Larry and Madeleine Cullen, to Alex's rented French country home. The couple, aristocrats, are silly and unremarkable except for one fantastical detail; Madeleine emerges from the car at the start of the visit carrying "a full-grown hooded falcon on her wrist"![39] Tower, the story's narrator, establishes a kind of kinship with the hawk, and the hawk becomes the enigmatic marker of his ambiguous sexuality as well as the explicit symbol of trouble in the marriage and a subtle but noticeable gender variance in Mrs. Cullen.

Cunningham, in his introduction to the *New York Review of Books* edition of *Pilgrim Hawk*, says humorously of the appearance of the hawk in the story: "Some readers may groan inwardly, as I did, when I first read about the hawk. Oh, I thought, a symbol. And the hawk is of course a symbol" (xii). As it turns out, the hawk both is and is not a symbol. Certainly, the hawk comes to represent the kind of wildness and freedom that marriage and wealth and social standing oppose and contain. But, more than this, it is a symbol for all that lies outside of the magic circle of power and privilege inscribed by a wealthy marital partnership—namely, animality, the Moroccan servants in the mansion, queers, and something the novel repeatedly calls "anarchy." The hawk, in fact, like Yeats's falcon, represents a spiraling sense of despair, loss, anxiety, and chaos that, in this story, defines the marriage specifically but indicates, as Yeats's poem does, a larger realm of disintegration. But the hawk is not only a symbol. The hawk in this novel, and in other narratives examined in this chapter, is sexuality itself or, rather, a fantasy of a sexuality that fuses man or woman with bird, links unruly desires to unruly political movements, and questions whether the falconer or the falcon has the upper hand.

In *Pilgrim Hawk*, Westcott's narrator casts the Cullens as conventionality itself—"they were self-absorbed, coldly gregarious, mere passers of time," and earlier "they were mere male and female of the species of well-to-do British which haunts the entire world" (13). The repetition of the word "mere" in these descriptions reduces the aristocrats to types, people unable to rise above their allotted place in the world, and Westcott uses the word "species" to reduce (or elevate) the Cullens to the status of the bird—a representative of a species, not specific at all. And just as the bird emerges from the chauffeur-driven car hooded and tethered, so the novella introduces the theme of sexuality in the first paragraph—"love and trouble" (3)—only to hood and declaw it by the end of that same paragraph with a declaration of marriage. Similarly, by the second paragraph the narrator has introduced the theme of perpetual motion or "peregrination" (3) as characteristic of aristocratic life in the 1920s only to still this movement in the present setting of the story, a time, the 1940s, when such mobility, freedom, and aimless travel are long gone. And, as if to emphasize the hooded and tethered nature of the relations between present and past, he conjures a past within which the forests close by were haunted by the call of hunting horns "which sounded like a picnic of boy sopranos" (xvii) but now only teem treacherously with antiaircraft guns and radio noise. What was once sexually and physically mobile is now fixed in place; what was once a hunting ground is now martial terrain; what was once open to desire is now subject to martial law. And as a soundtrack to this changing landscape, we have the horns which sound like "boy sopranos"—the young male soprano voice, as Benjamin Libertore's research shows, is resonant of histories of alternative sexuality. According to Libertore, the male soprano is a voice whose purity is predicated on the impending break that must shatter it and consign it to an out-of-reach past.[40] Similarly, here, the haunting call of the hunting horns echoes across an era of change and a shifting landscape. They offer a song from a past that is long gone, shuffled out of sight and sound by a new age of military might, classificatory precision, and a cleaving of the domestic from the wild.

The hawk in this story is no doubt a symbol for the narrator's unexplained bachelordom, and it represents an alternative to the repetitive cycle of love and trouble associated here with heterosexual marriage (in the Cullens, in the Moroccan servants in the household, and, looking ahead, in Alexandra's marriage to the narrator's brother). But it is a symbol not of something that exists but is hidden—the narrator's homosexuality, say, or even the wife's odd masculinity—

but of that which cannot be expressed at all, ever. (Eliot again: "In order to arrive at what you do not know / You must go by a way which is the way of ignorance."[41]) Mrs. Cullen explains that Lucy, her hawk, named for Walter Scott's tragic heroine *Lucia De Lammermoor*, was given to her by a Scottish gamekeeper who trapped the bird, hurting one of the bird's toes. The flawed bird, named for a mad, love-worn heroine who killed her husband while pining for her true love, now sits between husband and wife, a prosthetic extension (a contrasexual marital aid or barrier) of the wife's desire for an unnamed something more and the husband's inability or unwillingness to give it. The husband, indeed, we learn, hates the bird and will eventually try to set it free in order to recapture his wife. The bird meanwhile is indifferent to his male rival and only fixes the man with a stare characterized as "a slight natural bewilderment."[42] And it is not only her husband who dislikes the bird, Mrs. Cullen explains; their neighbors in Ireland also "don't like our having a falcon." The neighbor turns out to be Lord Bild, a Jew, new to wealth and the neighborhood and as disapproving of the bird as the loathsome Cullens are of him. The Jewish neighbor turns out to be only one of a series of racialized others in the text who are cast in opposition to the Cullens, who express fear of the bird and yet who, in the hierarchies established in the present tense of the book, are equivalent to the wildness that the bird represents. The Jewish neighbor, like the bird, is cast as threatened in some way: "He's a Jew furthermore; you can scarcely expect him to live and let live" (16). And the Moroccan servants, whom Alex had "found" in Tangier, are associated with a kind of general wildness, or fever, that is found in "the orient." Finally, the hawk is used as a reference point for some people Mrs. Cullen met in a "great madhouse in Dublin" who remind her of "hawks, exactly" (20). The bird, in this way, is both a fetish object for Mrs. Cullen—her phallus you might say—and a marker for all that lay outside the country house, the chauffeured car, the marriage, and even France.

Since the bird must be managed or "manned" in falconry lingo, and since Mrs. Cullen is the one doing the manning, the bird also represents a gender imbalance that plays out in the relations between the married couple and in the relationship between the heterosexual triangles that the novel creates and the lonely homo singles that it requires. As they sit together in awkward companionship in Alex's house, Mrs. Cullen "mans" the room by offering lore about falcons. The bird, she tells her trapped but somewhat charmed audience, experiences hunger much more urgently than other creatures, including humans, and this therefore makes it possible "to tame them and to perfect the extraordinary technique of falconry" (20). At this the narrator thinks of his own hungers, his failed attempt to be an artist specifically, and then, as the bird begins to "mantle" or spread its wings, he sees her as "an image of amorous desire" (22) and thinks of male desire as a hunger that can never be satisfied in marriage and of the "old bachelor" as lovelorn, worn out, defeated, and starving or, in his words "like an old hawk" (23).

Mrs. Cullen, in others words, a strong woman among weak men, is not just the master of the bird; she is a castrating because castrated presence. Just as Lucy, the falcon, had lost a bit of her toe in the gamekeeper's trap, so Mrs. Cullen has lost a bit of herself in the marriage, and the bird, standing as it does between her husband and herself, restores her to fullness and strength. Like a matched pair, Mrs. Cullen and Lucy become fused, in the sense that Arsić described fusion with reference to Thoreau. They are one, a bird becoming human or tame and a woman become animal or wild. The narrator confirms that women must be controlled at all times by their husbands or else one must hope they are worn down by the rigors of motherhood because "it is anarchy if they all flourish" (50).

It *is* anarchy, and the women in this narrative do flourish, and while the commentary on the story has tended to focus on the male bachelor, his unspeakable sexuality and his relation to the hawk, it is Mrs. Cullen in particular who here mans the bird, the husband, and the narrator. By the end of the narrative, moreover, in a clearly castrating move, she disarms her husband of a gun (it is not clear whether he intends to use it to kill the bird or himself), she also announces her intention to fire her chauffeur. And upon finding out that the narrator is not the love interest of the hostess, she lets him know that "I did not count, I was a supernumerary" (97). An old bachelor may well be like an old hawk, but the hawk in this story is not male, not old, and is very young and feisty. She smells blood and goes for the kill.

The falcon in *Pilgrim Hawk* is the circling predator waiting for the right moment to stoop down on its prey. It is desire itself, a potent force that must be kept in the dark, an urgent need that must be fed sparingly, and a wild thing that cannot be tethered for long. If the falcon for White was a phallus of sorts and represented a countersexual prosthetic appended to the inadequate human body, for Westcott it becomes more clearly recognizable as a figure for queerness, a queerness that cannot be folded into matrimony and that disrupts the organizations of bodies, social forms, and political structures over which the world, at the time of the novel, was about to go to war. This queerness, which is never constituted in the novel as gayness per se but only cast as a feature of the narrator's bachelordom and the wife's masculinity, finds expression here, as it did in White's writings, in the language of falconry, a language full of arcane terminologies, fetishistic accoutrements, and a vocabulary for wildness.

The falcon must be *manned*; it often struggles to free itself from human restraint in a mode called "bating" (37); the bird is tethered using a "creance" (98), from *croyance*, the French word for "faith." The creance indicates that the falconer lacks faith in his bird and so cannot let it fly free; a haggard is an older hawk, one trapped as an adult and therefore much more resistant to training. The accoutrements for training and flying the hawk involve handmade leather items—hoods and leashes, gauntlets and vests, bells and swivels, and sometimes even chaps.

In one of the very few essays to mention Westcott's novella in relation to a gay tradition of writing, Chase Dimock cites it as a reference point for Robert Duncan's 1968 poem "My Mother Would Be a Falconress." Noting that, in this poem Duncan seems to use the word *gay* to refer both to homosexuality and to its antiquated use—"gay . . . at one time referred to the sexually libertine lifestyle of men unencumbered by domestic duties"—Dimock comments: "I must also include reference to Glenway Wescott's 1940 expatriate novel *The Pilgrim Hawk* as a precedent for a gay writer to use the falcon-falconer relationship as an allegory for discussing sexual freedom. Thus, there was an already queer resonance with the image of the falcon circulating within the gay imaginary by the time Duncan wrote this poem. 'The Gay Falcon' was also the name of a 1941 B-movie starring George Sanders as Gay Lawrence, a.k.a. 'The Falcon,' a playboy and amateur detective."[43]

And so, Dimock's connection between Wescott and Duncan brings the hawk out into the open not as a symbol for the closeted gay man so much as a marker of mobility, an unclassifiable excess, singularity, and predatory desires that do not succumb to either the force of domestication or the tidiness of modern definition. The reference to falcons in gay literature, in other words, is not a code for *gay*; it is the symbol that Cunningham dreaded finding in Westcott's story.

Indeed, Duncan's extraordinary poem brings us full circle and imagines the gay man not simply in relation to a falcon, but as the bird itself. In the poem, Duncan imagines himself as a "gay falcon"—"gay," as Dimock has pointed out in both senses of the word—treading his mother's wrist, wearing a hood, and flying off to catch birds when given the command.[44] In this sense, Duncan is a kind of transitional figure between White's odd sexuality and the consolidation of a homosexual identity that follows in later writers. Duncan was himself a wild figure in San Francisco in the 1960s, an anarchist and a spiritualist with shamanistic leanings. Unlike White, Duncan had come out as homosexual early on and, in 1944, wrote one of the earliest contemporary treatises on homosexual rights: "The Homosexual in Society."[45] This essay, which was published in the anarchist journal *Politics*, edited by Dwight Macdonald, compared the plight of the homosexual to that of Jews and Black people and compared homosexuality to witchcraft in terms of the misunderstanding and fear it generated: "The law has declared homosexuality secret, inhuman, unnatural (and why not then supernatural?). The law itself sees in it a crime—not in the sense that murder, thievery, seduction of children, or rape are seen as human crimes—but as a crime against the way of nature. It has been lit up and given an awful and lurid attraction such as witchcraft was given in the 17th century."[46] Duncan struggled in this essay with both a distaste for the idea of being ghettoized as a gay person and a strong desire to be public about his desire. In the essay he expresses frustration that writers like Hart Crane would never be written about as gay and that, if mentioned at all, Crane's homosexuality was represented as a failing or a vice he had managed to overcome. Duncan's essay also argues with what he calls a "cult of homosexual superiority" and makes a claim for homosexuality not as a special kind of love, but as part of a larger struggle.

In "My Mother Would Be a Falconress," Duncan imagines himself in relation to his mother as a "gay falcon treading her wrist."[47] With his mother as both the handler and the mistress of life and death, the poet flies off to capture and kill small creatures and to bring his prizes back to her. He sits on her wrist with his hood covering his eyes and waits for the moment she releases him to "as far as her will goes."[48] At first he dreads that his mother will "cast me away," but eventually, like the child in a Winnicottian drama of attachment and separation, he is the one who draws blood and leaves his perch to strike out "from the blood to be free of her."[49] Yet even free of the mother, the poet remains in thrall to the methods of falconry and, despite having left her wrist, he still wears the falcon's hood and waits for his next chance to draw blood. Duncan's own mother, in fact, died in childbirth, and he was adopted by Edwin and Minnehaha Symmes, theosophists and spiritualists who, before adopting him, had consulted astrologers and who insisted on interpreting his dreams throughout his childhood. Later in life Duncan combined the first names his adoptive parents had given him, Robert Edward, with his birth mother's name, Duncan, and became Robert Duncan. Like White, he sat out World War II after announcing his homosexuality to the draft and getting a dishonorable discharge.

"My Mother Would Be a Falconress" circles around the themes we have associated here with ferality and domestication. The odd locution of the word "falconress" reminds the reader that the falconer (as per Yeats's poem) is usually male. But it also, by the same gesture, reminds us that a falcon is a female, not a male, hawk. In this poem, the gay male writer is situated as a falcon drawing out the femininity of his position in relation to a phallic, powerful, and dangerous mother and underwriting the whole setup with the use of "would" making everything conditional and uncertain. The poem is a gorgeous rendition of freedom and unfreedom, of constraint and release, of violence and belonging and offers a better, wilder rendering of modern sexuality than the ones we cleave to today with their moral orientation and their respectability. And I do not say that we should go back in time to these periods in which gay desire was unspeakable, or that we should be falcons/falconers too, but only that for every vulnerable thing that ends its life in the mouth of a predator, there is a predator who sits on the wrist in hooded silence.

Fierce

Some people want to run things, other things want to run.
If they ask you, tell them we were flying.
—Stefano Harney and Fred Moten, *The Undercommons*

At stake in the argument I have made here on behalf of a system of knowing organized around wildness rather than secrecy is a fuller set of vocabularies for desire and belonging. Paying attention to the wild attunes us to these ampler languages of carnality, of belonging, of sex than are immediately at hand in liberal or even progressive or queer frameworks. I have shown this, first, in relation to my recuperative account of the actual richness of attachment in the life of T. H. White, which writers have too quickly glossed over in their insistence on his homo-loneliness, and, second, in relation to a whole list of other writers who, like White, transferred a deep longing for relations beyond the human or at least beyond the normal, onto wild birds. But there is a third and much more social reason to pay attention to wildness as a sexual epistemology—it offers access to an alternative set of erotic economies and cultural practices associated not simply with white loners but also with Black queer subcultural life. And so, in this section, I want to turn to the uncoded multiplicity of relations referenced, if not actually figured, in a term like *fierce* for Black queer artists.

Over the past few decades, numerous challenges have been made to the epistemology of the closet, many of them by scholars working within a queer-of-color critique. Postcolonial queer theorists, such as Gayatri Gopinath,[50] have challenged the universality of the homo/hetero binary and have shown how often in non-Euro-American contexts queer life unspools alongside rather than to the exclusion of marriage and heterosexuality. In Black queer studies, as we saw in chapter 1, C. Riley Snorton argues that the closet is not simply a metaphor for secrecy in relation to Black life; it has become, instead, a way of depicting Black gay men in particular as deceptive about their sexual practices. Indeed, Black gay sexuality from the early twentieth century is all too often depicted as illegible, suspicious, and unknowable. Langston Hughes offers a perfect example of this illegibility. The concept of the "down low" represents Black queer life as subterfuge, but the illegibility of Black sexuality is not well explained in terms of deception or denial; instead, figures like Langston Hughes or Claude McKay, Chester Himes or Gladys Bentley, occupy an unsorted terrain, a terrain that is simultaneously extravagant, fugitive, and wild.

When writing about Black British filmmaker Isaac Julien's film *Looking for Langston* and the "affective labor" it performs, for example, Kara Keeling describes the way the film allows Langston Hughes's sexuality to escape the systems of classification that would cast Hughes as either hiding or unknowing.[51] Keeling writes: "The queer historiography of *Looking for Langston* is not invested in producing or asserting a historical truth that might become a ground for redeeming Hughes's homosexuality. Rather, it is important to understand the creative work that *Looking for Langston* does vis-à-vis Hughes's homosexuality as a type of affective labor that produces Hughes's homosexuality, puts it to use, and valorizes it rather than somehow redeeming it" (572). Keeling's reading is committed to the alternate reality that the film references but does not attempt to capture and that remains out of reach as, what she calls, "an impossible possibility" (566). When we read figures from the past, in other words, from within the strictures of our own reality, the temptation is to pull the pieces of the past into view so that they make sense *now*. Instead, this experimental film counsels us to leave the strange shapes of unresolved realities in fragments or, in Keeling's words, to valorize but not redeem.

Similarly, in her readings of Gladys Bentley, Saidiya Hartman places the singer within a genealogy of the wayward and the wild rather than trying to shoehorn Bentley into definitions of gender variance or lesbianism. In her chapter on the queer singer, pianist, and performer in *Wayward Lives*, Hartman imagines Bentley's life "as if it were an Oscar Micheaux film" or, more precisely, as if it were "select scenes from a film never cast by Oscar Micheaux."[52] The chapter opens with a series of hypothetical scenes from this unmade movie about Bentley, and through the imagined but nonexistent film we access a montage of Bentley's life. The imagined montage establishes Bentley's masculinity, his struggle with a mother who wanted a son, and his quest to become the son she wanted but could not embrace. This not-son, not-sufficient child of a not-good-enough mother leaves the family home to take his place in a queer world where he can "swagger" (194). Hartman uses Micheaux's visual strategies to establish the world within which a Black butch can be king, leading us into the club, into dance scenes, into the "collective movement" (196) of the chorus and simultaneously offering a reading of Bentley's biography and Micheaux's work. The song and dance scenes in Micheaux's films, she offers, like the force of music in Bentley's life, are "never inessential" (195). In these scenes, Hartman writes, "black virtuosity is on display. Then comes the chorus, and the dancing bodies are arranged in beautiful lines that shift and change as the flourish and excess of the dancers unfold into riotous possibility and translate the tumult and upheaval of the Black Belt into art" (196).

By describing Bentley as "an exemplary architecture of black possibility" (198), Hartman reorders entire systems of significance, placing song and dance way above work and property in this beautiful experiment of utopian reimagining. Hartman indicates as much by saying that while Bentley may not have been a revolutionary, he was instead a "brilliant performer" (197) to whom men and women were drawn. He was a bountiful source of pleasure and power, brimming with a secret knowledge of how to live. Looking after Bentley in this way, Hartman neither slots him into a queer historiography nor delineates the ways in which he does not fit there. Instead, she records his wayward, straying, wild mobility and refuses the urge to catalog or classify the errant desires of the king of Black nightlife.

Langston Hughes himself specifically used the language of the wild and established the space of the nocturnal as a way of recording his own relation to eccentric desire. *Looking for Langston* offers the night as a mysterious space of wild activity and queer dreaming, and instead of claiming Hughes, the film pays tribute to the night worlds he conjured and occupied. Shane Vogel has offered beautiful and detailed readings of "the queer poetics of Harlem nightlife" in Hughes's work via the language of the nocturnal and has also respected Hughes's carefully cultivated "sexual ambiguity."[53] Hughes's own reticence about naming his sexual preferences, like White's and many others, left open the possibility for critics (such as Arnold Rampersand) to ignore altogether any signs of a nonconventional sex life. And so, the open denial of queerness by straight readers forces the queer critic to either out Hughes or depict him as hopelessly closeted. Vogel, like Hughes, lets Hughes's work do the talking and, like Hartman, locates other epistemologies within the work itself. As Vogel writes: "Hughes 1920's poetry archives spaces and temporalities that seek to escape empirical confirmation and refuse identificatory foreclosure" (400). Instead of documenting gay life, Vogel proposes, Hughes's poetry creates, explores, and celebrates "closing time" (401) and "after hours" (400) spaces to provide counterhistories of illegal spaces and the illegible Black bodies that gather there. The most obvious example of a rendering of such spaces occurs in "Café 3 A.M.," where policemen and vice squad detectives show up to look for "fairies" and "degenerates" (401) who congregated in bars after the curfews established by the city to manage queer and Black and queer Black populations. Vogel notes that "operating between the gaps of established nightclubs, afterhours clubs shaped an expressive musical tradition as well as constituted modern subject positions" (407). Vogel's marvelous essay locates in Hughes's poetry not only the time-space of queer life but also a wild poetics that resists closure and locates alternative intimacies through "the anti-closural impulses of modern, avant-garde, and jazz poetry, forms within which the structural resources of closure are minimal" (417–18).

There is one other place, however, where we can look for these rhythms and alternative poetics of desire. Written in 1937, "The Genius Child" sings a "wild song" for the (Black) genius child who cannot be loved.[54] Hughes compares this child, a figure for alternate modes of knowing, wild embodiment, and fierce attachment, to a different order of things, to an eagle, a monster "of frightening name."

> This is a song for the genius child.
> Sing it softly, for the song is wild.
> Sing it softly as ever you can—
> Lest the song get out of hand.

And Hughes proposes at the end of the poem that there is nothing to be done with such a child, and so we must "Kill him and let his soul run wild."[55]

Hughes very specifically uses the figure of the eagle for this wild genius child:

> Can you love an eagle,
> Tame or wild?
> Can you love an eagle,
> Wild or tame?
> Can you love a monster
> Of frightening name?

The freedom that the hawk or eagle, the falcon or kestrel, has represented to early twentieth-century writers surely also speaks to the much more vexed and challenging project of Black freedom. In these lines by Langston Hughes, the eagle represents a desire that exceeds love, a monstrosity that exceeds naming, a wildness that exceeds sexuality. And while the poems by Hughes about the afterhours nightclubs locate Black nonnormative desire in queer temporality itself, a poem like "The Genius Child" avoids the language of homosexuality altogether in favor of the wild. Returning to Pete Coviello's argument in *Tomorrow's Parties*, that beyond the epistemology of the closet we find many terminologies that express desires spatially and economically rather than just in terms of bodily orientation, we can draw upon his concepts of the "extravagant" and the "unyarded," terms that could apply to the monstrous eagle in Hughes' queer imaginary.[56] Coviello describes the attempt by late nineteenth-century queer writers to navigate their way between new medical and legal codifications of desire and older systems of nuance and gesture. He cautions against reading all early sexuality as part of an inevitable drift toward the modern definitions we now prefer and, instead, seeks to apprehend less formalized desires in all of their ambiguity or, in his terms, errancy. "What if," he asks, "the queerness of any of these authors proposed, or yearned after, or otherwise intuited, fell somehow aslant of the languages of sexual specificity that were to come, with a newly legible homosexual identity in tow? . . . It may be, rather, that in their extravagance and errancy, their disappointment or dislocation—in their bracing untimeliness—many of these authors envision possibilities that the arrived future, whatever its other affordances, simply would not yield" (15). This terminology, the errant, the extravagant, and what Coviello, borrowing from Thoreau, calls unyardedness, describes a different orientation to orientation and an alternative approach to freedom that, like the anticlosure that Vogel locates in Hughes's poetic forms, seeks to express freedom using language and forms that exceed liberal frameworks.

The queerness in Hughes's oeuvre, as in the work of the writers Coviello writes about (Thoreau, James, Whitman), can never be located in explicit accounts of homosexual activity. And so, we find our evidence of sexual alterity in poems about night worlds or in memoirs of falconry, and the challenge is not to read these wayward archives straight, but to allow them to tell twisted tales of thwarted love, natural history accounts of decidedly unnatural passions, and oblique stories of unrequited love for inappropriate love objects. The an/archives of desire, in this sense, are replete with missed encounters, lost loves, failed romance, love, loss, and wildness.

Indeed, in a haunting essay on queer archives, Brent Edwards notes the vexation of trying to track down the meaning of a letter, a photograph, a note when the context has been torn away and the social world that may have given a fragment meaning has been lost, buried, or moralistically rejected. Citing *Minima Moralia*, Edwards takes up Adorno's image of the rejected pieces of formal history—namely, "the things that fell by the wayside"—and offers to read these things less in terms of total intelligibility ("muteness" in his terms) than in terms of a potentiality: "the remnants of an alternative history rather than the worthless shards left behind."[57] The desires of men and women from the 1930s in Europe had been fairly quickly drawn into a widely circulating discourse of sexual orientation (psychoanalysis), on the one hand, and sexual deviance, on the other.[58] But the lives of queer people in the 1930s did not submit easily and readily to the scientific, social, and medical explanations and the moral schemes that were used to make sense of nonnormative behavior. And even when white men and women and gender-variant people might have found refuge in the respectability of scientific terminologies, other communities may have taken far longer to use the new language of homosexuality to describe who they were.

The vernacular terms that still punctuate descriptions of Black queer life today hold these other histories within them. For example, Madison Moore's book *Fabulous: The Rise of the Beautiful Eccentric* implicitly draws on the formulation of dangerous and wild genius as expressed by Black bodies, and Moore has compiled the assortment of orientations named by what I am calling the epistemology of the ferox under the more contemporary Black queer vernacular heading of "fierce."[59] Drawing from an eclectic archive that includes the works of Balzac and Veblen and that moves from high-end designer boutiques and designers to installation art to voguers and drag queens, from Tina Turner and Grace Jones to Black dandies, Moore crafts a theory of the fierce and the fabulous that ranges easily between nineteenth-century Europe and twentieth-century New York as well as between critiques of capital and defenses of the art of appearance. Moore defines *fierceness* as part of a Black art of resistance and makes a specific claim on the fabulous from the perspective of Black subjects and Black culture. While fabulousness could and can and does emanate from some privileged subjects who are at odds with their own class status (he gives Edie Sedgwick as an example), Moore argues for a specific form of defiant fierceness that courses through Black performances of the fabulous. The emphasis in Moore's work is decidedly on urban spaces and temporalities—the nightclub, for example, plays a huge role in this mapping of the fierce, as it did for Hughes and does for Samuel Delany.

And while there is no obvious connection between the urbane and sophisticated Hughes and the reclusive and obsessive T. H. White, we can, within the epistemology of the ferox, locate these figures in nighttime spaces, in shifting and ambisexual relations of men, women, and aloneness, and in opposition to the insistence on definitional certitude. If we return momentarily to

Thoreau's understanding of the wild, we can see how it might offer a way of connecting, under the heading of the ferox, the intensely urban experiences of Hughes and the fierceness of Black performance to the solitary and remote existence of T. H. White. Thoreau proposed that under the ethereal light of the otherworldly moon, the village street becomes wild and history itself contracts so that "new and old are confounded."[60] Branka Arsić also comments extensively on the nocturnal in Thoreau's writings and wanderings and proposes that, for him, the dark houses another way of knowing and unknowing. But night worlds, Vogel proposed, have also been time-spaces for queer life—the lives of perverts that both hide in the dark and make the darkness into the setting for alternative forms of community or conversely into spaces of deep loneliness.

And while Hughes's contrary desires have been identified with wild nights in Harlem, for White, the nocturnal in 1930s rural England meant something rather different. While the nightclub represents a world where queers revel in subcultural pursuits, the nighttime for White was a space where he battled with his hawk, staying awake for long hours to try to accustom the hawk to his presence and to try to complete the process of "manning" him.[61] On one occasion, when he had lost sleep for days on end, White commented on the pleasurable side of willing himself to stay awake. He celebrated what he called "the extremely beautiful experiences of night denied to so large a percentage of civilization" (28). White then retreated to the barn to keep his lonely vigil and began again the confusing and useless pursuit of trying to tame and master a creature that will revert quickly, inevitably, eternally to a feral state. The shared space of the night for urban queers ("Café, 3 A.M.") and other genius wild ones makes connections across space between the different kinds of bodies that, in the 1930s, represented disorderly attempts to flee family, normativity, impending wars, class hostilities, and intense racial regulation.[62]

The epistemology of the ferox offers us not only a nonmedicalized and nonmoralizing relation to contrary desires and genders, it also opens onto other relations to life, death, animality, the wild, the strange, the inexplicable. Legislation that accompanied the shifts and changes in the organization of sexuality in the late nineteenth and early twentieth centuries did not make the huge definitional distinctions we now take for granted. In Sweden, for example, the term *sodomy* covered both same-sex desire and sex with animals, and both were considered illegal well into the twentieth century after previously being unregulated.[63] Again, the point here is not to make an argument for bringing outlaw forms of love into the warm embrace of recognition, but, rather, to see what forms of love, affection, being and knowing, feeling, making, intuiting, lusting, marking, and enjoying gave way, slowly and incompletely, under the sway of new definitional closure.

The figure of the hawk for White and Westcott, the falcon for Duncan, the peregrine for Baker, and the eagle for Hughes are not simply metaphors for flight and/or predation; they also stand as a reminder for them and for us that human-animal bonds and connections were once highly porous zones of interaction and communication. After all, in other times, such as the medieval period in Britain, as Susan Crane reminds us in *Animal Encounters*, people lived "in daily contact with domestic and wild animals."[64] The severed connection to the wild that inheres to our contemporary understandings of land, house, and home creates longing, curiosity, and desire. Some of these longings for the wild are expressed in the desire to find new objects to master—"some people like to run things"—while others are formed through the desire to escape—"some things like to run"—and the epistemology of the ferox holds these contrary desires in place even now as the homo/hetero binary begins to splinter and crumble under the weight of new ecologies of bodies and selves at the beginning of the twenty-first century.[65]

Becoming Feral

> Further back, there were times when we wondered with all our souls
> what the world was, what love was, what we were ourselves.
> —T. H. White, *The Once and Future King*

Helen Macdonald's book *H is for Hawk* ends as she completes her mourning for her father and her training of the hawk. Macdonald has flirted with the wild; she has participated in the ancient art of falconry, with its jesses and hoods, its fetish equipment, its playfulness, its unrequited love, and its quest for mastery. She has slipped in an out of the "exquisite, wordless sharpness of being a hawk" and has realized once and for all that the world of the hawk "and my world are not the same."[66] Along the way to this revelation that the wild must be left to the wild, Macdonald smartly and effectively narrates the histories of purity, nationalism, and fascism that flicker and in and out of the histories of falconry, wildness, and mastery. Macdonald has learned that national myths as well as fantasies of nature "work to wipe away other cultures, other histories, other ways of loving, working and being in a landscape" (261). Macdonald leaves the wild by the memoir's end, reconciles to the death of her father, ends her mourning, abandons the queerness that clings to a woman "manning" a hawk, and relinquishes her desire to use the hawk to "crossover" to the other side and "bring someone back" (280).

For his part, White, by the end of his memoir, has lost his hawk, failed in his attempt at falconry, sent for and lost a second hawk, set traps for more hawks without capturing them, and learned only that "no hawk can be a pet."[67] He fantasizes a reader for his narrative who would love an ending in which a peck at the window many years later reveals the return of Gos "looking sleek and happy, with his new wife peeping shyly at her toes and the cosy crocodile of babies lined up behind them" (208). But he conjures this scene of heterosexual romantic resolution only to sweep it aside without further ado: "Those things" he barks, "do not happen in the wild life led by hawks" (209).

Indeed, the contrast between Macdonald and White and between them and the Black forms of fierceness I have tracked in this chapter rests upon key distinctions between their various relations to the wild and the normative—in her book, Macdonald situates White as someone who gets too close to the wild, who suffers from wild desires, and who manipulates his hawk out of sexual frustration. She mourns; he is melancholic. What Macdonald accomplishes, in other words, White bungles. What Macdonald tames, White loses control of. The desire for the wild from which Macdonald gracefully withdraws strands White within a set of irresolvable desires. He can neither train his bird nor free it, and he remains tethered to the bird by his own desire for the feral.

In the terrain of the ferox, bodies flee, escape, hide, and seek. They express themselves not simply in same-sex or opposite-sex orientations, but through murderous desires, violent longings, flights from time, chaotic and illegible political associations, and deeply felt relations to animals and the wild. The epistemology of the ferox offers us not only the hegemonic system that, as Sedgwick proposes, produced the meaning of human sexuality in the early twentieth century but also the wild and odd systems it absorbed and erased. The desire to revert to a feral state that White expresses and that Gilles Deleuze and Félix Guattari might call "becoming animal" reaches for a world beyond the human, for relations to other animal forms of life, to emotional genres that exceed the cycles of wanting, needing, guilt, and regret that characterize human domesticity.[68] Deleuze and Guattari counsel us: "Always follow the rhizome by rupture; lengthen, prolong, and relay the line of flight; make it vary, until you have produced the most abstract and tortuous lines of n dimensions and broken directions. Conjugate the deterritorialized flows. Follow the plants: . . . Write, form a rhizome" (11). This exhortation echoes the passage from *The Peregrine*, with which we began, where Baker, some twenty years earlier than Deleuze and Guattari, explains how to approach a hawk as if you were one. The full passage reads:

> To be recognised and accepted by a peregrine you must . . . soothe the hawk from its wildness by a ritual of behaviour as invariable as its own. Hood the glare of the eyes, hide the white tremor of the hands, shade the stark reflecting face, assume the stillness of a tree. A peregrine fears nothing he can see clearly and far off. Approach him across open ground with a steady unfaltering movement. Let your shape grow in size but do not alter its outline. Never hide yourself unless concealment is complete. Be alone. Shun the furtive oddity of man, cringe from the hostile eyes of farms. Learn to fear. To share fear is the greatest bond of all. The hunter must become the thing he hunts. What is, is now, must have the quivering intensity of an arrow thudding into a tree. Yesterday is dim and monochrome. A week ago you were not born. Persist, endure, follow, watch.[69]

As we can see in all of these ferox texts, wildness must also be understood as a sense of time that opposes the temporality of "once and future" that defines sovereignty in White's Arthur narratives. Wildness, all of these authors tell us, lies outside of historical time and has no use for futurity either—the eternal present that defines a queer temporality for both hawk and human joins itself to the past not through traditions or the grand procession of history, but through an inherited sense of unknowing and disorder, through an enduring relation to those times when "we wondered with all our souls what the world was, what love was, what we were ourselves."[70]

Part II
Animality

There are three conditions which often look alike
Yet differ completely, flourish in the same hedgerow:
Attachment to self and to things and to persons,
  detachment
From self and from things and from persons; and,
  growing between them, indifference
Which resembles the others as death resembles life,
Being between two lives — unflowering, between
The live and the dead nettle.

—T. S. Eliot, "Little Gidding"

Animals Wild
and Tame

In a famous Monty Python skit a man (John Cleese) returns to a pet store with a parrot lying face up on the bottom of its cage. "I wish to complain about this parrot what I purchased not half an hour ago from this very boutique." "What's wrong with it?," asks the not-very-interested store owner (Michael Palin). "It's dead, that's what's wrong with it," says an indignant Cleese. "Nah," Palin responds, "it's just resting... stunned." The back-and-forth continues, and then Palin suggests that the parrot is "pining for the fjords," to which Cleese says, "Pining for the fjords?... This parrot is no more, it has ceased to be, it has expired and gone to meet its maker. This is a late parrot,... an ex-parrot."[1]

The "Dead Parrot Sketch"—immortalized in 2014 by Iain Prendergast's huge Norwegian blue sculpture of a parrot lying flat on its back in London's Potters Fields Park, announcing its own extinction and, at once, its continuity as a dead parrot— is a perfect symbol of our time, a time in which we are all already late, deceased, ex-humans masquerading as resting, stunned, or momentarily incapacitated. It speaks not only to the deadness of the parrot but also to the inertia of pet owning and the zombified relations between animals and humans that the pet holds in place. In a sense all pets are dead pets—ex-animals, prosthetic extensions of the human who owns them, stuffed toys wedged up against stuffed humans. Indeed, the pet is the very opposite of the wild bird that, as I discussed in chapter 3, various authors tried and failed to train.

In the remaining chapters, I explore two very specific relations to animals that emerge under the heading of wildness. In the first, we encounter narratives about the wild which figure wildness as animality and humanness as a form of relation that seeks to tame the wild. In the second, the desire for the feral that formed such a large part of the relations between proto-gay authors and the birds they tried to tame now becomes the desire for shared domesticity with the animals we call pets. These chapters investigate relations between children and wild animals, on the one hand, and adults and tamed animals, on the other. In one chapter, the child appears as wild, like the beast it tries to tame, and in the other, the adult's humanity can be discerned only in contradistinction to the animal it has already mastered. At stake in all of these representations of humans and their animal companions, furthermore, as Monty Python's dead parrot sketch implies, are questions about the meaning of life and death in relation to captivity and modern forms of domesticity. Accordingly, what I refer to as *zombie humanism* is a way of defining the human as alive only by positioning our humanity against other creatures that exist only as our prosthetic extensions. This was decidedly not the relation to animality taken up by the writers discussed in chapter 3, who desired to become feral, but the pet, unlike the falcon, is part of a postnatural world in which the human-animal relation shifts out of wildness and into domestication.

In the introduction to *Wild Things*, in relation to post- and antinatural forms of queerness, I recounted an episode in J.-K. Huysman's *Against the Grain*, within which the decadent antihero Des Esseintes orders a tortoise for his country home to serve as an ornament. The tortoise, which Des Esseintes had first glimpsed in a shop window in Paris, is to offset an Oriental rug whose rich colors, Des Esseintes fancies, would reflect nicely against the color of the tortoise's shell. When he orders the tortoise, has it delivered, and places it on his carpet, however, Des Esseintes finds that the tortoise does not serve the purpose he had in mind for it. "He therefore decided to glaze the shell of the tortoise with gold"! From there, he goes on to encrust the tortoise's shell with precious stones and then bejewel the shell with more and more stones and decorations until the tortoise expires from the weight of the material on its back. While of course the tortoise is not a pet in any sense of the word, this episode serves the bleakly humorous function of casting all creatures as mere accessories to human aesthetics—animals become decorative and literal objects of art, and as such, they shuttle, as the tortoise does here, between nature and culture, between life and death, between wild and domestic. Postnatural humanism, within which the human seeks to master animals and turn them into extensions of the human body or into objects for display or into beings that hover as the tortoise does, as the parrot did, between life and death, requires zombified forms of life. These zombified forms must also be located with an epistemology of the ferox, a form of knowing that parses out the differences between the wild and the domestic and lines up humanity and animality on either side of this shifting and porous divide. If for T. H. White the ferox was a terrain of desire that expanded well beyond the human, that extra-human element made up much of its appeal. White's sense that the hawk always returns to the feral state from which it has been coaxed offers him a model of potential permanent wildness that he cultivates in his own topographies of desire. But, more often than not, humans are not drawn into the wild by the animals they love and fear; rather, the animal is drawn into the domain of family life under capitalism, pulled out of the wild and into the warm embrace of domestic stability. If in earlier times the closet provided a sorting mechanism for desire that depended as much on ignorance as on knowledge, so the wild depends as much on the domestic as on the feral or untamable. The closeted gay figure was subject to the mechanics of an open secret. The housed or yarded wild animal—or wild human for that matter—exerts an appeal that lingers from another time and place within which it lived separate from the vagaries of property and the unspoken rules of family life established according to class- and race- specific mandates. The wild, increasingly, is a fantasy of before, a lingering trace of precapitalist logics of life and death; the wild, we imagine, still lives in the family pet, but it dies there too.

New investments in the uniqueness of the human that accompany disastrous environmental decline are dependent on and result in the production of zombie forms of life. Some of these zombified modes of living are routed through animals, others through humans, and still more through the production and circulation of systems dedicated to maintaining living death. And so, for example, as wealthy people invest in new technologies to extend life and maximize longevity, poor people manage with fewer and fewer opportunities for basic health procedures. And as middle-class people gentrify neighborhoods, low-income communities become increasingly precarious and slip in between housing markets. Jordan Peele's breakout hit of 2017, *Get Out*, offered a brilliant take on the racial politics of zombification and offered a horror film in which wealthy, old white people transfer themselves into young Black bodies, making the Black body into a kind of rentable space, a location rather than a person, a housing for the souls of white folks rather than a material space for Black life. And most of these processes of zombification, whether real or imagined, take the form, as they do in *Get Out*, of a benevolent patronage that reflects a deep belief that what is good for the rich and for white people will eventually trickle down into benefits for everyone else. In actual fact, the widening circuits of zombification result in what Ruthie Gilmore has called "premature" death for Black people, near extinction for certain animals, homelessness for poor people, and bare life for the incarcerated, the undocumented, and the animals with whom we live.[2] This dynamic of more life for the few and living death for the many articulates a version of the biopolitical divisions described so well by Michel Foucault and Achille Mbeme, Jasbir Puar, and others. But zombification produces not a hard-and-fast distinction between life and death, but new balancing acts between bio- and necropolitical regimes. Zombie humanism, accordingly, arrogates liveliness, dynamism, vibrancy, and resonance for itself and consigns all other forms of being to the status of inertia and stasis. Jane Bennett's work challenges this distinction by recognizing the vitality of many different forms of life. She writes:

> A life thus names a restless activeness, a destructive-creative force-presence that does not coincide fully with any specific body. A life tears the fabric of the actual without ever coming fully "out" in a person, place, or thing. A life points to what *A Thousand Plateaus* describes as . . . "matter in variation that enters assemblages and leaves them." A life is a vitality proper not to any individual but to "pure immanence," or that protean swarm that is not actual though it is real: "A life contains only virtuals. It is made of virtualities."[3]

In this formulation, liveliness extends way beyond the human and can be located in the slow processes of rot, the fast transmissions of data, the motion of matter-energy. Bennett's book, *Vibrant Matter*, offers a theory of life that abandons the centering of the dynamic human in an otherwise inert world and instead proposes to build a vocabulary for "the active powers issuing from nonsubjects" (ix). If we move with Bennett away from the "figure of an intrinsically inanimate matter," we can understand the activity of living as a force "that does not fully coincide with any specific body" and can contest the "earth-destroying fantasies of conquest and consumption" (ix) that coexist with human-centric visions of a universe populated by live subjects and dead or zombie objects. Bennett's redefinition of life through her conceptualization of vitalism therefore allows for more ecologically minded theories of the human, of world, and it troubles the otherwise too easy boundary we erect between life and death. We could extend Bennett's insights into the divisions between lively and inert to argue that whatever dares to move or to share in lifelike motion gets represented as living death, walking dead, or as not dead because it was never living. Indeed, this is how we think of the animals we farm for food, but it is not how we think about the animals we live alongside for comfort. Zombie humanism signifies, then, in the production of states of life, states of death and states of living death that are projected onto others in order to leave the human situated securely in a warm glow of purposeful being and heroic survival.

In this zombie economy, the pet occupies a high place in the hierarchy of liveliness—it is not living dead like the cattle we slaughter or the chickens we raise; it is warm, real, and alive. It's liveliness depends absolutely on its being tethered to us, its "species companion," and its survival depends on its ability to please us or to answer to our anthropomorphic call for companionability in the forms we mandate—a pet can nip and chew but not bite and scratch; it can whimper or purr but should not bark or whine; a pet must learn obedience and eat and shit when we say, and it must adapt to a carceral reality in exchange for not being eaten.

The practice of harnessing other life-forms to the human has been promoted and celebrated by Donna Haraway and others as an example of a decentering project in which the story of evolution and the narrative of life itself knocks the human out of its orbit and places it in empathic and unselfish relations to other creatures. Haraway herself talks about a human co-history with the dog and about coevolution that must be written as an "ontological choreography," a dance between and among species and not one that features only human dancers.[4] While Bennett would add that such an ontological choreography would have to recognize the presence of all kinds of vibrating life forms, my emphasis on zombie humanism would also note that the dance is still created, enacted, and performed by humans with animals, pets, and other things as props rather than coplayers.

As the "Dead Parrot Sketch" illustrates, the human-pet relation is romanticized by this framework of "companion species" and better understood in terms of another order of zombie humanism within which the human makes a kind of stuffed animal out of the pet and then plays out dramas of dependency, emotional entanglement, and protection in relation to it. Within zombie humanism, all wildness—human/animal/vegetable—becomes fodder for an economy of voracious human consumption. And, so, the human tells herself she is saving the animal as she enslaves it; she tells herself that she is most alive when she makes death a distant reality. And, most importantly, the human doubles down on the concept of the human—a concept that, as we saw in relation to Frank Wilderson's work in the introduction to part I, presumes white benevolence—when in relation to a beloved animal. This sets up the human as white, the animal as other, and the whole cycle of signification that establishes itself around the universal white subject can be rebooted from there.

This is the version of the human that Monty Python always pokes irreverent fun at—it is a version that must die and become extinct in order for large portions of the world to survive. It is also a model that presumes that intimate contact with animals is, first, good for humans; second, good for animals; and, third, totally distinct from and at odds with sex with animals. The animals we love and live with are safe in the human home, we tell ourselves, to the extent that we do not abuse them, we feed them well, we let them outside every now and then, and, most importantly, we refrain from having sex with them.[5] In the engagement with wild things discussed in chapter 4, we will see that an erotic glow continues to emanate from the human-animal dynamic, and in chapter 5 on pets and/as zombies we recognize that the taboo on bestiality has blossomed into an array of activities conducted physically between animals and humans that stop short of what we would call sex but also retain a distinctly erotic charge.

Previous chapters have shown how the wild animal in particular has served as a love object for certain sexual loners who desire not simply the animal body per se but the ferality they read into that form of embodiment. For some, the proximity to wildness is erotic and compelling, and unlike relations to other humans, it is never subject to the domesticating tendencies of marriage and child-rearing. In the introduction, I mentioned the legal shifts that separated bestiality from same-sex sex under various sodomy laws in Europe and the United States. In some ways, scholars have never properly investigated why those two forms of desire were lumped together under the heading of crimes against nature, nor have we considered why we now believe that laws against same-sex sex are vestiges of an earlier, less tolerant society but that statutes against sex with animals are just and right. Gabriel Rosenberg investigates just this web of thorny questions and comes up with some very surprising answers. In "How Meat Changed Sex: The Law of Interspecies Intimacy after Industrial Reproduction," Rosenberg follows the trail of legislation that seeks to identify, prohibit, and punish sex between humans and animals.[6] Rosenberg argues that the very laws that strictly prohibit human-animal sexual contact must simultaneously legitimate and legalize human-animal sexual conduct for the purposes of animal husbandry and within the context of the meat industry. This contradictory function of antibestiality legislation creates a sovereign distinction within the law between bestiality that must be forbidden for reasons of sexuality morality and human-animal sexual conduct that may be deemed necessary for the production of meat. According to the article, bestiality laws operate according to the dictates and needs of capital rather than according to any form of sexual morality.

Sex between humans and animals was clearly part of the repertoire of early modern societies. Why else would legislative clusters criminalizing purported crimes against nature include such activities under the heading of sodomy? Rosenberg notes, indeed, that very recent repeals of crimes against nature (CAN) legislation had the unwitting effect of legalizing both homosexual acts and sex acts between humans and animals. Other scholars have previously investigated this odd grouping of homosexuality and bestiality under the sign of sodomy, and Jens Rydstrom's *Sinners and Citizens* argues that concerns about bestiality in rural Sweden gave way to worries over same-sex penetrative sex as populations moved, in the early twentieth century, from the countryside to the cities.[7] But no one before Rosenberg had written this kind of biopolitical account of the production of animal life (through human-assisted artificial reproduction) for death (within the industrial production of meat) in relation to the legal prohibition of bestiality.

Rosenberg looks at three distinct strands of the legislation on bestiality and meat production. In one line of inquiry he lays out the recent history of bestiality and explains how and why the repeal of CAN legislation first decriminalized bestiality and then recriminalized it with the exception of human-assisted artificial reproduction of animals. Given how much sexual contact is required between humans and animals in order for successful animal husbandry to occur, it would have been very easy, Rosenberg proposes, for cattlemen and farmers to be prosecuted by animal rights advocates or others under bestiality laws. Supplemental legislation therefore had to be written and circulated in order to prevent meat producers from being charged with unnatural and perverse contact with the animals they bred to kill. In a second strand, though, Rosenberg explores the politics of what he calls "the agricultural exception" to the ban on human-animal sexual contact and details the kinds of contacts between humans and animals that make up contemporary mechanized animal reproduction.[8] He also shows, in this section, how the laws banning bestiality in effect produce a sovereign right to distinguish between often identical acts between humans and animals while producing animals as "like children" (482) in their silence, their inability to consent to sexual conduct, and their need of protection. In the final section Rosenberg unpacks the contradictions of a social order that condemns sex between humans and companion animals while industrializing sex for the purpose of producing meat and streamlining the reproduction of more animals to kill (stimulating life for death). Here Rosenberg mounts a critique of Giorgio Agamben's theory of speciation in *Homo Sacer* and *The Open* through a close and astute reading of the cult film *Zoo*, about a group of men who meet to engage in penetrative sex with horses. Arguing for a historically specific understanding of Agamben's "ontotheology," on the one hand, and for the differentiation of animals closed to sex (pets) and animals opened to sex (meat animals), on the other, the author builds to a powerful conclusion: "The bestialist, the farmer, and the livestock animal are coherent subjects of law only within the context of the system of industrial meat that has emerged in the past half century. And rather than figures of opposition, the bestialist and meat farmer are situated as mutually constituting categories, figures who are distinguished not by their sometimes functionally identical relations to animals, but, in fact, by their relations to biocapital reproduction" (489).

Using a combination of queer theory, legal argument, and an engagement with theorists of bare life and biopolitics, Rosenberg weaves a powerful case for considering meat agriculture as a form of trans-speciative procreation. Without digging into the culture of pet owning and all of its affective and physical contradictions, Rosenberg reminds us that the difference between animals we love and animals we eat is not about companionship, but about capital. In this respect, not only is this essay a fascinating account of the history of bestiality laws, but it contributes to what I am calling here the biopolitical management of life and death as it functions through our relations to animals and through the production of zombified forms of life and living death. Work like this that foregoes conventional animal rights narratives and investigates the possibility that bestiality laws are not for protection of animals, but for the maintenance of the financialization of livestock populations, punctures many dearly held views on human-animal love, lust, and labor. And once we begin to acknowledge the tangled relations between pet owning and meat production, it will be much harder to claim that the cat or dog we saved from the animal rescue center confirms the good intentions of the pet owner.

Furthermore, this contextualization of pet owning in relation to meat production and in opposition to bestiality offers traction for projects by scholars, like Zakkiyah Jackson, who want to separate out discourses of pet ownership from their often seemingly intuitive connections to slavery precisely because of the reinvestment in the category of the human that such comparisons allow.

Rather than simply settling for a critique that reduces humans to the status of animals under slavery, Jackson takes aim at the version of the human that such an equation allows. In the essay "Losing Manhood: Animality and Plasticity in the (Neo)Slave Narrative," Jackson argues that "in the case of slavery, humanization and captivity go hand in hand."[9] Here Jackson brilliantly refuses the concept of a process of "humanization" that undoes the violence of slavery and instead proposes that "slavery is a technology for producing a kind of human" (96). She makes the connection to wildness clear in an astonishing passage that lays out the relations between transformation, plasticity, humanity, and concepts of *becoming* as they are bundled together within an epistemology organized to insist upon human projects of building and mutating, making and constructing: "The black(ened) can only be defined as plastic: impressionable, stretchable, and misshapen to the point that the mind does not survive—it goes wild. We are well beyond alienation, exploitation, subjection, domestication, and even animalization; we can only describe such transmogrification as a form of engineering. *Slavery's technologies were not the denial of humanity but the plasticization of humanity.*"[10] *It goes wild.* The concept here of a Blackness out of mind and reduced to body does not lead to the conclusion that humanization saves, but rather that *redemption itself is the problem.*

And yet, if the analogy between pet owning and slavery is deeply suspicious, so too is the insistence on the lack of connection between humans and ferals. The category of the feral, indeed, is often just the prelude to a massacre in that it firms up discontinuities between the animals we love, the animals we eat, and the animals we classify as pests in order to justify their extermination. And while *the feral*, as demonstrated in chapter 3, exerts its own erotic pull on humans, it also takes its place within systems of racialization that, as Jackson asserts, reinvest in the construction of the human. Indeed, as Fiona Probyn-Rapsey confirms in "Five Propositions on Ferals," "the 'feral' should remind us that the language of species is entangled with the language of race."[11] And that, furthermore, the same systems of classification invented by Carl Linneaus to know and master the so-called natural world produced, at the same time, a shadow system of classification for the unnatural, the racially diverse, the unproductive, and the criminal.

Building on the deconstruction of the benevolence of the human at which both Rosenberg and Jackson take aim, this section of *Wild Things* distrusts the hard-and-fast distinctions between pets and other animals in which Euro-Americans have become invested and asks not just where the wild things are, but what happened to them and when and why they ceased to be wild, when and why they became taboo as sex objects but compulsory as love objects, and how and why we misunderstand the wild animals we watch from a distance, the tame animals we admit to our household, and the forms of humanity that make such distinctions meaningful. Even a brief survey of bumper sticker speech confirms that the investments people make in dogs and cats in particular are based on some supposition that a domestic relation to an animal makes you a better person: "The more people I meet, the more I like my dog"; "Dogs are people too!"; "Kids are for people who can't have dogs"; "Who rescued who?"; "Dogs have owners, cats have staff"; "Beware of people who dislike cats"; "Furry lives matter"; and so on. The next two chapters will dig deep into such belief systems and propose that owning animals does not make you better, nicer, kinder, gentler, more benevolent; it just enmeshes you much more deeply in the production of living death.

FOUR

Where the Wild Things Are

Humans, Animals, and Children

Wild—Not under, or not submitting to, control or restraint; taking, or disposed to take, one's own way; uncontrolled. Primarily of animals and hence of persons and things, with various shades of meaning. Acting or moving freely without restraint; going at one's own will; unconfined, unrestricted.

—Oxford English Dictionary

We speak of the child as wild and monstrous.

—Kathryn Bond Stockton, *Growing Sideways*

Let the wild rumpus start!

—Maurice Sendak, *Where the Wild Things Are*

I concluded my book on failure, *The Queer Art of Failure,* with an iconic scene from *Fantastic Mr. Fox* in which the fox and his friends, on their way home from defeating the farmers using guerrilla warfare, catch a glimpse of a wolf in the wild. In that book I made an argument for creative failure as an oppositional force to the conformity of success and proposed the archive of children's animation films as a collection of anarchist fabulations designed to appeal to the chaotic viewership of the child who is situated differently in relation to time and space. Mr. Fox for me was an example of a creature who opts out of the civilized, upwardly mobile world in favor of a shared relation to reward and punishment. In *Fantastic Mr. Fox* the wild sometimes comes in the form of an encounter between the semidomesticated and the unknown, speech and silence, motion and stillness, and sometimes it comes without warning, as in the wolf scene. But ultimately the wild is an affective space where temporality is uncertain, relation is improvised, and futurity is on hold. Into this space walks a figure we cannot classify, who refuses to engage us in conventional terms but speaks instead in a gestural language, one that finds solidarity, connection, and, yes, hope in the continued commitment to the dark, the lonely, and the wild. The wild of the animated film, however, and this is what engaged me in *The Queer Art of Failure*, is also a vision of the shared reality of animal and child (the very relation, we may recall, that Stravinsky called up in order to explain the audiences for his music). In this chapter, I explore concepts of the feral that inhere to shared correspondences and differences between animals and children. And the wolf, as it did in *Fantastic Mr. Fox*, becomes a dense transfer point for fantasies of animality, wildness, darkness, and anarchy.

For example, as discussed in the introduction to part I, Maurice Sendak's *Where the Wild Things Are* opens with Max dressed in wolf's clothing and defying the law of the parent while identifying with the stuffed toy and the animals and wild things beyond the family home. It is significant that his chosen outfit is a wolf costume and the stuffed toy is a kind of dog. The opposition between wild and domesticated is clearly rendered in their opposition.

The wolf also makes a startling appearance in a beautiful book about rewilding projects in Europe in an era of environmental collapse. In *Feral: Rewilding the Land, the Sea and Human Life*, British environmentalist George Monbiot provides a wide-ranging critique of the mismanagement of green spaces and offers a far-reaching proposal for rewilding or allowing nature "to find its own way."[1] In an echo of contemporary anarchisms, Monbiot insists that his project has "no end points" (10); instead he proposes that Europeans cease to manage nature and, on behalf of "an unmet need for a wilder life" (13), engage new forms of environmentalism that neither imagine that they can go back to some earlier moment of pristine wildness nor embrace a new primitivism. Instead, Monbiot offers both lyrical and practical solutions to the wastefulness of contemporary uses of space. The feral, for him, is an imaginative as much as a scientific project and requires the recognition of the beauty of untidiness, the necessity of disorder, and the charisma of the wild animal. In relation to the appeal of the wild animal, he offers the example of the wolf: "I want to see the wolves reintroduced because wolves are fascinating and because they help to reintroduce the complexity and trophic diversity in which our ecosystems

CHAPTER FOUR

are lacking. I want to see wolves reintroduced because they feel to me like the shadow that fleets between systole and diastole, because they are the necessary monsters of the mind, inhabitants of the more passionate world against which we have locked our doors" (117).

The juxtaposition in Monbiot's argument for the reintroduction of wolves does not simply depend on a rational ecological argument but also makes a more fanciful case for the creature as evidence of "complexity" on the one hand and a more "passionate" world on the other. In another section of his book Monbiot reminds us that not so very long ago truly marvelous creatures roamed the earth and often crossed paths with humans. In the Middle Ages, humans could be excused for believing in monsters and miracles given the wide range of monstrous creatures they could expect to encounter over the course of their rather short lives. Nowadays, of course, in many urban areas around the world wild creatures are squeezed into smaller and smaller tracts of land while human development eats up all of the space, all of the land, and tries to eliminate the possibility of any confrontation between the human and the animal unless it takes the form of pet ownership. Monbiot remarks: "The absence of monsters forces us to sublimate and transliterate, to invent quests and challenges, to seek an escape from ecological boredom" (139). His treatise, a passionate manifesto as well as a pragmatic how-to book, despite its power and wisdom, still invests in a fairly clear separation of the human from the animal or what Jacques Derrida called "the beast and the sovereign."[2] In what follows, we go in search of wild things and find they are closer than we thought.

The beast in Derrida's *The Beast and the Sovereign* is not exactly the same as the animal; nor is it simply animal nature expressed within a human form. The beast, for Derrida, appears as part of a gendered dyad—*la bête, le souverain*— and plays the role of the feminine, the subjugated, the silent, the wild and un-ruly, the criminal, the raw, the pack, the people, the ferocious, the feral. Der-rida tracks the role of the beast as other to the sovereign through a series of ar-cane and folkloric references, through references to wolves and foxes, through close readings of Defoe's *Robinson Crusoe* and Heidegger's seminars, and in relation to a roguish refusal of the law. The beast and the sovereign are alike as well as different—they both stand outside the law, they wield power and violence, and they represent the chaos that can be unleashed by the exercise of either too much power (absolute or solitary sovereignty in Crusoe's case) or too little (as in the case of Friday or Poll, the colonized objects of Crusoe's rule). The beast and the sovereign are neither woman and man nor subject and ruler; they are, rather, the poles of governance in a system in which some have all and many have nothing.

This zero-sum calculation of rule shifts, as Michel Foucault has shown, in the contemporary period into a dispersed set of relations to power, some of which are historically conditioned by race and class while others are sedimented in temporal and spatial relations. The terms *child* and *animal* are part of this sedimentation — they mark a seemingly unchangeable outside to power and could even be considered part of a wild world that the adult human forsakes in order to be "free."[3] As adults enter into the realm of marriage, reproduction, work, compliance, and, ultimately, docility, they also give up on another space, one governed by wild emotions, rebellion, and refusal. In what follows, we will track the child into the space of the wild and see what relations between bestiality and sovereignty s/he calls into being. "Let the wild rumpus start!"[4]

Sovereign? Beast?

The sovereign is not an angel, but, one might say, he who plays the sovereign plays the beast. The sovereign makes himself the beast, has himself the beast, sometimes in the most troubling sense of a zoophilia or even a bestiality the historical symptoms of which we would need to inventory, detect, or even interpret.... And then the supposed sovereign subject begins, by an invincible attraction, to look like the beast he is supposed to subject to himself (and we already know, having often — last time too — verified it, that in the place of the beast one can put, in the same hierarchy, the slave, the woman, the child).

—Jacques Derrida, *The Beast and the Sovereign*

Resisting from the start any intimation that the sovereign and the beast are diametrically opposed, Derrida reminds us that the sovereign, unlike God, is no angel. He is not innocent or beyond flesh. The sovereign does not sit in opposition to the bestial; rather, he owns the beast. He has decision-making power over the lives of the bestial (the slave, the woman, the child, the animal), but in order to deploy this power he must make decisions that are not obvious or inevitable and that therefore reside in the realm of the irrational, the unlikely, the unthinkable. In order to operate as sovereign, in other words, the sovereign descends into the territory that seemed to belong to the bestial. But Derrida also reminds us that there is also an erotic charge to the relation between sovereign and beast, a charge that lingers in the term *bestiality* and that conjures a forbidden sexual relation that only requires prohibition because it is likely and dangerously possible.

This exact relation of a dangerous erotic encounter between the bestial and the sovereign informs an art piece by Ines Doujak that in 2016 was at the center of the controversial decision by the Barcelona Museum of Contemporary Art (MACBA) to cancel a show based on *The Beast and the Sovereign*. Doujak's piece, *Not Dressed for Conquering*, depicts a three-way sodomitical encounter involving former Spanish king Juan Carlos, Bolivian feminist and labor leader Domitila Chúngara, and a dog/wolf figure. This explicit image is what led the director of MACBA to withdraw the artwork from the show and to fire the curators, Paul Preciado and Valentin Roma. Of course, the obscenity depicted in Doujak's work is in no way extraneous to the understanding of power that Derrida advances. In his seminars, power stages certain encounters within which an array of positions can be taken. Sovereignty, like bestiality, is allegorized rather than inhabited by a figure like the king, and bestiality is symbolized by rather than attached to the animal. Furthermore, the attributes of all of the positions within this field of power can be switched around, and pleasure and power and conquest form a dense network of relations, erotic connections, and map contradictory relations to desire, domination, and duty.

By censoring the piece, the MACBA director read obscenity literally onto the artwork instead of abstractly seeing how its explicit nature brings out the erotic charge already present within relations of power and revealed the way these relations structure hierarchies and ensure the dominion of certain groups. In other words, the chain of command and the chain of being, here rendered as a literal sexual scene of penetration and as a series of sexual conquests, tend to enter into representation free of the taint of eros and scandal. Doujak's artwork, with its title that plays on human and animal nudity, names the frisson of conquest as sodomitical. As a title, *Not Dressed for Conquering* could imply that the figures in the sculpture are dressed inappropriately for the business of conquest or that they are not dressed at all or that they are refusing to dress for conquest. The whole piece also puns on the well-known image of "the emperor has no clothes" and literally and figuratively exposes the naked body of the sovereign. In its nakedness, the sovereign is vulnerable, human, and the last part of a chain that begins with the wolf. After all, in the three-way depicted by the sculpture it is the wolf that occupies the powerful position of fucking but not getting fucked. The middle figure in this sequence also commands our attention; breaking with the male chain of homoerotic power, Chúngara appears here sodomizing the king of Spain. The king's abjection is completed by the insertion of a mouth gag, in the form of green plants, but is also implied by the fact that he is fucked by a woman. The fact that she is also sodomized here, by a wolf, could indicate her own subjugation, and yet Doujak represents Chúngara and the wolf as upright, as potential partners, while the king is on all fours and bent over. Part of the controversy over the image certainly issues from the compromising position of the king, but the power of the sculpture to shock must also emerge from this staging of bestiality without judgment. If Chúngara and the wolf are connected in their project to humiliate and defeat the king, then the spectacle of bestiality serves not as a scene of subjugation for Chúngara, but as a statement of solidarity between the feminist and the wild creature she does not seek to control.

Doujak's artwork renders visible and explicit the relations and tensions that attend to even the most seemingly allegorical representations of animal-human interaction. The configuration of the beast and the sovereign, as Derrida proposes, would seem to be oppositional—the sovereign is not the beast and rules the beast; the beast is ruled by the sovereign, and this arrangement confirms and enacts sovereign power. But, as time goes on, Derrida offers, "the sovereign makes himself the beast, has himself the beast."[5] The sovereign turns beast, the beast turns sovereign, and the brutality that distinguished the world of animals from the world of humans becomes the common ground for a new set of disturbing relations. While Doujak's artwork relays the relations between man, woman, and animal through the figure of conquest, by adding another figure, the child, we find new constellations of power, pleasure, rule, and submission. In what follows, I offer two examples of well-known cultural texts that bring out the same kinds of tensions, frictions, and erotic scenes within a shifting association of sovereignty and bestiality as they link to child bodies, to animal bodies, and to wild adults.

In the first example, *Where the Wild Things Are*, the bestial is a realm beyond the family but accessible by the child alone. It is not a place for children, but a realm where the child can be king and adults face their own ruin. Max, the small boy who sails for days to reach the wild things, feels himself to be free in the world of adults who do not seek to rule him and feels powerful in the space where instead he occupies the place of the sovereign. But ultimately Max finds that being king is not preferable to being ruled and that the place where the wild things are lies beyond the place where the ruined adults seek guidance. In the second example, Yann Martel's *Life of Pi*, the narrator grows up in proximity to a zoo in Pondicherry, India, and learns hard truths about the relations between humans and animals. Martel writes in the voice of Pi: "Well-meaning but misinformed people think animals in the wild are 'happy' because they are 'free.' . . . This is not the way it is. Animals in the wild lead lives of compulsion and necessity within an unforgiving social hierarchy in an environment where the supply of fear is high and the supply of food low. . . .

What is the meaning of freedom in such a context?"[6] Like Robinson Crusoe, an obvious literary relative of Pi and Max, both boys find themselves in a wild place with a wild thing for companionship.[7] And both discover that wildness is not the territorial equivalent of freedom. The wild, we are reminded throughout both texts, is not simply the result of the absence of rules; wildness has its own regulatory regimes, its own concept of order, and its own hierarchies and modes of domination.

The wild, we will see in these narratives, as it functions in relation to discourses of civilization and social stability, also depends heavily on distinctions between animals, children, and adult humans. But, what makes this distinction so legible, so seemingly intuitive? What is it that children and animals exemplify that the adult human does not? What wildness do children and animals express and inhabit, and what happens to our conception of this wildness in relation to adult humans? Is maturation a process of taming, and is childhood a human experience of the wild? And what versions of the adult human oppose wildness? What versions inhabit it? More precisely, how and when and where does the wild become a construction of racial otherness that depends for its signifying power on temporal models of the primitive, on the one hand, and bestial constructions of desire and culture, on the other?

Where the Wild Things Are

And let's not forget the wolves. I insist on the forgetting as much as
on the wolves and the genelycology because what we should not stint on here
[*foire l'iconomie de*] is the economy of forgetting as repression, and some logic of the
political unconscious which busies itself around all these proliferating productions
and all these chasings after, panting after so many animal monsters, fantastic beasts,
chimeras, and centaurs that the point, in chasing them, is to cause them to flee, to
forget them, repress them, of course, but also (and it is not simply the contrary),
on the contrary, to capture them, domesticate them, humanize them,
anthropomorphize them, tame them, cultivate them, park them,
which is possible only by animalizing man and letting so many symptoms
show up on the surface of political and politological discourse.
—Jacques Derrida, *The Beast and the Sovereign*

And let's not forget the wolves. In *Where the Wild Things Are*, a beautiful and seductive story of childhood rebellion and exploration, the child-animal-wild continuum names a set of relations that cordon off the home from the world, that situate love alongside violence, and that link mobility to freedom and sequestering to ruination. Sendak introduces us to world threatened by a catastrophic conflict between mother and child, burdened by the phallic power of the absent father, and soaking in the child's inevitable encounter with rejection and departure.

The child in this story, Max, may not have been raised by wolves, but he is, at any rate, wearing a wolf suit and making enough mischief that his mother calls him a "wild thing."[8] In response to his mother, and while embracing his wildness, Max says "I'll eat you up." For his punishment, Max is sent to bed without supper, and as he stands in his room, alone and hungry, a world grows around him and then an ocean and then a boat, and he sails off, "in and out of weeks," until he arrives "where the wild things are." The wild things, part human and part animal, "roared their terrible roars and gnashed their terrible teeth and rolled their terrible eyes and showed their terrible claws." When the wild beasts see that Max is not afraid of them, and when he tells the creatures to "be still!," the wild things make Max their king and celebrate with a wild rumpus. Eventually Max gets sick of being king and "the most wild thing of all"; he is lonely and wants to be loved and fed. And so, home he goes, lured by the smell of his mother's cooking, and he reenters the home, perhaps in the absence of any other truly wild space to go.

Sendak, who died in 2012 at the age of eighty-three, was the child of Jewish-Polish immigrant parents who moved to Brooklyn in the 1920s; he was also gay. Indeed, queerness limns *Where the Wild Things Are* and resides within the implicit critique of the family and in the marginalized spaces to which the wild things have been banished. Publication of the book certainly raised concerns for some parents, and initially it was excluded from some libraries in 1963 despite being very well received (the book won the Caldecott Medal in 1964). The grotesque figures that make up the world of the wild, and the anger that propels the small protagonist to join them, along with the implication that there are worlds of rejected people just beyond the space of the domestic, go some way toward identifying both the disturbing quality of the book and the queerness that underlines its narrative. Max's status, in his wolf costume, as half boy–half animal, as partially wild, confirms the unsettled arrangement of desire and embodiment that might constitute the precondition for queerness. Wildness, in this book, sometimes functions as a synonym for queerness, but at other times it names a mode of being that lies outside of the systems of classification that nest human bodies into clear and nonoverlapping categories. Wildness names the potential of certain forms of desire to stray beyond the boundaries of family and home. For this reason, Sendak's gayness, while not an explicit part of his storytelling, props up the human-animal-child dynamics in much of his work that are notable for their eccentricity.

Sendak's Jewishness also played a role in his conjuring of the wild. Sendak saw childhood not as an experience of "sweetness and light," but as a dark experience of anger and rage as well as cruelty.[9] Sendak supposedly modeled his wild beasts on his older Jewish relatives who, according to him, were unpredictable and a little threatening because they were always offering to "eat you up." In an interview with the *Guardian* published in 2011, Sendak told the journalist, "The monsters from *Wild Things* were based on his own relatives. They would visit his house in Brooklyn when he was growing up ('All crazy—crazy faces and wild eyes') and pinch his cheeks until they were red. Looking back, he sees how desperate they all were, these first-generation immigrants from Poland, with no English, no education and, although they didn't know it in 1930, a family back home facing extinction in the concentration camps."[10] The article continues: "Sendak's picture books acknowledge the terrors of childhood, how vicious and lonely it can be." Sendak, who understood himself as a lonely child of desperate parents, never tried to soften the edges on life for his child readers, and they loved him for it. He never apologized for the menace his story presented, a menace that emerged from the intimate space of the family itself. Sendak refused the sentimentality that shrouds so much of children's literature and offered his small antiheroes up to the darkness, to the monsters, to the wild.

Max, meanwhile, after a day of being bad and all dressed up in his wolf suit, inspires his mother's wrath. She calls him a "wild thing," to which he responds by saying "I'll eat you up!," and "so he was sent to bed without eating anything."[11] In his bedroom that fateful night, as he lay estranged from his mother, at odds with the world, wild in his aloneness, a new world grows around him—first a forest sprouts, the vines hang from the ceiling, and finally "the walls became the world around." When an "ocean tumbled by with a private boat for Max," he sets sail across time and space until he arrives where the wild things are. The wild things do their wild thing routines—"they roared their terrible roars and gnashed their terrible teeth and rolled their terrible eyes and showed their terrible claws." The repetition of "terrible" here magnifies the threat that the monsters perform and partakes in a state that Adriana Caverero names as part of "horrorism."[12] *Horrorism*, for Caverero, describes modern violence that numbs the human, stills it, undoes it. But more than this, horrorism is violence that issues from the very people and institutions that claim to protect. Offering the mother as an obvious example of a figure who can either care for the child or destroy it, Caverero proposes that care and harm are nestled within the same social function. The monsters Max encounters, then, are the unleashed creatures of the maternal unconscious, the beasts who represent the mother's deep ambivalence toward the child—shall I eat it or let it eat? Shall I kill it, silence it, or help it to thrive? But Max has his own magic trick and rather than be stilled by the wild things he tames them by returning the gaze and "staring into all their yellow eyes without blinking once."[13] The child's gaze is terrifying in its unwavering and all-seeing control. He knows he must still or be stilled, see or be seen, rule or be ruled, eat or be eaten. And so, in this Hobbesian state of nature, in a world of violence and wildness, Max does the only thing possible as child sovereign. He calls for a riot, he authorizes confusion and disorder, he indulges his orientation to chaos. "And now," cries Max, "let the wild rumpus start!"

In one domestic space, the home, the child performs wildness in response to an adult; and in the realm of the wild things, Max presides over the wild things who threaten, in response, to eat *him* up. And because he shuttles between the order of the oedipal household, where his mother rules, and the ruined world of the wild, where no one is in charge but him, he knows the parameters of the real—he sees that either you settle in to the domestic prison you have been offered or you set sail for another, potentially more violent, terrain. The wild here is not a place and not an identity; it is neither sanctuary nor utopia. The wild is not heaven, hell, or anything in between; the wild is the space that the child and adult share in their antipathy to one another. The wild is entropic, cruel, and violent; it is, in the words of T. S. Eliot in "East Coker," "the way of dispossession" in which "in order to arrive at what you are not / You must go through the way in which you are not. / And what you do not know is the only thing you know / And what you own is what you do not own / And where you are is where you are not."[14] Eliot and Sendak are saying something similar here—they both recognize that only the "movement of darkness on darkness" can lead to knowledge;[15] only in the wild rumpus can monsters recognize each other; only in negation can the child know that it must represent and fail to represent innocence. When the mapping of innocence onto the child fails, indeed, and the failure is inevitable, we speak of the child as wild and monstrous.

In the context of Sendak's children's book, the child is never made to shoulder the burden of innocence. Here, he knows what is expected and refuses to perform. And so, in the story, the wild is a shifting landscape that depends on an odd geometry of human, child, and animal arrangements. When the child is king, adults are ruined; where adults are wild, children cohabit uneasily and precariously with them; where children are wild, adults enforce

CHAPTER FOUR

rules and regulations. Wildness, in other words, is a set of relations, a constellation really, within which bodies take up roles and scripts in relation to one another. At home, Max is the wild thing because he defies his mother and because he issues the cannibalistic threat to "eat her up." Far from home, Max is not wild because he meets the creatures who are; these wild things are survivors, ruined adults who have been cast out of the space of the domestic and the tame and who have found the violence of the wild preferable to the violence of the domestic.

Like an embodiment of the amoral, the wild things stand in opposition to what Nietzsche calls the "disgrace" of the domesticated human who must use morality and clichés to cover over their true feelings of anger, outrage, disappointment, and fear. This tension between the wild side of human nature and the civilized or domesticated side comes to the surface in book 5 of *The Gay Science*, where Nietzsche writes:

> Now consider the way "moral man" is dressed up, how he is veiled behind moral formulas and concepts of decency—the way our actions are benevolently concealed by the concepts of duty, virtue, sense of community, honorableness, self-denial—should the reasons for all this not be equally good? I am not suggesting that all this is meant to mask human malice and villainy—the wild animal in us; my idea is, on the contrary, that it is precisely as *tame animals* that we are a shameful sight and in need of the moral disguise, that the "inner man" in Europe is not by a long shot bad enough to show himself without shame (or to be *beautiful*). The European disguises himself *with morality* because he has become a sick, sickly, crippled animal that has good reasons for being "tame"; for he is almost an abortion, scarce half made up, weak, awkward.[16]

Even allowing for the instability of translation, this is an outrageous passage and one that contributes to the readings of Nietzsche as invested in a model of superior and inferior beings. But, actually, Nietzsche, like Freud, is trying to poke at and challenge the moral order requiring that man, however wild he may be, perform his goodness in quotidian interactions. Conventional wisdom opposes the wild to the tame in terms of a wildness that must be dressed up and covered, suppressed and denied. But for Nietzsche, the wild animal in European man represents an order of being that does not require the alibi of morality to cover over his violent orientation to the rest of the world. The "tame" here is the name for the vexed relation between goodness and exploitative violence that continues to define dominance. Lashing out at "the herd animal," Nietzsche fears not the predator, but the prey: "It is not the ferocity of the beast of prey that requires a moral disguise but the herd animal with its profound mediocrity, timidity, and boredom with itself" (295). Nietzsche depicts this herd animal in terms that connect disability—"sick, sickly, crippled"—to the status of the nonhuman—"animal"—and both to the liminality of the "abortion" (295). In this way, Nietzsche's own logic doubles back on itself and reinvests in the very binary of wild/tame that he seems to want to question. While we might see value in critiquing the herd animal or the prey for its "mediocrity," and while we might want to see a potentially decolonial violence unleashed in the figure of the predator, the ableist characterization of the tame human as also "crippled" reinvests in a colonial power sequence and, perhaps, declaws the critique of domestication that Nietzsche offers.

The Nietzschean "things" that Max meets are wild because they can never go home, because they no longer believe in the falsehoods of family and community, and because they refuse to disguise their wildness, their ruination, and their place in a violent order of things. The wild things are not dressing for conquest, Doujak might say. They are naked, exposed, committed neither to covering up their wildness nor to performing civility. They are wild, they are angry, and they will not be tamed. What was understood to be disturbing about Sendak's book in the years after it was published, however, has changed over time. In the late 1960s, Bruno Bettelheim critiqued *Where the Wild Things Are* in *Ladies' Home Journal*. Bettelheim claimed that Sendak's book played upon a child's fear of being abandoned by one's mother. And, a critic for *Publisher's Weekly* worried that "the plan and technique of the illustrations are superb. . . . But they may well prove frightening, accompanied as they are by a pointless and confusing story."[17] Child readers did not find the story pointless, reminding us that children read differently and see the relation between image and text with different eyes, and while some children may have found the book frightening, it has been experienced by millions of children as a book that delivers a pleasurable thrill. Sendak responded to criticism of his work in *The Art of Maurice Sendak*, in which he was quoted as saying, "I wanted my wild things to be frightening."[18]

Some forty years after its original publication, Sendak's beloved book was turned into a film of the same name by Spike Jonze (2009). In this film version, a different kind of threat emerges. If the original book made some people worry about a tale of abandonment, the film draws out the sadness and melancholia of the wild and those who live there. In an odd, family-unfriendly film peopled with puppets and humans, Jonze was able to convey the weightiness and the burden of wildness. For a start, the puppet heads worn by the puppeteers in the film, and created by the Jim Hensen Company of Muppets fame, were literally too heavy and required some careful balancing by the puppeteers who wore them. Eventually the scenes with the puppet heads were reshot using CGI. Second, Warner Bros. was not happy with how bleak the film was and wanted Jonze to reshoot; however, Jonze insisted on sticking to the mood he had established for the characters and Max and sacrificed high-volume audiences by refusing to make the film into just another adorable kids movie with a clear moral frame. Finally, the decision to use puppets rather than animate the wild things surely contributed to the film's conjuring of a level of discomfort for the viewer. Sendak refused to sanction an animated version because he felt that animation would make the wild things cute and Max adorable, and the whole wild rumpus would lose its menacing edge.

Ultimately in *Where the Wild Things Are*, the wild, despite the promise of the title, is not a destination, and nor is it an identity. Rather the wild is the un/place where the people who are left outside of domesticity reside—small children, animals, and ruined adults, an anticommunity of wildness. We find survivors, humans who have lost all belief in the concept of humanity as something noble, empathetic, and uplifting and for whom concepts like order, civilization, goodness, and right mean nothing and fail to provide the protection they imply. For the wild things, the violence of the world has been revealed, and nothing can ever be the same. The connection between Max and these survivors is their unvarnished view of the world, their understanding that the world is brutal and violent and that it will eat you if you do not threaten to eat it. These fantasies of incorporation, moreover, are both fantasies of power and recognitions of the way that power works incorporatively, vertiginously even; power is not something to have or to wield, Max learns the hard way, it is something that will swallow you whole, absorb you into its organic system. The "thing" in "wild things" surely distances being from subjecthood and conveys an object like status to the bodies of those who are ruled and rejected.

Life of Pi

Sexuality is most often held to be bestial in itself; sexual desire is the beast in man, the most boisterous and most avid, the most voracious beast.
—Jacques Derrida, *The Sovereign and the Beast*

Where the Wild Things Are must surely have been a huge influence on Yann Martel's *Life of Pi* (2001). And yet, Martel never directly credits Sendak with providing some of the inspiration for this story of a young boy lost in the wild with creatures he cannot control. However, in several interviews, Martel does reveal that a direct influence on *Life of Pi* was a story by a Brazilian author, Moacyr Scliar, titled *Max and the Cats*.[19] In Scliar's 1981 novella, a young Jewish boy, Max Schmidt, leaves Germany for Brazil just as the Nazis are coming to power. He flees Germany on a ship that has zoo animals in the hold, but the ship goes down as part of an insurance scam and Max finds himself in a lifeboat with a black Jaguar. Max in *Max and the Cats* surely cites Max in *Where the Wild Things Are*, and both books reference Nazism and the Holocaust as part of the backdrop against which the struggle between boy, animal, and wildness takes place. But Scliar's book also makes slavery into one of the crucial reference points for his allegory of the wild, the tame, the free, and the brutal.

The insurance scheme in *Max and the Cats* that dooms Max's ship quotes implicitly the infamous case of insurance fraud that became the basis for M. NourbeSe Philip's book of poetry, *Zong!* (2011). In 1781, according to the legal records Philip consulted, the captain of a slave ship named *Zong* threw 130 slaves, many of them sick, overboard in the hopes of collecting the insurance money on his jeopardized "cargo."[20] The legal case that followed, *Gregson v. Gilbert*, holds within it and in the language of the law, the story of an unspeakable crime. While the legal court ruled that there were no grounds for murder charges, the company was able to accuse the ship's captain of fraud. In the case that followed, and in highly rationalized legal language, the murdered slaves were reduced once more to goods, property, and things. In an attempt to recover damages for lost cargo, and to hold the captain responsible for recklessly disposing of "property," the case never addressed the real crime of ownership that animates the whole endeavor. In a brilliant crafting of alternative history, Philip took the language of the legal briefs and reworked the bloodless narrative told there into a wild text of sorrow, outrage, mourning, and silence. At times in *Zong!* words fall apart—the first piece is the complete fragmentation of the word "water" (3)—and at others, a legal brief is turned into song—"of / water / rains &, dead" (8). The words that first appeared in the legal brief take on new life. They are made wild by their disruption, and as they spill off the page, they come to stand in for the outrage that the legal brief rationalizes, the live bodies that tumble into the ocean and the fragmented legacy that the loss leaves in its wake. Indeed, the wake for Christina Sharpe marks more than just the symbolic trace of a ship's passage through water: it is thick with the activity of traumatic loss; it troubles historical time. The wake is a cradle and a grave, in her terms; it is the afterlife of slavery.[21]

The analogy in both *Max and the Cats* and *Life of Pi* between the zoo animals in the hold of the ships upon which Max and Pi travel and slaves forces a recognition of the forces of financial speculation that have thrown Pi and Max into these stark, allegorical confrontations with the wild and reminds the reader in both cases of the disposability of some human life. But while *Max and the Cats* figures the wild as a space in which the predations of animals are preferable to the predations of humans (Nazis, slave traders, capitalists), in *Life of Pi* the wild is a pedagogical space from which Pi learns to recognize the indifference of the animal to human life and the phantasmatic nature of human investments in their own goodness. Pi repeatedly imagines himself as "saving" the tiger with whom he shares the lifeboat, but in the end, the tiger's indifference (a rehearsal of the indifference that the glare of the hawk conveyed in an earlier chapter) reduces Pi's efforts to the kind of moral kinesthetic that Nietzsche describes as part and parcel of modern investments in the good.

In *Life of Pi*, a teenage boy raised by parents who own a zoo in Pondicherry, India, is journeying from India to Canada with them and his brother and various animals from the dismantled zoo when, after the ship goes down in a storm, he finds himself lost at sea on a small lifeboat with four animal companions—a zebra, a hyena, an orangutan, and a Bengal tiger named Richard Parker (after the hunter that captured it). After the storm, only Pi and these four animals manage to escape from the wreckage; once saved, Pi, like Max in *Where the Wild Things Are*, finds that he is both sovereign ruler of his new community and in danger of being eaten by his fellow beastly survivors. As the little community bobs around on a large, wide ocean, beset by hunger, thirst, waves, wet, cold, and heat, an animal drama plays out in small as each creature struggles to stay alive. And when, finally, only Pi and the tiger remain, the standoff between human and nonhuman animal modes of living commences. A kind of erotic connection develops between Pi and Richard Parker such that it is no longer clear as to who rules, who preys upon whom, who desires whom, who would eat whom, and when all is said and done, who will survive.

Pi's experience with animals in the zoo in India in no way prepares him for this encounter with animals outside of their cages. While he has resolved that both the zoo and the wild have rules, restrictions, hierarchies, and routines, the rules in the zoo were legible to him while the rules of the wild remain opaque and inscrutable. He knows that the wild is not equivalent to freedom but bears a different relation to freedom than does the zoo. To the extent that we entertain fantasies of the wild as the other of the zoo, we do so in relation to the long afterlife of slavery. After slavery, indeed, understandings of freedom have evolved against and in opposition to incarceration and forced labor, and to the extent that they have done so, notions of freedom actually require the prison/zoo/asylum, as Foucault has shown, in order to have a material presence. But, as so many theorists of slavery and its aftermath—Saidiya Hartman, Christina Sharpe, Fred Moten, and others—have argued, we have to search for ways to imagine freedom separate from the epistemological framework of enslaved/free—if we do not, then the very society that fostered slavery comes to define the parameters and the nature of freedom. As Lisa Lowe puts it in her book *The Intimacies of Four Continents*, "freedom" within modernity offers a narrative of the overcoming of slavery that is part of a civilized order of things.[22] In reality, she proposes, freedom is an ideological invention that ushers in new forms of exploitation. Lowe writes: "Liberal forms of political economy, culture, government, and history propose a narrative of freedom overcoming enslavement that at once denies colonial slavery, erases the seizure of lands from Native peoples, displaces migrations and connections across continents, and internalizes these processes in a national struggle of history and consciousness" (3). With remarkable economy Lowe summarizes the structures of thought that encapsulate freedom and slavery as opposites while occluding the fact that the same system that enslaved peoples is now representing its own righteousness in terms of a narrative of emancipation. While Lowe calls this structure the "intimacy of four continents," I use the term *zombie humanism* (see next chapter 5) to name the structure by which capture and rescue are issued from the same source.

For Lowe, Frantz Fanon represents one strand of anticolonial thought that has confronted the negation of Black humanity represented by colonial rule. And she notes that Fanon argued for a kind of neo-Marxist analysis of the colonial condition. In *The Wretched of the Earth*, Fanon comments on the limits of Marxism in relation to racial colonialism and argues for a shift away from thinking in terms of the development of class struggle out of the alienation of labor and toward a consideration of the violent dehumanization of Black populations on which colonial rule depends.[23] Crucial to this dehumanization, Fanon explains, is the development of a "zoological" (7) lexicon for the Native other. Fanon writes of the colonizer: "He speaks of the yellow man's reptilian motions, of the stink of the native quarter, of breeding swarms, of foulness, of spawn, of gesticulations. When the settler seeks to describe the native fully in exact terms he constantly refers to the bestiary" (33). Nineteenth-century European narratives of evolution and progress provided the framework for colonial legitimation such that European man could place himself at the head of a new great chain of being anchored now not by God at the top and the devil at the bottom, but by the white man at the top and the animal at the bottom. Seeing clearly this new order of things, Foucault's "untamed ecology,"[24] Fanon comments: "The native knows all this and laughs to himself every time he spots an allusion to the animal world in the other's words. For he knows that he is not an animal; and it is precisely at the moment he realizes his humanity that he begins to sharpen the weapons with which he will secure its victory."[25]

It is tempting to see in Fanon's comments on the animalization of the Native a new human/animal binary that, despite its appearance in an anticolonial context, still works within the same logic of the total opposition between human and animal. But in fact, we notice in this passage that the recognition of humanity in Fanon does not depend on the same hierarchical order that exists within colonial systems. The Native, he says, realizes his humanity through the process of knowing he is NOT an animal. And so, his humanity requires the otherness of the animal, the wildness of the animal, and establishes a connection of sorts between the exploitative regimes that govern human-animal relations alongside those that render the colonized as savage.

These ideas about freedom, colonialities of power, race, animality and power, not to mention violence and wildness, play out in complex ways in *Life of Pi*. The novel imagines freedom in the passage with which we began less as a wide-open space that opposes the limitations of the cage and more as an arena governed by different rules. Furthermore, different locales impose different rules upon subjects, and so, while the zoo creates a human-animal hierarchy that gives the human sovereign power over the animal, the novel explores ways in which the open ocean establishes a new set of rules, dynamics, and power relations. *Life of Pi*, with its allegories of cohabitation, power, and survival, reimagines the wild, happiness, and freedom as contingent and interdependent.

As a teenage boy, Pi resides in a space in between childhood and adulthood, and as an allegorical figure he represents the quest for freedom and mediated relations to power. Pi, his name apparently referring to irrational numbers and calculus, seems to embody the calculations we make to situate ourselves in relation to space, danger, ferocity, and boredom. But in fact, as he tells us early on, Pi was not named for the famous number that symbolizes semiotic function itself, but for a swimming pool—a piscine—where he swims religiously with a friend of the family. The pool is opposed, in the novel, to the ocean, and like the zoo in relation to the wild, it offers a contained environment in which to practice, to become disciplined, and to orient oneself in relation to constraints and boundaries. The heterotopic spaces of the novel—zoo, hotel, ship, ashram, colony—are all opposed to the wild, which is represented as a "spread out" version of the house and a realm where survival trumps all other values and motivations.[26] As Martel writes: "Animals in the wild lead lives of compulsion and necessity within an unforgiving social hierarchy in an environment where the supply of fear is high and the supply of food is low" (18).[27]

Survival, both of these stories seem to propose, turns us wild, forces us to interact along the lines of animals in an economy of scarcity and danger. And in the game of survival, Pi learns quickly in the lifeboat that the human can win only if he domesticates the animal with which he is confronted. Pi comes to this realization when he is confronted with Richard Parker's ferocious, uncaring gaze: "I had to tame him. It was at that moment that I realized this necessity. It was not a question of him or me, but of him *and* me. We were literally and figuratively in the same boat. We would live—or we would die—together" (216). Pi then transforms the boat into a mini zoo and attempts to train the tiger to keep its distance, to live in a mutual bond of necessity, and to function as a large, dangerous pet.

Pi and Richard Parker, existing precariously in the same boat, allegorize the relations between the child and the animal within human relations. In fact, the child is a kind of liminal figure through whom we can visualize our relation to animals. As a preadult, prenormative, preregulated creature that must be domesticated, potty trained, put on a schedule, fed, walked, waked, and washed, the child approximates an animal companion especially in the years before it can speak. And for the child, as for the animal, the opposition between home and the wild/world is not simple, not a binary, not a choice between the caged and the free; for both, the wild and the domesticated offer different modes of living.

In *Life of Pi*, Pi makes an error in relation to the big cats in his father's zoo, and he presumes that the animals recognize him and regard him with sympathy. His father teaches him a hard lesson one day in order to alert him to the necessary distance that must be maintained between humans and wild animals, and while Pi uses this lesson to survive the lifeboat ride with Richard Parker, he also ends up forgetting the lesson and fully expecting the tiger to acknowledge the dangerous intimacy they have shared. When Pi and Richard Parker part ways, the question with which we are left is whether the animal has been domesticated or trained at all or whether the boy has become wild.

The opposite of the pet or domesticated animal is the wild child or the child raised by animals. The wild or feral child emerged as a concept in the eighteenth century after children raised by animals and living separate from human community were discovered on the outskirts of several European towns and villages. These children were often described as impervious to human training; they resisted or were unable to master language acquisition, and they retained a preference for raw food and nakedness. Some of these narratives have been dismissed as folktales, others have been explained in terms of the mental or developmental impairment of the child in question, and still more have become the stuff of colonial fantasies that imagine the primitive, such as the classic *Jungle Book*.

But the category continues to hold a certain appeal if only because, whether raised by wolves in the wild or in urban Germany, the feral child is seen as an outlaw, un/trainable, outside of language, order, domesticity, and the law. As such, many different theorists have addressed the category of the wild child as a limit case in terms of definitions of the human. Kalpana Rahita Seshadri, for example, in *HumAnimal*, reads the wild child through Derridean notions of linguistic dispossession and in relation to Giorgio Agamben's ideas about the law and language.[28] Seshadri situates the wild child, who is without language or law, as "that which surprises the law" (165). As such, the wild child, she claims, "appears in between sense and understanding, expression and indication, inside and outside" (165). Seshadri goes on, however, via Agamben, to make the leap from the mythical feral creature raised by animals to the ordinary infant. The infant, like the wild child, is also without language, also stands outside of speech, sense, and the law. And the infant, as Agamben argues in *Infancy and History*, precedes speech, thereby marking the split that constitutes the human—not the separation between speaking and not speaking, but the opposition between such terms as *langue* and *parole*, language and speech. Agamben writes: "Animals do not enter language, they are already inside it. Man, instead, by having an infancy, by preceding speech, splits this single language and, in order to speak, has to constitute himself as the subject of language—he has to say I."[29] And so, the wild child as a kind of mythic form of extended infancy represents both, as Seshadri puts it, "the experience of the human being at its most original and contemporary condition"[30] and the symbol of a mode of being that both precedes language and contests the law that language instantiates. The wild child, in simpler terms, is wild because it cannot speak, has not become a subject of ideology (yet), and therefore cannot be constrained, incorporated, or even known. The internal structure of the child cannot be mapped by an external world that requires language for its knowledge.

But what neither Agamben nor Seshadri address adequately is the way the wild child, despite being prehuman, has already been inserted into a racial order of things such that the wildness and the immaturity have already been coded in relation to a set of signifying systems that merge the human with temporal and affective markers of progress and development and leave the nonhuman firmly in the realm of the primitive and the racially other. Just to give one obvious example of this racial marking, consider François Truffaut's 1970 film *L'Enfant Sauvage*, in which a kindly doctor and his housekeeper collaborate in their efforts to raise a "wild boy" who emerges mute and wounded from the forests of rural France. The boy struggles to learn to speak and never does enter the social order completely. While Truffaut cast himself in the role of the doctor, he struggled to find a child for the wild child role until an assistant, scouting for potential child actors, looked to the schools in Marseilles and selected there a young Roma boy, the nephew of a well-known Flamenco performer, Manitas de Plata. The casting of Jean-Pierre Cargol in the role of the feral child perfectly captures the racial presumptions about speech, civilization, wildness, and the human that are absent from much of Agamben's work. As Alex Weheliye has shown, polemically and persuasively indeed, "bare life and biopolitics discourse largely occludes race as a critical category of analysis," and as a consequence, much of the work that travels under the heading of the biopolitical, he proposes, continues to orbit around the master-subject of liberal critique, a supposedly race-neutral and abstract figure but in reality a blanched extension of white liberal humanism.[31] Weheliye is also clear on how this racial model of the human plays out in animal studies, commenting at length:

> Moreover, posthumanism and animal studies isomorphically yoke humanity to the limited possessive individualism of Man, because these discourses also presume that we have now entered a stage in human development where all subjects have been granted equal access to western humanity and that this is, indeed, what we all want to overcome. It is remarkable, for instance, how the (not so) dreaded comparison between human and animal slavery is brandished about in the field of animal studies and how black liberation struggles serve as both the positive and negative foil for making a case for the sentience and therefore emancipation of nonhuman beings. (10)

Animal studies, in other words, relies on a false claim about human equality in order to emphasize the unequal relations between humans and animals. In this regard, the wildness of the child can never stand as a racially neutral facet of a preadult subject without language; rather, as shown in both *Where the Wild Things Are* and *Life of Pi*, the lonely queer Jewish child in one and the colonized and then diasporic subject in the other, take up a relation to wildness in terms of a childish refusal of adult worlds but also within a matrix of racialization that situates child, wild, and animality beyond the pale of white humanness.

The potential of the wild child, however, as these texts also demonstrate, exceeds its enclosure within such systems of signification. And in the implicit ties between the unscripted nature of the infant/wild child's desires, we can begin to understand the wildness of the child and the queerness of the animal. The wildness of the child, as for the animal, lies in its lack of susceptibility to adult human inscription—its tendency, in other words, to follow other rules and commit to other forms of life. The feral child remains outside of the human community because it simply cannot be trained to be human in the form we demand (speaking, walking on two feet, manners, clothing). If it cannot be trained, it cannot become heterosexual, domestic, housed, and oriented to money and hygiene. What I am calling wild here, then, is the part of the child/animal that resists incorporation into white and heterosexual norms (enacted through language) and that, in this resistance, calls the conventions of so-called civilized worlds into question.

Where the Wild Things Are, like *Life of Pi*, finds the wild to be a place of precarity and danger; it contains equal parts freedom and constraint, companionship and alienation, expression and inhibition. Because the wild has been produced as the other to the home and the zoo, it can only be a place of ruin and sadness. But what if the wild were truly wild? What if freedom meant something apart from being tethered to imprisonment? Whether we cage animals or watch them in the wild, Martel suggests, we misread them and their relations to freedom, will, and survival. And through those misreadings we are able to overcome contradictions and irrationality and see the animal as everything we are not. If we see the animal as other, it is because its otherness confirms our orderliness, rationality, and significance. But if, as children do with animals, we identify with the other, make faith with the other, and acknowledge in the other our own pathetic insignificance, our mortality, our vulnerability, then we come closer still to the wildness that is not the opposite of freedom after all, but just a quest to survive another day.

When Pi says goodbye to Richard Parker he wishes the tiger well and says: "You have known the confined freedom of the zoo most of your life; now you will know the free confinement of a jungle,"[32] to which the tiger with the hunter's name says nothing but instead turns and walks away with not even a backward glance. The tiger, clearly, prefers the "free confinement of the jungle" to the "confined freedom of the zoo" (361), even as Pi prefers the confinement of the pool to the expansive openness of the ocean. What the tiger knows and tried to convey to Pi while they were on the lifeboat is that the wild may well not deliver on its promise of unlimited potential, but while the wild, like the ocean, can be unforgiving, rough, merciless, he, the tiger, will always choose the wild over confinement with a human, even if his life depends on it. The animal, in this regard, knows something about the wild that Pi seemingly cannot access and that Richard Parker seemingly cannot communicate. In this gap between Richard Parker's choice to slip into the jungle and Pi's desire for some evidence of a bond that will continue to tie the two together lies the real answer to the question of where the wild things are.

CHAPTER FOUR

FIVE

Zombie Antihumanism at the End of the World

Wild—Fierce, savage, ferocious; furious, violent,
destructive, cruel. See also wild beast.
—*Oxford English Dictionary*

Many die too late, and a few die too early. The doctrine still sounds strange:
"Die at the right time!" Die at the right time—thus teaches Zarathustra. Of course,
how could those who never live at the right time die at the right time? Would
that they had never been born! Thus, I counsel the superfluous. But even the
superfluous still make a fuss about their dying; and even the hollowest nut still
wants to be cracked. Everybody considers dying important; but as yet death is no
festival. As yet men have not learned how one hallows the most beautiful festivals.
—Friedrich Nietzsche, "On Free Death," in *Thus Spake Zarathustra*

And what the dead had no speech for, when living,
They can tell you, being dead: the communication
Of the dead is tongued with fire beyond the language of the living.
—T. S. Eliot, "Little Gidding"

Wildness, various critics have proposed, is a realm of the monstrous, excess, extravagance, freedom, unspeakable desires, death, life, and illegible territories in between. The wild, for contemporary culture, is a fast-evaporating concept, a terrain that barely exists, a category of life lost to knowledge and a disintegrating future horizon of potential. As in other moments of cultural and political and ecological crisis, we have fashioned monsters to embody what we cannot name, to frame what we have come to fear, and to banish what we cannot tolerate. If Frankenstein's monster represented an early nineteenth-century fear of hybridity and untrammeled scientific experimentation, not to mention concern about multitudes and the power of feminine creativity, by the end of the nineteenth century it was the vampire that came to stand for, all at once, popular unrest, threats to national identity posed by immigrant populations, forms of perverse sexuality, and new forms of capitalism that sucked the life out of everything. Both of these monsters remain potent figures for unregulated science and unregulated greed, but they are joined in the late twentieth and early twenty-first centuries by the zombie, a figure part human and part animal, wild and unruly, racialized as Black or Native, and part of an increasingly polarized class system representing a deepening confusion over the distinction between life and death. The zombie's particularity, after all, is that it continues to live on after death.

The popularity of the metaphor of the zombie, not to mention zombie films and TV shows, evidences deep anxiety in contemporary Euro-American culture over things that refuse to die, on the one hand, and things that occupy a realm between life and death, on the other. As medicine seeks to extend life beyond the body's actual capacity—think pacemakers, for example—and as debates over abortion remain intractable over the status of the unborn child in relation to the category of life, the boundary between life and death becomes porous in new ways. In addition, the daily news of disappearing species, of new viruses and threats to complex ecosystems, puts the larger category of *life* into question and raises the possibility that earth is already in a zombified condition of living death.[1]

In "Little Gidding," T. S. Eliot proposed that there are "three conditions" in modern life that "often look alike" while differing completely.[2] The three conditions are first, an investment or attachment to self and others and things, second, a detachment from the same, and third, indifference to people and things. This indifference, he noted, "resembles the others as death resembles life" (55). This enigmatic formulation of a third space between attachment and detachment names not only the kind of relentless force of the zombie, indifferent to right or wrong, but also seems to describe the indifference to the human that was characteristic of the feral creatures discussed earlier in relation to falconry. That indifference to human effort, human kindness, and human love inhered to the wildness of the falcon (and the tiger in chapter 4). The feral creature expresses neither gratitude nor loyalty to human companions and responds to them only because of an urgent need to be fed. In the household pet, feral indifference gives way to dependence, and dependence grows from the two-way attachment between human and animal. The human trains the pet to be dependent, and the pet trains the human to get its food and clean up its shit.

Zombification has become a potent figure for operations of lawless capital, for undocumented populations living between nations, for incarcerated populations hovering between bare life and death, and even for luxury real estate projects used for investment purposes rather than to house people. And, of course, the specter of zombie apartment buildings devoid of residents gives rise to its opposite, the nightmare of massive homeless populations, priced out of affordable dwellings and driven into tent cities and nonviable spaces of precarious existence. In this chapter I explore the trope of the zombie in relation to the ever-fading boundary between the domestic and the wild. The household pet, to give one ubiquitous example, is not wild nor totally domesticated, not simply an extension of the human, nor wholly other. The pet is a piece of the wild, zombified and coddled, that we sneak into the family home to splinter domesticity, on the one hand, and to extend its carceral reach, on the other. The pet, indeed, takes its place within a history of the objects against which humanist discourse has understood itself as good, benevolent, sentient, and empathetic. This version of humanism defines itself against the zombie even as it invests in a version of care that renders the animal, like other forms of objecthood that preceded it, a form of living death.

My Zombie, My Pet

There are few more depressing spectacles in city life than the crouching stance of a dog on a leash about to relieve itself on the public footpath. This happens millions of times a day as avid pet lovers walk their beloved dogs to the end of the street and back, urging them to do their business so that the smug owner and the pampered pet can return to the small apartment from whence they came. Once home, the pet will return to the bed, the sofa, or the floor to snooze the day away, and the owner will check another item off their to-do list and hurry off to another busy day in the city. New York City and other big cities are rapidly turning into dog loos while city parks are being transformed from places for adults or children to play, zones for cruising, or teenage hangouts into dog runs where highly strung city animals sniff butts under the adoring gaze of their human companions.[3] In Los Angeles, furthermore, the dog run near Silver Lake reservoir has nicely covered areas where dogs and dog lovers can find shade. Around the bend from there, the picnic areas for solo humans or human groups are wholly without shade and for this reason are devoid of people.

I begin with this complaint about dogs in the city precisely because pet critiques have become almost taboo in and beyond academia and because I want to propose that domestic pet owning is akin to the circus, the zoo, and the animal shelter in terms of the treatment, the abuse, and the training of animals. The previous chapter recalled stories about humans misreading the wildness of the creatures with which they resided and showed how the wild stays wild and how what is domesticated becomes something else, something not human, not animal, not exactly living. And the pet, I will propose, is only the latest creature we have rendered as a prosthetic extension of our mortal bodies. As an accessory, a fetish, an improper object of love and intimacy, the pet—unlike the wild birds, as discussed earlier (see chapter 3), unlike the wild things in *Where the Wild Things Are*, and unlike the tiger in *Life of Pi*—is a zombified figure of the blurred boundaries between life and death in contemporary culture. The zombie figures with which we surround ourselves both comfort, by giving evidence of a world (of living death) that extends our world, and horrify, by existing within a new postreligious realm of space and time, a horrifying space created by the vertiginous activity of capitalism that swirls opposition into compliance, help into sacrifice, and life into living death.

In what follows I will further propose that far from being sites of love, pet cultures are rife with violence and that the intimacy and affection many people cultivate with their animal friends lures them into a false sense of benevolence that blinds them to the way in which the domestication of animals is central to the hierarchies that sustain human exceptionalism. The term "pet," John Berger offers, was originally a word of Scottish or Northern English origins implying a diminutive and beloved creature—a child or animal. It may have been a Geordie term of endearment for women and children that evolved into usage for small animals kept at first in wealthy households and only later, in the late twentieth century, becoming ubiquitous. Indeed, as Berger suggests, our obsession with keeping and indulging household animals grew as our appetite for the public display of large animals—elephants and tigers and lions—waned.[4] Like household technologies that draw labor from outside the home to inside, like personal devices that move communication from the public to the private, the pet represents the transition of animal contact from uncontrolled spaces known as the wild and controlled spaces like circuses and zoos into disciplined spaces of home and hearth. As such, the privatization of the relation to animals—pet owning—should be placed alongside many other contemporary shifts of space, labor, intimacy, and feeling rather than being cast within universal narratives affirming pet owning as timeless. While we are fairly critical nowadays of the zoo, we have not fully extended that critique of capture and display to pet owning. But as pet owners we also imprison animals, we discipline them, we force them into intimate labor on our behalf, and we transform them from independent creatures, "critters" to use Donna Haraway's quaint vocabulary, into prosthetic extensions of ourselves.[5]

In other words, we zombify animals and, in turn, insist on our own humanity. This process can be thought of in terms of a zombie antihumanism within which the zombified other represents both the limits of the human but also a force hostile to the human. We can certainly see such a force in relation to the zoo with its ambivalence about wildness and its desire for caged and tamed animals. As was shown in chapter 4, the zoo in *Life of Pi* was a place of mutual respect. Yann Martel writes: "A good zoo is a place of carefully worked-out coincidence: exactly where an animal says to us, 'Stay out!' with its urine or other secretion, we say to it, 'Stay in!' with our barriers. Under such conditions of diplomatic peace, all animals are content and we can relate and have a look at each other."[6] But this notion of a two-way benefit is revealed to be a naive investment in the goodness of humans and the gratitude of animals, notions that are upended by the confrontation between Pi and Richard Parker on the open sea. By the end, we come to see the zoo, like the colony, as being a heterotopic space where experiments in freedom and incarceration are conducted and animals serve the dual purpose of shoring up concepts of human decency and confirming a system of scientific classification which begins with the distinctions between human and nonhuman animals but ends with racial distinctions between humans. Alibis for the zoo, however, are easily ruptured. In *Life of Pi*, Pi learns the hard way not to believe in human benevolence, and in Frederick Wiseman's famous documentary *Zoo* (1993), the viewer watches in horror as the violence of the zoo reveals itself from behind the veneers of entertainment and science. *Zoo*, like much of Wiseman's work, is a nonpedagogical, nonnarrative documentary of institutional life, here captured via images from a few days at the Miami Zoo. Early on in the film, bored and unmoved spectators watch as an irritatingly chirpy animal wrangler sings orders to a group of terrorized elephants. The majestic creatures are pulled out of their natural lumbering style and asked to be quick, peppy, and agile. They are made to circle around, to stand on blocks, to change directions, all at a clip that defies one's sense of elephant temporality. The very size of the elephants argues against this kind of activity, but somehow the skill of the trainer actually depends on defeating the animals' inclinations while pushing and pulling their massive bodies into poses and actions at odds with their bulk.

Given this sadistic introduction, it should come as no surprise that in the frames that follow the camera tracks a series of mishaps and bizarre occurrences that do not lead us into a confrontation with animal life, animal death, and animal logics but, rather, force us to come face to face with the meaning of the human: the human emerges out of the sunny openness of the zoo as a murderous, sadistic set of impulses, with the impulse to know funneled through the impulse to capture, train, and discipline. The desire for relation to animality is channeled through a desire to reduce the animal to object status—nothing of the quirkiness of this or that creature can make it through the harsh regimens of feeding, cleaning, and performing that make up the schedules of the zoo animals. When a baby rhino is to be born to a stoic mother rhino, the TV cameras line up along the parkway trying to get the right angle on the big event. Wiseman, in his quiet and unobtrusive way, also sets up to film the birth. The labor continues into the night, and finally the huge Rhino pushes out a birth sac and a baby rhino tumbles to the ground but makes no movement. The human handlers come into the pen to see what has happened, but the calf is stillborn and does not respond to human efforts to revive it. The mother rhino ambles off while the humans debate whether the mother did everything she could to get the calf out in a timely fashion.

As Laura Marks notes in the chapter on "Animal Appetites" in her book *Touch*, the scene of the stillborn birth is quickly followed by a soulless autopsy in which the rhino's head is severed from its body and the carcass is splayed and displayed as an audience looks on. Marks writes: "The death of the rhino kid is sad because it is a failed investment, as is made clear by the distress at a board meeting later. The animals are useful only as spectacle, and the zoo pays dearly to keep them in shape for that reason. . . . A film cannot set up a different kind of relation between humans and animals unless the local ecosystem encourages it in some way. In *Zoo* it is an all or nothing relation: Animals are mirrors or they are meat."[7] While *Zoo* works beautifully as an example of what Marks calls haptic cinema, a cinema that escapes the logic of mastery and gives itself over to the materiality of the image, her critique of animals as commodities needs to be taken a little further. What Wiseman's nonnarrative cinema allows, in fact, is a human confrontation with the horror of the human subject of white liberal thought, the zombification that humanism demands and depends on—the stillborn kid represents much more than a failed financial investment; its sadness is the pathos of the human, the cruelty of the human, the impossibility of life in the vicinity of the human—*Zoo* and the stillborn rhino remind us that we may not survive the bloody impulses of the human, and the dead rhino is like a prehistoric creature displaying the gory details of its own extinction and a warning of other extinctions just on the horizon.

To counteract such uses of animal life perhaps we should consult animal scientist Temple Grandin, who uses her own autism to try to establish more humane livestock procedures. Grandin opposes Giorgio Agamben's language-based distinction between humans and animals and proposes instead that animals think in languages that are not readily accessible to humans and are potentially not translatable but are languages nonetheless. Arguing that communication among animals develops not simply among creatures of high intelligence but, more urgently, among creatures with many predators, who use language as a mode of survival and develop elaborate warning systems to alert each other to danger (she gives the prairie dog as an example), Grandin proposes that language use correlates to vulnerability. She writes: "If language naturally evolves to serve the needs of tiny rodents with tiny rodent brains, then what's unique about language isn't the brilliant humans who invented it to communicate high-level abstract thoughts. What's unique about language is that the creatures who develop it are highly vulnerable to being eaten."[8] In other words, language should help us understand risk, vulnerability, danger and not rationalize our efforts to make the world safe for ourselves and dangerous for everything else.

Grandin's claim to be able to intuit how animals think leads her to eccentric and counterintuitive accounts of animal behavior. But it also aids her in her role as a livestock consultant who has developed a system bringing together animal welfare concerns and slaughterhouse practices. Grandin has become well known for advising farmers and meat industrial plants on how to lead cattle to the slaughter without startling them into a panic stampede. Making animal slaughter more efficient is an odd way of showing concern for animal welfare, but Grandin justifies her work saying: "I think we can eat meat ethically, . . . but we've got to give animals a good life."[9] In this case, a good life means a good and a calm death, but it does not imply a critique of the meat industry, and this is where Grandin and animal rights activists part ways. Grandin has faced protesters at her lectures around the country, and she has been accused of collaborating with an industry that many people feel is unethical in terms that go way beyond slaughterhouse etiquette. Indeed, while Grandin devises pathways that sooth the animals as they walk to their doom, and claims to have removed the distractions that caused them to bolt or stampede, she herself may have been mistranslating the animal behavior. What she reads as a simple fear mechanism may have been anger. What she reads as neurotic jitters may be animal apprehension of the mechanism of death. What she reads as calming may be the equivalent to a shower before a gas chamber.

Animal studies is fairly unequivocal nowadays in its condemnation of the zoo and industrial meat production. Jason Hribal, for example, has written essays and books on animal resistance to the confinement and display techniques indulged by zoos and circuses. Lori Gruen has written about the questionable "ethics of captivity," and Anat Pick has written about creaturely poetics that exceed human attempts to know the animal.[10] While humans have transported massive animals around the globe for the past three hundred years or more to show them off to adoring and engaged audiences under the big top of the circus or the fake habitats of the zoo, this practice has recently come to a much-applauded end. In 2017, Ringling Bros. and Barnum & Bailey Circus closed up shop. Many reasons were given, including competition to the charms of the zoo and the circus offered by such online attractions as *Pokémon Go*, the cost of transporting animals and people around the globe, and a general dwindling interest in the tricks performed and the animal training. But the biggest reason for the end of the circus seems to have been a general opposition to the mistreatment of animals. While many accounts of animal abuse cast the animal as a passive victim, scholars have recently wondered whether in fact animals have the capacity to fight back.

Hribal's book, *Fear of the Animal Planet: The Hidden History of Animal Resistance*, catalogs in great and unrelenting detail the multiple cases of animals, mostly elephants, that, having been mistreated and exploited by drunken and cruel trainers, reach a breaking point and run wild, often directing their anger and rage at the trainer himself and ignoring and even avoiding children and other audience members while doing so![11] Hribal claims various forms of agency for animals and uses James Scott's influential model of "weapons of the weak" to classify various forms of animal actions involving refusal, immobility, and menace as "everyday forms of resistance." At one point in his "history from below" of animal agency, Hribal transforms the singsongy narratives associated with animal nursery rhymes into a catalog of revolutionary refusal: "Donkeys have ignored commands. Mules have dragged their hooves. Oxen have refused to work. Horses have broken equipment. Chickens have pecked people's hands. Cows have kicked farmers' teeth out. Pigs have escaped their pens. Dogs have pilfered extra food. Sheep have jumped over fences."[12] As with other forms of subaltern refusal, forms that Gayatri Spivak famously situated as embedded in something other than speech, these modes of resistance have been read by trainers, owners, animal rescuers, pet owners, and the media as isolated instances of an animal gone bad. Using human logic that situates everything that refuses mastery within the category of anomaly, we have told stories about animal uprisings that demonize, pathologize, and render incomprehensible these animal-authored acts of violence.[13] In actual fact, there is nothing surprising about animal resistance whether it comes from a pet, a circus animal, or a barnyard creature. What is more surprising is that animals regularly do NOT resist.[14] But however much we may thrill to stories of Jumbo or Nellie hurling a mean man into the air and then stomping him, as a society, I am willing to guess, we are less engaged by the spectacle of rogue pets.

The Secret Life of Pets

> Liberated forever, domesticated never.
> —Snowball, *The Secret Life of Pets*

As discussed in chapter 3, something about the human desire for feral birds of prey exceeds the simple explanation that that gay desire has been redirected through wildness. The desire directed at the hawks and falcons was not a stand-in for something else; it exemplified a deep and erotic longing for wildness itself. Nor was the desire directed at domesticated animals, or pets, a substitute for the love of a significant human other. T. H. White, in fact, on the death of his dog Brownie, wrote in his journal, "It means that I died last night. All that is me is dead. Because it was half her." And, he continued, "She was the central fact of my life."[15] The love of the animal does not stand in for a more proper love; the dog *is* the (im)proper object of desire and affection that White has chosen. While at least one response to this kind of devotion is to consider the pet-lover to be in denial, another, as was the case with White, is to suspect the author of unbearable loneliness, which is increasing in contemporary life; the idea of sharing one's life with an animal rather than a human seems to have extraordinary appeal. What was a sign of eccentricity in the 1930s has now become accepted as a reasonable retreat from human intimacy into animal bonds.

In an essay on the shifting boundaries between bestiality and zoophilia, the eroticization of animals and the love invested in animals, Kathy Rudy claims that the strong taboo against sex with animals makes it acceptable to harbor deep affection for them. However, she goes on, given that queer and feminist theory has challenged any simple understanding of what constitutes sex, it becomes harder and harder to tell the difference between pet owning and bestiality. Rather than adjudicating a constantly shifting boundary then,

Rudy, from her position as a lover of dogs, says: "There is not an adequate name for the kind of life I lead, the way my desires organize themselves around animals." Noting also that while in the past, gay and lesbian sexual orientations may have been seen as impossible, now, "such ideas seem silly or quaint, almost forgotten."[16] She concludes: "But can people like me even hope for such liberation, when choosing animals as partners or companions doesn't really even have an adequate name?" (604–5). Leaving aside for a moment the notion of a distant and quaint homophobia that has thoroughly dissolved into "liberation," Rudy's desire for recognition for her love of her dogs both partakes in the desire for wildness that we have been tracking and departs considerably from it. While the desire for wild animals, and the identification with them in the past, represented a strong urge in a human to become feral, and located a set of desires that exceeded the classificatory power of the homo/hetero binary, this zoophilic love that Rudy describes seems to involve something more akin to domestication. White and J. A. Baker and even Helen Macdonald did not seek to pull the wild bird into their world but hoped instead to become part of the bird's world. But Rudy and other zoophiles, by taking their pets into the beds, into their very human environment, acclimate the animal to their own rhythms and habits rather than the other way around. In fact, what Rudy describes as an odd and apparently unclassifiable desire—the deep love for a pet—is all too commonplace. And while we could ask whether the love for the pet exceeds the love for other humans, we also might at least fantasize about whether all this domestication is good for the animal being housed and sheltered, loved and fed, groomed and walked.

At least one animated film for children tries to imagine the experience of pet owning from the perspective of the pet and in so doing, tiptoes into the territory of the pet gone rogue rather than offering a cheery narrative about a properly sensible and domestic household animal. In *The Secret Life of Pets* (2016) a group of pampered pooches, fat cats, enterprising hamsters, and rage-fueled rabbits move back and forth between animal and human worlds.[17] In the human world they are toys for their busy humans, and their role is to adore the human and attend to her and exist only for her. In the animal world, they play with each other, sneak out the windows of the apartment complex to check on each other, and jockey with each other for alpha status. But there is another world in this film, an underworld, an animal undercommons where abandoned pets are gathering and plotting to attack and kill the humans who so cruelly flushed them away (and, indeed, *Flushed Away* [2006] is the name of another such film with a very similar theme).[18]

Figure 5.1   The Secret Life of Pets (2016).

In *The Secret Life of Pets*, a guerrilla force of abandoned pets agitate for revolution. These former pets want to make war on humans and plan to rise up from the sewers, where they currently reside, in order to encourage other animals to join them in the fight against human tyranny. In this underground world, the angry pets reverse the transition from wild to domestic, and their revolutionary aspirations are cast in the logic of the film as part and parcel of becoming feral again. Within the same logic, however, domesticated pets go feral not by choice or after a fugitive dash to freedom, but because they lost the love of their human companions. The film thus opens the door to revolution by critiquing pet owning only to close it again by reasserting the value of the pet-human relationship over and above relations between and among animals. As mentioned earlier, the possibility that animals might be capable of resisting their lot as pets or food, as sources of affective labor or commodification, has been entertained by a number of different thinkers in and beyond animal studies. Dinesh Wadiwel, for example, proposes that in terms of the transformation of chickens into food, "the use of chicken catching machines only demonstrates the implicit resistance of chickens to human subordination."[19] Wadiwel goes on to argue that "even domesticated animals are always already wild" (528), and their resistance to training, discipline, and human brutality must be thought of not as moments where that training fails, but as the outcome of constant opposition to capitalist attempts to commodify them and extract their labor.

The intimate and industrial labor that animals perform in urban, Western societies makes a decisive split between animals we pamper and animals we eat and implies that while industrially farmed animals might resist, pets do not. And while Rudy and others imagine that the pampered animals are engaged in a love relationship with their human minders, the endeavor nonetheless takes place within what she names as the framework of human exceptionalism. This framework, fostered within a decidedly Western context, as many critics have pointed out, situates the pet as a substitute for the (white) child and then exercises all manner of paternal oversight on it. The idea of any connection between wild animals, farmed animals, and animals in the household, meanwhile, hardens into a firm boundary, and the pet shifts decisively from the realm of animality and wildness into the warm embrace of the domestic. With a very few exceptions, furthermore, there seems little likelihood of a reversal of domestication in which a tame animal may go wild.

But in other cultural contexts, the possibility of domestic animals becoming feral seems more possible and even likely. In a wonderful exploration of human-animal relations in South Asia, Radhika Govindrajan describes animal intimacies and what she terms, "interspecies relatedness" in India; in one chapter, for example, she offers the story of a domesticated pig that turns feral with catastrophic results on local villages.[20] With chapters on myths and social practices around bears, goats, monkeys, cows, and pigs, and within a compelling ethnographic set of stories, Govindrajan situates human relations to animals firmly in the context of colonialism. In the chapter on pigs, a woman tells Govindrajan to watch out for wild boar that have been attacking people in the village. The local people were terrified of the wild pigs but could not cull them because they are protected, as wild animals, by the state. But when Govindrajan asks where the boar came from, since apparently they are a new addition to this ecological landscape, a long tale unfolds about an animal research center close by that had been established by the British. The villagers claim that thirty years earlier a pregnant sow, a domestic pig, had escaped from the center and run off into the woods, where it had given birth and begun a lineage of wild boars. "The trouble started then," says one person, "because that domestic pig went wild" (121). Govindrajan uses this story to lay out the function of wildness in a colonial frame. There, in the central Himalayas, she offers, the stories she hears about pigs gone wild, bears who claim human lovers, and so on attest to "the uneven and arbitrary nature of wildness, the colonial logics of which remain in force in postcolonial conservation laws in India" (122). Wildness in this context is far from the feral world of another species flying free; it is a cultivated form of life produced by a network of co-

CHAPTER FIVE

lonial operations that set themselves up against some forms of wildness while protecting others.

The Secret Life of Pets does not feature a pig gone wild, but it does have a bunny that has transformed into a feral rabbit. With a nod to George Orwell's *Animal Farm*, the rabble-rousing, radical rabbit is named Snowball. Having been abandoned by his human family, he has now become an angry and powerful leader in the animal underground! Indeed, the film follows in the footsteps of many other stories and films that imagine animals that are pushed to their breaking point and organize themselves into revolutionary groups to confront the brutality of the human. In *Animal Farm* the animal hierarchies reestablish a power system that can only be read as human, and in *Planet of the Apes* the acquisition of language is cast as the building block for imagining resistance. Lacking lofty purpose and willing to renege on their own political trajectories, animated films about revolt, such as *The Secret Life of Pets*, unlike counterexamples, such as *Fantastic Mr. Fox* and *Chicken Run*, flirt with open rebellion against the human while settling for an anarchism born of rejection and hurt feelings and returning to the status of man's best friend. But there are moments in the film where the critique of the human is made explicit—in one memorable instance, for example, Snowball (voiced by Kevin Hart and played as a Black Panther–style revolutionary) riles the animals up, urging them to kill their owners and refuse their roles as pets. Counteracting the surface narrative of mild neglect with which the story opens (pets are expected to live their lives waiting for the return of their owner) with the specter of animal discontent, the underground pets propose the menace of a pet scorned. The film, ultimately, proposes that the pets that wait for us at home, nip at our heels, and sleep beside our beds may be as in love with the human as the human is infatuated with the pet. But, maybe, just maybe, the pet is plotting its escape, its revenge—survival, in other words, on its own terms.

Whose Streets? Dog's Streets

A recent film from Hungary takes up the cause of the abandoned pet and turns it into the site of an animal uprising. *White God* (2014), which offers a tribute to Samuel Fuller's film *White Dog* (1982), imagines the mistreated household pet not as Fuller did, as a vehicle for the transmission of socially abhorrent ideologies like racism, but as a representative of social unrest. You would have to go back to Alfred Hitchcock's *The Birds* (1963), I think, to find a more vivid representation of animal uprising than the one we witness in Kornél Mundruczó's *White God*. In the film, a teenage girl, Lili (Zsófia Psotta), is abandoned by her mother, who has a new partner and leaves for an unspecified amount of time. Lili and her dog, Hagen, are taken in by her reluctant father, who works, significantly, as a slaughterhouse inspector. The father is not enthusiastic about having the girl and the dog in his building and then finds out that he must pay a "mongrel" tax on the dog because it is mixed breed.[21] Under pressure from his neighbors in the building to get rid of the dog, and to the dismay of his child, the father leaves the dog by the roadside. The film now follows the fortunes of Hagen as he befriends a smaller white dog, escapes from butchers and animal pound workers, but then eventually is caught by a homeless man who sells him to a dog-fighting business. In a montage sequence we watch the dog experience brutalization as the trainer readies him for fighting. The trainer starves him, beats him, teaches him to fight, and then puts him in the ring. After Hagen kills another dog in his first fight, he escapes and runs through the city. Once again humans catch him, and this time he is placed in an animal pound where he agitates with the other animals, including the white dog he befriended earlier, to rise up against their human guards. The cinematic sequences of the loosed dogs running through the streets are shocking and beautiful. Often filmed at a dog's eye level, the film imagines the perspective of the dog and justifies scenes of shocking violence, in which dogs kill humans, through this dog's-eye view.

The dog has been the object of our most fervent and passionate claims for human-animal bonds. Donna Haraway's *The Companion Species Manifesto: Dogs, People, and Significant Otherness*, for example, urges readers to take dog-human relationships seriously and to contemplate the "significant otherness of the dog" while joining human lives to dog lives.[22] Offering a quirky and compelling account of the domestication of the dog, Haraway argues that we should understand the human-dog relation in terms of coevolution and as a love relationship that we experience as unconditional but that stops short of sexual engagement. She writes about kissing her dog and engages with many other narratives in which the dog is a human being's natural companion, but Haraway, like most other commentators on the dog, refuses the possibility that the human-animal bond is in any way erotic or in any way imposed on the animal.[23] Ultimately, Haraway is unable to create a new entity out of the human-dog relation. What she describes as a companionate dynamic ultimately defaults to human logics, and the dog receives training, sleeps in a human bed, and guards the household.

Another critic similarly offers seemingly new ways of thinking about animal-human love. Colin Dayan, in *With Dogs at the Edge of Life*, also claims to write from the dog's perspective. Dayan's book, a passionate and personal narrative about dog owning, pit bulls, and the law, tries to use the human-animal relation to reveal the limits of a human-centric relation to life.[24] The book manages all at once to both conjure the kinds of relations to animals that are presented in the hawk narratives in chapter 3, relationships that embrace the feral and reveal the arbitrary nature of human loves and desires, and to fetishize dogs and disparage public fears of violent dogs. In one chapter, for example, she compares the state management of dangerous pit bulls to Nazi euthanasia programs! As the book progresses, Dayan begins, by her own admission, to identify with animals, over and against humans but within a framework that, like Haraway's, is Christian: "I am still lost in the life of dogs. Everything I know of the spirit, I learned from them" (24). Haraway says something similar: "I believe these theological considerations are powerful for knowing dogs, especially for entering into a relationship, like training, worthy of the name of love."[25] For both of these writers their belief in the relationship between God and dog, which in English is embedded in the shared letters of the words, expresses an ineffable relation to spirit and relies on all kinds of Christian assumptions about human goodness, the fall, compassion, and the centrality of the human. At one point, for example, Dayan, on a trip to Haiti, sees dogs everywhere: dogs in the streets, dogs without masters, without humans. Rather than see these wandering dogs in terms of a different relation to ownership (this is Haiti, after all, site of the first slave rebellion), she worries about one dog in particular, a puppy being trained to guard the house: "Left alone on the grey, stone floors with nothing inside, the dog has no bed, no blankets, nothing at all." Dayan worries about the dog, obsesses about its welfare, and then declares: "I become a dog. I am the thing that brings me pain."[26]

Against this notion of the dog without comfort I want to think about human comfort as the very thing that the dog must refuse and that the human must not offer. I want to recognize not the pathos, but the power of the abandoned dog because it registers and represents what *The Secret Life of Pets* is unwilling to pursue—namely, the violent refusal by animals of human stewardship. While cultural critics like Dayan have practically dismissed *White God*, noting the film's attempt to capture the dog's point of view but also casting it as an extended metaphor for the treatment of Hungary's minority populations, in fact, *White God* exceeds its director's intentions and offers much more than an allegory for human suffering. As we see in one of the final scenes that reunites the dog and Lili and that evokes the ending of *Life of Pi*, the dog regards its former human companion with indifference and is willing to simply run her down or run over her on the way to freedom. The dogs' sprint through the streets of this Hungarian town eschews the heroic and the triumphal and instead cleaves to the elemental: the finale proposes an animal revolution composed of the exclusion of human involvement, loyalty between animals (the dog is the dog's best friend), the absolute indifference to human love or contact, and the taking back of abandoned zones in the city where dog catchers cruise for animals. The bond that the dog, Hagen, shared with a young girl at the start of the film has been completely eradicated by the film's end, and all he does by way of acknowledging their former connection is forbear from savaging her. The film ends with a clear question that I believe lies at the heart of what we might reasonably call animal anarchy: What if we are not the authors of revolution, but the masters who must be overthrown?

Zombie Apocalypse Now

Here they came, the ambassadors of nil.
—Colson Whitehead, *Zone One*

The spectacle of dogs charging with purpose through the streets of a small town, and even the comical scenes in *The Secret Life of Pets* in which abandoned pets mass together to plan to overthrow their masters, are reproduced in countless zombie films from the past fifty years where the dead refuse to stay dead and instead rise from their graves to amble through the streets, the countryside, the cemeteries, the shopping malls, and all the other spaces of modern life where life and death are supposed to occupy comfortably separate terrains. The animals who rise up in the films referenced above are certainly more lively than zombies, but they still occupy the category of living death in relation to their human companion, who decides everything for them and who deploys them as a prosthetic extension of the good life. If we return also to Monty Python's dead parrot as representative of pets in general, we might ask whether all pets are always already dead, in the sense of no longer independent of the humans to which they are now attached, permanently and fatally. I propose that the household pet is a zombie form of life, that is, barely living and existing only according to the dictates of a human master while harboring its own deadly desires. Turning away from the zombie pet, in this section I survey the field of zombie representations to see how a long tradition of horror that passes not only through the circus and the slide-show but also through slavery, becomes reanimated in our current craze for zombies. Building on the narratives within which an animal transitions from wild to domestic but threatens to become feral again and rise up against the human, the zombie narratives examined here engage capitalist and racist fantasies of harnessing the labor power of the living dead, but they also betray deep anxieties about the possibility of a zombie revolt. For zombies as for the rogue pets, power lies in numbers.

In Haitian traditions the word *zombi* means "spirit of the dead" and represents the fear of former slaves that they would be brought back from the dead and enslaved anew. But in the spate of representations of zombies by white colonial explorers like William Seabrook in the 1920s and 1930s, the figure represented a kind of naturalization of slavery and enforced labor. In *White Zombie* (1932), Bela Lugosi plays an evil white Haitian voodoo master who offers to help a white settler in Haiti marry his love object, Madeline. The voodoo master is protected and served by a zombie army of Black Haitians, slaves essentially, and the practice of voodoo in this film is cast as a threat not to Black sovereignty, but to white womanhood. Other zombie films of the first half of the twentieth century include *Revolt of the Zombies* (1936), also by the Halperin brothers and involving another white woman rescue narrative, and Jacques Tourneur's *I Walked with a Zombie* (1943), which concerns the entrapment of a white woman by a man who would rather see the woman dead than lose her to a rival. So, early Zombie films engaged the material of slave revolt but quickly transformed it into another iteration of white masters and Black subservient bodies. But in terms of the very present specter of slavery and, even more horrifying to white audiences, of the revolt of former slaves, these zombie films took on clear racial overtones and set the stage for the next wave of films.

The zombie, like the pet, hovers between life and death, pain and pleasure, subject and object. Zombies and pets confirm the difference between humans and other nonhuman animals, and they register that difference in deeply racialized terms. And so, while heeding Zakiyyah Jackson's warnings against simply mapping animal captivity onto human captivity, a relay of connections between the household pet, the walking dead, and the history of slavery is made available through contemporary zombie narratives. Wildness, as I have proposed several times in this book, is both the name for certain civilizational discourses that want to universalize white humanity against the backdrop of Black bodies, colonized bodies, and animal bodies but also understood as the force of an anticivilizational, oftentimes Afro-pessimist, refusal of the category of the human altogether. And so Jackson notes, following Saidiya Hartman, that "humanization and captivity go hand in hand."[27] The human, in other words, is not, within an Afro-pessimist rendering of racial order, a goal, a horizon of possibility, an answer to a problem. Rather, the human and its metaphysical rationales for existence depends on key forms of personhood that uphold white supremacy—namely, ownership, presence, will, enlightenment. For example, if a Hegelian formulation of Blackness assigns to it a "wild and untamed state"[28] and locates Blackness outside of history altogether, thereby reserving rationality, harmony, equality, and goodness for the white human, then it is the category of the human itself, as Calvin Warren proposes, that must be destroyed: "Black freedom then," he writes, "would constitute a form of world destruction."[29] And while Warren finds an acceptable version of world destruction to be part of a Heideggerian formulation of the relationship between *Being and Nothing*, with "nothing" holding the place of Blackness, we could look beyond Heidegger for more powerful renderings of nothing. We could look to the zombie.

In George Romero's 1968 classic *Night of the Living Dead*, reactivated bodies rise from the dead. Unlike a previous generation of zombie films that engaged narratives of Black slaves and white masters but that stopped short of mapping zombies onto slave revolt, Romero's film reanimated a deep and broad archive of racial animus.[30] Critics have interpreted the zombies in this film as a figure for multiple forms of horror from the US's white supremacist past—the zombies can be read both in terms of the return of the undead past of American slavery and in relation to the Vietnam War.[31] But the most obvious reference for the night terrors in the film, and a reference that could not have been missed in 1968 by the film's first audiences, was contemporary Black political rage. Indeed, the historic casting of a Black man, Duane Jones, in the lead role led to an unmistakable connection in *Night of the Living Dead* between the restless zombies roaming the Pennsylvania countryside for flesh and the afterlife of slavery. The first zombie attack comes quickly in the film as a white couple, Barbra and Johnny, who turn out, in a twist worthy of Edgar Allan Poe, to be siblings, visit the grave of their dead father. A strange man approaches them, lurching and stumbling. Johnny tries to protect his sister when the stranger attacks her and is quickly killed. Barbra runs to a farmhouse where a Black man, Ben (Duane Jones), helps her to safety. As the night progresses, another white couple arrive in distress at the house, and, finally, the small group discover a white family, mother, father, and daughter, in the basement. The daughter, Karen, has been bitten; the father, Harry, is angry and armed; the mother, Helen, is torn between assuaging her husband and caring for her daughter. This infected group allows for multiple readings of the toxicity of the white family, the violence of the law of the father, and the complicity of the mother in a corrupt social order. Ben, on the other hand, is a solo figure, without an ally or a partner, without community or allegiance. He has been severed from his social context, and in his aloneness, the film implicitly sets him apart from white society. And so the racial allegory plays itself out through confrontations within and among the people in the house and, beyond that, between the beleaguered group inside the house and the growing threat of zombies outside. And, in another frame of reference, there is news on the radio of "armed posses" roaming the countryside trying to beat back the zombies.

The film sets up a number of dynamics that become foundational to later zombie narratives. First, the violence outside, represented by the zombies, is mirrored inside by violent dynamics among the band of survivors. Second, in the zombie film, white families come under attack and engage in outrageous violence, often with impunity, in order to defend themselves. Finally, new forms of collectivity emerge, shatter, and reemerge as human survivors are beset over and over again by waves of zombie violence. Many contemporary zombie narratives present opportunities to rethink kinship, social relations, racial politics, and so on, but in most, a white supremacist, patriarchal order asserts new forms of order that are all-too-reminiscent of the old ones they replace. All of these dynamics play out in *Night of the Living Dead*, and the group in the house close ranks around whiteness, familial units, and patriarchal authority. Only Ben, the Black hero, thinks beyond the restoration of order; only Ben survives the zombie attack.

Night of the Living Dead allowed for both Black vengeance and rage (Ben slaps a white woman and kills a white man), and it showed how white racial paranoia racializes all sources of threat as Black and violent. Harry repeatedly challenges Ben and aims his gun at him, seeing him as the internal version of the zombie threat. And while Ben calmly takes the initiative and offers plans to escape, he is never embraced by the other humans. If there is any doubt about the way the film's white people see Ben as a threat rather than as their salvation, it is snuffed out in the film's still-shocking final sequence where the rescue squad made up of police and citizen vigilantes arrive and casually shoot Ben, the only survivor of the zombie rampage, reading him as a zombie when he runs out of the house, arms raised.

The inability of the cops and white vigilantes to distinguish between the heroic Black man and the zombies in the film that launched a contemporary fascination with the living dead seals the barely disguised relation between Blackness and zombification. While this connection could be no more than one more racist trope within the landscape of monstrosity, it may also function as a more complex signifier of racial anger—the zombies, after all, constitute a restless collectivity of refusal. They are the embodiment of the "world destruction" formulated by Calvin Warren and others. And zombies were a potent enough figure of Blackness to influence Black novelist Colson Whitehead's foray into the zombie genre. The apocalypse in his novel *Zone One* combines elements of George Romero's zombie films with more contemporary concerns about viruses, environmental ruin, and end days. For Whitehead, however, racial animus is one place to begin in explaining the continued appeal of the zombie. In an online interview Whitehead commented on the appeal of the horror genre, identifying a pleasure rooted in the spectacle of the ruination of the social order. And, he continues: "Then comes the George Romero 'Living Dead' trilogy, with its template for the slow-moving zombie. The blaxploitation movies I saw as a kid provided one example for a black hero, and *Night of the Living Dead* gave me another one. Black guy on the run from hordes of insane white people who want to tear him limb from limb? What's more American than that? It's like T.G.I. Friday's, and Pez. The movies stuck with me."[32] Whitehead's novel is a stylish rendering of the zombie genre, one that uses the trope of zombie apocalypse not simply to offer a panoply of terrors but also as a platform for existential questions about life and death, the mundane nature of life under capitalism, and the undying legacy of white supremacist violence. The zombies are not just the living dead in *Zone One*; they are, in Whitehead's words, the "angry dead," "the ruthless chaos of existence made flesh."[33] Watching the zombies pour out of a bank, at one point, Whitehead writes: "Here they came, the ambassadors of nil" (306). In a world ruined by the desire for everything, the zombie comes to preach the silent gospel of nothing.

Every zombie represents a critique of the human. The zombie must not be read as simply the human emptied of will or subjectivity; the zombie is a kind of parahuman force, a collective subject reaching from beyond the grave to exact bloody revenge from regimes of law, order, and truth. The zombie is part of a wild otherworld suppressed by white, rational thought and returning to partial life in order to dispossess humans.[34] If zombie narratives represent a kind of Afro-pessimist spectacle within which white humans are on the run from restless, violent, vengeful, parahuman entities who seek not to become human, but to destroy humanity altogether, how does the (white) human imagine its own survival? Increasingly, concepts of the human depend on white racial fantasies of extended longevity (even in the face of diminished environmental capacity), technologically enhanced futurity, and a maximized relation to survival. This, at least, is the premise of the neo-eugenicist endeavor dubbed transhumanism.

Transhumanism

From slavery to current day sweat shops, certain forms of labor have established relations between individualized owners/managers/humans and masses of people cast as zombified by the repetitive labor assigned to them and by their seeming lack of consciousness. Zombie narratives turn on these oppositions between the many and the few, so much so that not a few costumed protestors at Occupy Wall Street showed up in zombie costumes, sometimes to represent zombie bankers, cogs in the financial machine, and at other times to represent zombie workers, passive victims of the market. Zombie forms of living death crop up everywhere nowadays, proliferating as the concept of *living death* comes to describe everything from runaway markets (zombie capitalism) to runaway politicians (zombie Trump) to destitute populations. And even as living death becomes a feature of the super-capitalist landscape, so do new financial ventures emerge offering to save us from the very conditions that capitalism has created. These fantasies of redemption come in the form of neocolonial ventures in which Europeans or Americans seek to intervene in global crises that they themselves have created or in the form of new, pseudo-scientific fantasies of de-extinction and transhumanism.

Early transhumanism was a concept used by eugenic thinkers like Julian Huxley, (1887–1975). Huxley's brother Aldous was the author of *Brave New World*, a terrifying look at a dystopian near future in which reproduction and death is controlled by the state. Julian Huxley was less fanciful than his brother, and he concentrated on science not science fiction—although, given his beliefs on racial difference, you could say it was science fiction of another kind. In 1957 Julian Huxley coined the term *transhumanism*—a word that, for him, described the obligation of the human to improve himself, his terms of embodiment, and his social condition.[35] Prior to World War II, Huxley espoused notions of racial inferiority and superiority; in the postwar period, when such ideas had been revealed in all of their disastrous violence, he moved away from the idea of racial improvement and toward human improvement—hence transhumanism. In a contemporary context, eugenics also plays a big role in fantasies of manipulated reproductive potential and in imperial notions of de-extinction. Against the futurist fantasies of transhumanism, I pose a zombie antihumanism within which the living, the dead, and the living dead struggle against the constraints not simply of the body, but of the tight webs made up of race, class, gender, and sexuality that continue to bind us to certain corrosive and enduring narratives laden with hierarchies and deadly fantasies of domination.

Such projects are multiplying as the demand for some kind of meaningful response to climate change and species extinction mounts. As an example, we could turn to de-extinction projects. Fantasizing the technological reversal of extinction, de-extinction projects preserve the ruinous incursions of humans into the habitats of endangered animals that reduced animal populations to extinction in the first place. But they do so while imagining themselves as the salvation of animal life. An example can be found in a link on the site of a new venture by Stewart Brand (editor of the *Whole Earth Catalog*). Brand's organization, The Long Now Foundation, represents itself as "counterpoint to today's accelerating culture and help make long-term thinking more common."[36] This sounds unremarkable enough, but nested in their list of projects we find a connection to another, more pernicious organization, called Revive & Restore, which describes itself as a project designed to "enhance biodiversity through new techniques of genetic rescue for endangered and extinct species."[37] Revive & Restore announces:

> Thanks to the rapid advance of genomic technology, new tools are emerging for conservation. Endangered species that have lost their crucial genetic diversity may be restored to reproductive health. Those threatened by invasive diseases may be able to acquire genetic disease-resistance. It may even be possible to bring some extinct species back to life. The DNA of many extinct creatures is well preserved in museum specimens and some fossils. Their full genomes can now be read and analyzed. That data may be transferable as working genes into their closest living relatives, effectively bringing the extinct species back to life. The ultimate aim is to restore them to their former home in the wild.[38]

Notice that there is no sense that the same forces that have invested in a "rapid advance of genomic technology" may also be responsible for the rapacious clearing of habitats and polluting of environments that resulted in the extinction of these species—this text merely attributes the disappearance of animals to "the loss" of genetic diversity and diseases. There is also a highly optimistic sense that once "we" have "rescued" these creatures from extinction, "we" will simply pop them back into their "former homes" in the "wild," which presumably still exists somewhere and awaits their return.

These reawakening projects, with their Christian rhetoric of revival, their fantasies of raising Lazarus from the dead, their seemingly innocent languages of resurrection, and so on, spend little time on the question of why species become extinct and whether they would be brought back only into new forms of endangerment. Instead, such projects prop up the mode of humanity that depends on these cloned, zombie forms of life. And such dynamics between salvation and endangerment define much more than just animal populations. Similar language has been used to justify colonial settler violence against Native populations. Indeed, what I am calling zombie antihumanism builds upon Jodi Byrd's formulation of "Zombie Imperialism" at the conclusion of *Transit of Empire.*[39] For Byrd, zombie imperialism eliminates over and over again the figure of the Indian—first the Indigenous peoples are destroyed and removed, then the memory of their removal is erased, and finally the state represents them as extinct through some mysterious process of evolution. Indians who appear in the here and now are represented as zombie-like figures, back from the dead, threatening and hungry, slow and violent. "Zombie imperialism," writes Byrd, "has emerged as the post-racial, liberal democratic apocalyptic vision of pluralistic cosmopolitanism gone viral" (225).

The "zombie" in "zombie imperialism" refers to the "back from the dead" process within which the violent, brutal erasure of peoples, animals, and things is re-narrated in the present as a form of heroic rescue, but it also refers to the liminal status of those peoples and animals cast, all at once, as both in need of rescue and as threatening. But another way of understanding these zombie discourses would be in terms of the biopolitical mandate described by Foucault as a clean technology of governance—in new strains of the biopolitical, the state mandates life at all costs for some and consigns others to death and living death. And so, at a time of limited resources (drought, starvation, scarcity), we develop ever more elaborate technologies for the reproduction of the wealthy. And where once eugenic discourses sought to control the reproduction of so-called undesirable populations, the state now seeks to facilitate and maximize the reproductive potential of so-called desirable groups. This switch from negative to positive power is what Foucault identifies as central to the biopolitical.

Living Death

In opposition to the de-extinction fantasies of zombie imperialism, then, I offer a zombie antihumanism, an alternative form of fantasy that finds nothing to save in the human and imagines in the zombie a new form of collective life. Today, North American and British popular culture is flooded with zombies in films and in popular TV series that conjure different future nightmares of destruction and impending extinction. At the same time, academia is similarly teeming with analyses of zombies, zombie anthologies, all kinds of books with *zombie* in the title (*American Gothic Zombie: The Rise and Fall (and Rise) of Zombies in Popular Culture, Not Your Average Zombie, Zombie Culture*, and so on). And popular literature from self-help books to parenting advice to economies also has overemployed this ubiquitous epithet (*Parenting in the Zombie Apocalypse, Economics of the Undead, Zombie Economics*). Like vampires before them, zombies are a viral monster, and in our era of viral digital media the concept of the living dead is so infectious that people seem fairly ready to admit that the zombie apocalypse is already upon us, and we are it!

The feeling of proximity to zombie apocalypse has surely contributed to the incredible and long-lasting success of AMC's *The Walking Dead* in the United States. Based on a comic book by Robert Kirkman, the series focuses on a police officer, Rick Grimes (Andrew Lincoln), injured in a gunfight and placed in a coma, wakes up in the hospital and slowly discovers that while he was out the human world has been overrun by "walkers." The show never actually uses the word *zombies*, but the term *walkers* conveys the same sense of a shambling, unstoppable mass of flesh. Rick leaves the hospital to go in search of his wife and child and quickly finds himself trapped. Only the intervention of another survivor, Glenn Rhee (Steven Yeun), allows Rick to escape a horde of walkers. Glenn then introduces Rick to the others in a small group of human survivors, and in this group he finds his wife and child and his best friend, another policeman (allowing for a good cop/bad cop scenario to unwind), Shane. This core group, an expanded family, fills out at various points along the way until the series settles on a group of anywhere between ten and twenty people who offer special skills, provide emotional support, or become cannon fodder, depending on the plot's needs. As the series continues, however, the postapocalyptic landscape quickly turns into the "Wild West," and at least in the early seasons, you would think that only white heterosexuals were able to survive the apocalypse! As with earlier zombie narratives, the white family is the source of immense violence as it sacrifices everything around it on behalf of its own survival. The western feel of the series is intensified by the way the walkers are represented: like the Indians in cowboy films, they always arrive en masse and look otherworldly because they are so different from the white pioneers (they are often half naked and wear feathers or scraps of clothing, for example), but the walkers, like the Indians, are also bent on the destruction of the white survivor community.

As the humans in *The Walking Dead* adapt to their bleak, new reality and learn how to survive by picking off the walkers one by one with a well-placed blow to the skull or by outrunning them, postapocalyptic life offers new terrors—brutal humans bent on enslaving other humans, internecine struggles within the group, incipient fascism, and resource management. As the power brokers emerge, the sheriff, Rick, takes on a messianic role, and as a deified presence he is able to slaughter humans and walkers alike with impunity. Rick, indeed, exemplifies the humanism that zombies oppose as his humanity depends on the reduction of everyone around him to either enemy if human or vermin/feral if walker. The precise problem with this moral division emerges

Figure 5.2   The Walking Dead (2010–).

in season 3, when the human survivors end up in a prison. Recognizing that the former prison now represents the best shelter from the living dead (its design prevents incursions or escapes), the group begin to set up a new home there. But they quickly realize that the prison is already inhabited, by former prisoners who do not know what is happening outside their walls, and they drive out the other living dead, the remnants of an actual prison population, in order to stake their claim to the territory they once used to cordon off the lawful from the criminal. While the TV show never waivers in condemning the prisoners and casting them as outsiders rather than fellow survivors, the audience of the show might be able to discern the continuity between the walking dead on the streets and the living dead behind bars. Zombies in *The Walking Dead* quickly emerge as a wandering subaltern; they are literally the unhoused, the hungry, the excluded, the expendable, the sick, the dying, the disabled, and the ignorant. Their strength lies in their numbers, their weakness is connected to their slowness, and they have to be killed twice—one time to inhabit the liminal category of the dead alive and a second time in order to be sacrificed to the higher good.

In a UK show that ran for several seasons the zombies are far less gory but just as obviously a cross section of marginalized populations. *In the Flesh* aired in 2013–14 on BBC Three and used the conceit of an apocalyptic event called

The Rising, possibly an environmental disturbance, during which everyone who had died that year (2010) came back from the dead as zombies. The reanimated dead terrorize the population, and then, as suddenly as it began, the event ends, and the nation must round up the reanimated zombies. Postapocalypse, the government decides to try to rehabilitate the zombies, and they are now cast not as monsters, but as people suffering from partially deceased syndrome. Sufferers are treated with drugs to prevent them from remaining "rabid," in the show's parlance, feral in ours, and they wear makeup to fit in with the general population and receive therapy to manage their memories about the terrible things they may have done or seen while rabid. The goal of all this is to bring the deceased back into the ranks for the living after the mayhem of The Rising. In the United Kingdom, the framework within which the partially dead are rehabilitated combines the ruins of a welfare system with nationalist mandates to assimilate. But the central figure in this show, a gay teen suicide brought back from the dead, aptly named Kieran Walker in a nod to *The Walking Dead*, refuses the humanist attempts at rescue and redemption that his community offers him and represents an irresolvable tension between autodestruction and the biopolitical mandate to choose life over all else. Indeed, Victus, the white nationalist party who believe that the "rotters" should be rounded up and shot, situates itself as "pro-living," and this creates a standoff between the pro-living and what comes to be the Undead Liberation Army.

The biopolitical schemes of life, unlife, and death in *The Walking Dead* and *In the Flesh* are quite different. While *The Walking Dead* subscribes wholeheartedly to an old-fashioned humanism countered by a zombie antihumanism, as I have termed it, where the only life that counts is human life and everything else is reduced to raw material for human thriving, *In the Flesh* offers a critique of the human and comes down on the side of the undead. The undead in the British show are consistently opposed by groups of white militias; they are hunted and caged, rejected, and shot. In addition, the main character, Kieran, is a gay man who literally chose death over life and thereby, even before The Rising, offered a deep critique of his family and community and decided that death was preferable to a kind of un-life in a small homophobic and xenophobic world. Living death in *In the Flesh* is not the return from the dead, but the unbearable organization of life and the living on behalf of the normative, the bigoted, the secure, and the wealthy.

Flesh here, of course, also conjures the division between bodies and flesh, a primary division created by slavery and then installed within what Hortense Spillers calls "an American grammar" or a symbolic structure dedicated to the construction of racial division. The exact relations between humans and zom-

Figure 5.3   In the Flesh (2013–14).

bies in zombies narratives from *Night of the Living Dead* to *In the Flesh* mimics this original division between bodies and flesh, white and Black, human and wild. And in the system of naming, Spillers notes, the structure repeats: "Dominant symbolic activity, the ruling episteme that releases the dynamics of naming and valuation, remains grounded in the originating metaphors of captivity and mutilation."[40] In both *The Walking Dead* and *In the Flesh*, bodies chase flesh across a ruined landscape. But in both narratives, the zombies, an elemental antihuman force of restless and endless violence, threaten at every moment to symbolically and physically reveal the vulnerability of both the human body and the humanist grammar out of which it emerges. Zombies are not simply mindless ids, not only rapacious appetite in motion. Zombies represent the return of the dead that imperial powers have sacrificed, mutilated, severed, and brutalized on behalf of maximized life, profit, and massive wealth for the very few. Contemporary obsessions with zombie forms, like nineteenth-century obsessions with vampires, recognizes in this monstrous form the end of era, and if the era in question at the close of the nineteenth century was a form of capitalism, as the twenty-first century mints its own monstrous symbolism, the end it imagines is not of an era, but of the human itself.

No Future

Zombies are the millions of bodies that exist between life and death in this era of impending extinction. They are the pets with which we live, the animals we have hounded into extinction, the world we have tethered to human concerns. The question is not life or death, but lives and deaths and everything in between. The living, walking, suppurating dead are those bodies we have assigned to the gray zone between the good life and bare life—they include the incarcerated, refugees, the hungry, the terminally ill, the sick and dying, the very young and very old, the homeless, the drug addicts, the endangered species, the mentally ill, the disabled, the starving, the dispossessed, the occupied, the unsaved, unremembered, irredeemable, illegible, illegitimate undead. The undead are hungry, they are angry, they are sick, and they are tired. And while you may look upon them with horror today, tomorrow, you will no doubt try to save them in order to redeem a seriously compromised sense of your own humanity. But in the end, it is not you who can save the zombie; it is the zombie that will decide whether we live or die and whether survival will have been worth it.

The Ninth Wave

Wild—Of the sea, a stream, the weather, etc. Violently agitated, rough, stormy, tempestuous, "raging"; hence *fig.* or *gen.* full of disturbance or confusion, tumultuous, turbulent, disorderly.

—*Oxford English Dictionary*

We cannot think of a time that is oceanless
Or of an ocean not littered with wastage
Or of a future that is not liable
Like the past, to have no destination.

—T. S. Eliot, "The Dry Salvages"

Wave after wave, each mightier than the last,
Till last, a ninth one, gathering half the deep
And full of voices, slowly rose and plunged
Roaring, and all the wave was in a flame.

—Alfred Lord Tennyson, *Idylls of the King:
The Coming of Arthur*

A nautical myth proposes that sets of waves at sea gain progressively in intensity until, by the ninth, they have reached a climax of water, weight, height, and force. The ninth wave is the obliterating force you always knew was coming; it is the wave you cannot see behind, the one that is about to crush you, and it is the wave that has gathered momentum by sucking up "half the deep."[1] However huge the seventh and eighth waves in a set may be, it is the ninth wave, the myth goes, that will swallow you up or spit you out. The ninth wave either delivers you to your fate or dashes you to your doom; it determines whether you are among the drowned or the saved: the ninth wave delivers us to the shore or hurls us toward death. But of course, the ninth wave is also just a myth. While some sets of waves may result in huge swells by the ninth wave, others will have dissipated by then or will still be building. Waves are hard to judge, hard to predict, and by their very nature, unruly and wild. We like myths such as the ninth wave, which has now become the name of art projects, blog sites, and all kinds of poetic projects precisely because we want nature to be (ac)countable somehow. We want to believe in a realm called nature, where waves come in sets, storms at sea have patterns, and kings arise out of the depths to walk on the land and restore order. But the wild has other plans for us.

In Tennyson's description of the ninth wave in *Idylls of the King: The Coming of Arthur*, the wave bursts into flames as it delivers the future King Arthur to the shore. As the poem continues, this epic ninth wave takes on the force of myth, magic, and mayhem as it represents the swelling political momentum that is to deliver Arthur to the English throne so that he can enforce his sovereign power against the chaos of lawlessness that rules the land. As Tennyson puts it:

> For many a petty king ere Arthur came
> Ruled in this isle, and ever waging war
> Each upon other, wasted all the land;
> And still from time to time the heathen host
> Swarm'd overseas, and harried what was left.
> And so there grew great tracts of wilderness,
> Wherein the beast was ever more and more,
> But man was less and less, till Arthur came.[2]

And so, even the wildness of the sea is tamed by the coming of the king, and the seemingly random progression of waves gives way to the pattern and order that the sovereign represents and restores.

Perhaps the most famous myth-making around the ninth wave, other than Tennyson's of course, came in 1985 in the form of a concept album by British singer Kate Bush. Many of the concepts of the wild that jostle for space in this book can be found in that album, and so I want to add Bush to my archive of the wild, both for her otherworldly, dystopian visions of a dark world where the free spirit, the hound of love, is persecuted and hunted down but also for her ability to conjure strange new worlds where we can make it rain, where the fox escapes the hounds but dies anyway, where the sky itself holds peril and promise, where we are all lost at sea. Indulge me.

In 1985, her career stalled by poor sales of her previous album, Bush released her fifth record, *Hounds of Love*, and overnight went from being a quirky young singer to an international cult star. *Hounds of Love* is a mesh of fantasy, menace, melancholy, and loss, and it alternates between the heat of the chase, the hunt, and the capture, all of which filters through its instantly popular set of singles on side one and the conceptual work on side two, which features a cycle of songs titled "The Ninth Wave."

With such classics as "Running Up That Hill" and "Hounds of Love" (the title track), the album begins dramatically: a driving beat, lush arrangements, strings, and Bush's singular voice, which, once heard, can never be forgotten. The voice is not exactly operatic, not simply a soprano; it is a female falsetto—a woman impersonating a woman: this falsetto is why the neo-soul singer Maxwell, who has a pure male falsetto voice, could cover "This Woman's Work" effortlessly and why others simply cannot come close to performing her songs let alone covering them. The female falsetto at its worst is grating and shrill, but at its very best it shreds all emotion that comes its way; it deepens loss, heightens despair, burdens expectation, breathes possibility, and hushes opposition.

Once we get to "Cloudbusting" we are actually no longer running up that hill, but heading down, out of the trees and into the ocean. But "Cloudbusting" is itself the liminal and the climactic song on the album—built around a book Bush read by Peter Reich about his father, the kooky and wild Wilhelm Reich, who believed that repression and lack of orgasms was to blame for mass delusion, fascism, neurosis, and even drought! "Cloudbusting" refers to Reich's dream of building a machine that could channel bioelectric waves to open up clouds and release the rain—an obvious metaphor for orgasm, flows of liquid relief, and the unleashing of repressed material. When she opens the song with the line "I still dream of Orgonon," Bush is referring to the house that Reich built and lived in in Maine. The song tells the story of building a machine to drain the clouds and to bust through the barrier between life and dreams—"just saying it could even make it happen."[3]

This wild album brims with the kind of energy that Paul Preciado refers to in *Testo Junkie* as *potentia gaudendi*, a force of pleasure, power, and pain; the source of liberation and subjugation all at once.[4] "I just know that something good is gonna happen."[5] But it also turns dark as soon as you flip the album over and begin the sequence titled "The Ninth Wave."[6] This side of the album turns away from the hydraulics of desire, the gushing, transmitting, circulating force of potential jouissance, and swings onto the dark side—shifting from a sky full of clouds to a wild ocean of unpredictable moves and rogue waves. Fishermen are told to "get out of the water," and even the usually soothing sounds of the "shipping forecast," a naturally poetic text that for decades has been recited every evening on the BBC, becomes the harbinger of doom.

"The Ninth Wave" veers between determined apocalyptic outcome and wild, random futurity, between lunar travel—"Hello Earth"—and oceanic voyage, between death and new life, between desire and loss.[7] The song cycle is a reminder to always flip the album over, to look for the darkness as well as the light, to experience the sense of loss and abandon that is as much a part of life as it is a part of death. Kate Bush can be the irritating falsetto on "Wuthering Heights," but she can also offer us "And Dream of Sheep," a song made up of equal parts resignation, hope, and poetry—here it is the poetry of the shipping reports, the hope that the lost soul will be found, the resignation to the fact that she is lost. As the album winds to a close with "The Morning Fog," a new day is born, another life is extinguished—the song refuses to rescue the swimmer lost at sea, the fishermen, the boats tossed by the storm: we all succumb, it says, to love, to death, to the ninth wave.

It is impossible after Christina Sharpe's lyrical, devastating study *In the Wake: On Blackness and Being* to ignore the dense relations that gather in the water (and in the weather) between Blackness, violence, obliteration, and a temporality that comes after and is awash with trauma.[8] The wildness of the wave and the spectacle of the boat tossed upon high seas cannot be a neutral image in the wake. Throughout this book, I have attended to a proximity between Black bodies and wildness—a wildness that sits outside of civilization, a wildness that refuses and resists the order of things, a wildness that offers unpredictable and undead refusals to the regimes of representation that seek to swallow up difference altogether. Blackness and indigeneity indeed are cast within Euro-American modernism as a form of wildness that must be conquered and as a restless force of living death that can be tapped for labor, physical and symbolic, but that must also be held at bay. But through the lyrical force of a disordering prose, Sharpe also links Blackness to the wildness of the water, the "multiple registers of the wake" (20). "In the wake," Sharpe writes, "the semiotics of the slave ship continue" (21). These semiotics can be found in Sendak's *Where the Wild Things Are*. Max's journey to where the wild things are, a journey that, as I noted earlier, turns all too quickly from a voyage away from family, sense, and order into a colonial opportunity for conquest, rule, and command, a voyage that also leaves a wake. And the wild things who find themselves in the wake are left with the deeply uncomfortable knowledge that Max's departure, by boat, his return to the home, the nation, the white family, signals his shift from wild thing to sovereign being. Just as Max becomes white, male, and adult by leaving the wild things behind, so the wild things stay wild in his wake and guarantee his survival by sitting uncertainly within their own. The calculation of time, space, domestic, and wild that allows Max to come and go determines that wild things must stay where they are and that the place where they live will be wild as a consequence of their presence. This book has tried to interrupt the voyage to where the wild things are and has tried to imagine the end of the world that depends on an exiled wild.

Speaking of the temporality of the wake and citing Toni Morrison's *Beloved*, Sharpe writes: "We, Black people, exist in the residence time of the wake, a time in which 'everything is now. It is all now'" (41).[9] And the ninth wave too is here now. In this present tense crowded with racial histories, life continues in its backwash and adrift in its refuse-strewn wake. "We cannot think of a time that is oceanless," T. S. Eliot proposed in 1941, "Or of an ocean not littered with wastage." He continues, "Or of a future that is not liable / Like the past, to have no destination."[10] We can now think of a future that is all ocean; we can imagine an ocean full of garbage; we live with a future severely curtailed, and we acknowledge a past that has delivered us here and now. Our world is not the promise that wildness held out to us and that was courted and inhabited by queer thinkers in the early years of the twentieth century; it is a disaster of our own making and one that will take a complete revolution to reverse. The lines of Eliot's poetry that have introduced many of the sections of this book feel urgent and right, molded to this moment, activated anew by the tumbling future into which we have fallen. If the *Four Quartets* were written both in a state of anxiety about the impending war and as a meditation on finality, they also seem, presciently, to be focused on a looming environmental crisis. The theme of temporal foreshortening is not only a personal reflection on death and dying, on mortality in a time of war; it also focuses on a world that is disappearing before Eliot's eyes. A world in which time expands, nature forms a foundation, and the human fuses with wildness slips from view and is replaced by perpetual death ([And the time of death is every moment]), cyclical movements that spin to a conclusion ("Feet rising and falling. / Eating and drinking. / Dung and death"), and massive changes in climate and context ("Where is the summer, the unimaginable Zero summer?").[11] Eliot, certainly one of the odd, wild figures in this book who defies the classifications of sexuality that we have settled on, also speaks as a man who knows that time is up. With the poet's ability to look beyond his own mortality and toward a more menacing finality, he provides a soundtrack for apocalypse.

> There are other places
> Which also are the world's end, some at the sea jaws,
> Or over a dark lake, in a desert or a city—
> But this is the nearest, in place and time,
> Now and in England.[12]

There are other places that are also the world's end, and we have found them, inhabited them, and settled them. And if the former center of empire should be established as the most bleak of such places, now and in England, in a summer of soaring temperatures, in a world tempted again by fascist solutions to intractable problems, then we, too, like Eliot, may find ourselves at "the intersection of the timeless moment" in the space of "never and always."[13]

The wild, in this book, has been a journey out of order and into the swift ever-changing currents of the ocean. Wildness has conjured anarchy, embodiment beyond identity, zombies, and other forms of living dead. It resides in our past and forms the unknowability of the future still to come. Wildness is neither utopia nor dystopia; it is a force we live with and a way of being that we are organizing out of existence. If the wild has anything to tell us, it is this: unbuild the world you inhabit, unmake its relentless commitment to the same, ignore the calls for more, and agree to be with the wild, accept the wild, give yourself to the wild, and float or drown in its embrace.

Introduction to Part I

1 Maurice Sendak, *Where the Wild Things Are*, 50th anniv. ed. (New York: HarperCollins, 2013).

2 Michel Foucault, *The History of Sexuality*, vol. 1, trans. Robert Hurley (New York: Random House, 1985), 101.

3 Catriona Mortimer-Sandilands and Bruce Erickson, "Introduction: A Genealogy of Queer Ecologies," in *Queer Ecologies: Sex, Nature, Politics, Desire*, ed. Catriona Mortimer-Sandilands and Bruce Erickson (Bloomington: Indiana University Press, 2010), 1–50.

4 Mortimer-Sandilands and Erickson, "Genealogy of Queer Ecologies," 21.

5 Eduardo Kohn, *How Forests Think: Toward an Anthropology beyond the Human* (Berkeley: University of California Press, 2013), 41.

6. Sylvia Wynter, "Unsettling the Coloniality of Being/Power/Truth/Freedom: Towards the Human, after Man, Its Overrepresentation—an Argument," *New Centennial Review* 3, no. 3 (Fall 2003): 257–337.

7 J. Kēhaulani Kauanui, "'Savage' Sexualities," in *Paradoxes of Hawaiian Sovereignty: Land, Sex, and the Colonial Politics of State Nationalism* (Durham, NC: Duke University Press, 2018), 153–93. Kauanui writes: "A range of sexual practices drew sustained attention and caused alarm among missionaries and eventually Hawaiian chiefs. . . . Prior to Christianization, Indigenous practices were diverse and allowed for multiple sexual possibilities." Missionaries "also crafted severe penalty regimes for those caught 'backsliding' into 'heathendom.'" Although Kauanui reads a very different archive than I do—she is concerned with the legal archive of Anglo-American colonization in Hawai'i, and I am drawing on Anglo-American modernism, the language of the wild, the heathen, and untamed possibilities abound in both contexts and around the same time.

8 Hayden White, "The Forms of Wildness: An Archaeology of an Idea," in *Tropics of Discourse: Essays in Cultural Criticism* (Baltimore: Johns Hopkins University Press, 1986), 151.

9 Patrick Jarenwattananon, "Why Jazz Musicians Love 'The Rite of Spring,'" NPR's *Deceptive Cadence*, May 26, 2013, https://www.npr.org/sections/deceptivecadence /2013/05/26/186486269/why-jazz-musicians-love-the-rite-of-spring.

10 See Kent Monkman, "The Casualities of Modernity," lecture for the Penny W. Stamps School of Art & Design, University of Michigan, streamed live April 2, 2015, accessed October 2019, https://www.youtube.com/watch?v=sDFAKcptgZA.

11 Macarena Gómez-Barris, "A Fish-Eye Episteme: Seeing Below the River's Colonization," in *The Extractive Zone: Social Ecologies and Decolonial Perspectives* (Durham, NC: Duke University Press, 2017), 91–109.

12 Jane Bennett, *Thoreau's Nature: Ethics, Politics, and the Wild* (Lanham, MD: Rowman and Littlefield, 2002); Kohn, *How Forests Think*, 94; Branka Arsić, *Bird Relics: Grief and Vitalism in Thoreau* (Cambridge, MA: Harvard University Press, 2016).

13 Bennett, *Thoreau's Nature*.

14 Michel Foucault, *The Order of Things: An Archaeology of the Human Sciences* (1996; reprint, London: Routledge, 2002).

15 T. S. Eliot, "East Coker," in *Four Quartets* (New York: Harcourt, 1943), 23. Hereafter, the names of poems from this source and the pages quoted from them are presented in parentheses.

16 For more, see Carole Seymour-Jones, *Painted Shadow: The Life of Vivienne Eliot* (New York: Doubleday, 2001), and Louis Menand, "The Women Come and Go: The Love Song of T. S. Eliot," *New Yorker*, September 22, 2002, https://www.newyorker.com /magazine/2002/09/30/the-women-come-and-go.

17 See Eve Sedgwick's *The Epistemology of the Closet* (Berkeley: University of California Press, 1990) and David Halperin's *One Hundred Years of Homosexuality and Other Essays on Greek Love* (New York: Routledge, 1990), among others.

18 On these other models of sexuality, see Benjamin Kahan, *The Book of Minor Perverts: Sexology, Etiology, and the Emergences of Sexuality* (Chicago: University of Chicago Press, 2019). Kahan goes so far as to propose that we may have focused too much on sexual epistemology in our efforts to provide a history for sexuality, and in so doing, he claims, we have ignored other, often racialized, histories of the body that are less easily located in the abrupt and decisive turn to personage that Foucault narrates ("the nineteenth-century homosexual became a personage"). Kahan turns to etiology, or the examination of the causes of certain sexual orientations, to reveal a far less clear shift from behavior to personhood and shows "how an explosion of 'unrationalized'—which is to say multiple and conflicting—explanations of sexuality came to exist simultaneously." The minor perverts of Kahan's title are the thousands of behaviors that doctors and sexologists diagnosed and then rushed to treat in the nineteenth century.

19 Foucault, *History of Sexuality*, 43.

20 Peter Coviello, *Tomorrow's Parties: Sex and the Untimely in Nineteenth-Century America* (New York: NYU Press, 2013), 3.

21 Foucault, *Order of Things*, 303.

22 The noted exception, Paul Preciado's *Countersexual Manifesto*, was translated into English and published in 2018 by Columbia University Press with an introduction by me. Preciado begins his manifesto with the following line: "Countersexuality is not the creation of a new nature, but rather the end of Nature as an order that legitimizes the subjection of some bodies to others."

23 See Joan Cadden, *Nothing Natural Is Shameful: Sodomy and Science in Late Medieval Europe* (Philadelphia: University of Pennsylvania Press, 2017), 4.

24 Cadden, *Nothing Natural Is Shameful*, 4.

25 Parliament of England, *Buggery Act: An Act for the Punishment of the Vice of Bugerie* (1533), accessed January 13, 2020, https://www.bl.uk/collection-items/the-buggery -act-1533.

26 Eve Kosofsky Sedgwick, *The Epistemology of the Closet* (Berkeley: University of California Press, 1990), 44.

27 Susan Sontag, "Notes on Camp," in *Against Interpretation and Other Essays* (New York: Farrar, Straus and Giroux, 1966), 48.

28 Oscar Wilde, "The Decay of Lying," in *Intentions: The Works of Oscar Wilde*, Edition De Luxe (New York: Brainard, 1909), 7.

29 The necessity of occupying the terrain of the unnatural explains the dominance of the trope of theatricality in Oscar Wilde and other late nineteenth-century writers associated with contrary desires.

30 Oscar Wilde, *An Ideal Husband* (London: Leonard Smithers and Co., 1899).

31 Joris-Karl Huysmans, *Against the Grain [Á rebours]*, trans. John Howard (1884; Project Gutenberg E Book, 2014).

32 Oscar Wilde, *The Picture of Dorian Gray*, Edition De Luxe (New York: Brainard, 1909).

33 Percy Bysshe Shelley, *Mont Blanc: Lines Written in the Vale of Chamouni* (1861), excerpted, accessed January 14, 2020, https://www.poetryfoundation.org/poems/45130 /mont-blanc-lines-written-in-the-vale-of-chamouni.

34 Timothy Morton, *Hyperobjects: Philosophy and Ecology after the End of the World* (Minneapolis: University of Minnesota Press, 2013), 4.

35 Macarena Gómez-Barris, *The Extractive Zone: Social Ecologies and Decolonial Perspectives* (Durham, NC: Duke University Press, 2017), 4.

36 Wilde, *Picture of Dorian Gray*, 16.

37 See new work by Branka Arsić on the popularity of stuffed tortoises in the nineteenth century!

38 Radclyffe Hall, *The Well of Loneliness* (1928; reprint, Ware, UK: Wordsworth Editions, 2005).

39 Annamarie Jagose, *Inconsequence: Lesbian Representation and the Logic of Sexual Sequence* (Ithaca, NY: Cornell University Press, 2002).

40 Hall, *Well of Loneliness*, 138.

41 Jordy Rosenberg, *Confessions of the Fox* (New York: One World, 2018), 136. This book imagines, with historical precision, that Jack Sheppard, the notorious English thief and jailbreaker of the eighteenth century, memorialized in John Gay's *The Beggar's*

Opera (1728) and generally described as a small but strong man, was actually a trans*
person.

42 Jack Halberstam, *Female Masculinity* (Durham, NC: Duke University Press, 1998).

43 Frantz Fanon, "The Fact of Blackness" (1952), in *Black Skin, White Masks*, trans.
Charles Lam Markmann (New York: Grove, 1967), 109.

44 Fred Moten, *In the Break: The Aesthetics of the Black Radical Tradition* (Minneapolis:
University of Minnesota Press, 2003).

45 Mel Y. Chen, *Animacies: Biopolitics, Racial Mattering, and Queer Affect* (Durham,
NC: Duke University Press, 2012).

46 C. Riley Snorton, *Black on Both Sides: A Racial History of Trans Identity* (Minneapolis: University of Minnesota Press, 2018), xiv.

47 Lindon Barrett, *Blackness and Value: Seeing Double* (Cambridge: Cambridge University Press, 1999).

48 Frank B. Wilderson III, *Red, White, and Black: Cinema and the Structure of U.S. Antagonisms* (Durham, NC: Duke University Press, 2010), 74.

49 See Stephen J. Mexal, "The Roots of 'Wilding': Black Literary Naturalism, the Language of Wilderness, and Hip Hop in the Central Park Jogger Rape," *African American Review* 46, no. 1 (2013): 101–15. In this article on the "language of wilderness," Mexal provides a clear and historically situated account of how and why this term was affixed to the accused men and how it resonated through racial histories of Central Park, as well as Black literary discourse and hip hop. The rape, media commentators claimed, was part of a known set of practices indulged by Black youth and operating under the name of *wilding*. The men were cast by the police, by politicians, and by the media as rude intrusions on the hallowed grounds of Central Park. Having left their neighborhoods of the Bronx and Harlem, they were already out of place and were cast as trespassers, as criminals even before they were attached to a crime, and they remain criminal in the minds of many despite having been exonerated. Mexal's essay on the Central Park Five does much more than a documentary by Ken Burns on the topic to explain how and why five young Black men could be randomly arrested for rape. Mexal traces several lineages for the use of the term *wild* in this case: First, it appears within what Mexal calls American literary naturalism to define otherness in terms of savagery and brutishness. Second, it appears in African American literature by Richard Wright and others to "explore the discursive nexus of criminality and the language of wilderness." Wright's representations of Black masculinity reveal the circular logic by which Black bodies are culturally constructed using the language of wildness and then must deploy the same stereotypes in order to reveal the marks of their construction. Third, wildness conjures the fear of Black populations that drove urban planning in the 1980s and that set the stage for the mass delusion that allowed the term *wilding* to accrue meaning so quickly and with such force in 1989. Donald Trump, already a real estate mogul at this time, was so sure about the guilt of the Central Park Five that he took out full-page ads in the *New York Times* arguing for the death penalty for the men and conjured the specter of "roving bands of wild criminals." Finally, the wild, Mexal proposes, was part of the original justification for the removal of en-

tire neighborhoods in the 1840s, when Central Park was in the planning—residents of the area were cast as part of a poor and nonwhite wilderness that, like other parts of the country, needed to be razed, cleared, and settled. Given this background, it was all too easy for the media and the police to cooperate in the production in 1989 of a practice of wilding associated with lawless groups of Black and Brown men and representing a major threat to the white populations in the city who were beginning to benefit from an economic boom. Wilding entered the vocabulary of urban terror as, in Mexal's words, "a terrible word from a strange new language" (102). Mexal goes on to explain how the term *wilding* was lifted from a popular rap hit of that year by Tone Loc, "Wild Thing." But the term *wilding*, he proposed, actually appeared at least a year earlier, in 1988, in a song by Ice-T titled "Radio Suckers," wherein the rapper describes an urban scene of police surveillance and entrapment. Ice T describes his neighborhood in Los Angeles in the song in terms of "Gangs illin', wildin' and killin'" but then goes on to suggest that "guys will stop wildin' if you stop that crap." In other words, here, too, Black wildness is the product of and the response to police violence.

50 Saidiya Hartman, *Wayward Lives, Beautiful Experiments: Intimate Histories of Social Upheaval* (New York: W. W. Norton, 2019), 227.

51 Wilderson, *Red, White, and Black*, 23.

52 Kara Keeling, *Queer Times, Black Futures* (New York: NYU Press, 2019).

53 Karen Barad, "Transmaterialities: Trans*/Matter/Realities and Queer Political Imaginings," *GLQ: A Journal of Lesbian and Gay Studies* 21, nos. 2–3 (2015): 394.

54 Wilderson, *Red, White, and Black*, 36.

55 Donna J. Haraway, *Staying with the Trouble: Making Kin in the Chthulucene* (Durham, NC: Duke University Press, 2016).

1. Wildness, Loss, and Death

1 Joseph Conrad, *Heart of Darkness* (1902; reprint, Claremont, CA: Coyote Canyon, 2007); T. S. Eliot, "Little Gidding," in *Four Quartets* (New York: Mariner, 1943), 59.

2 Eliot, "East Coker," in *Four Quartets*, 23.

3 Conrad, *Heart of Darkness*, 7.

4 Gayatri Chakravorty Spivak, "Can the Subaltern Speak?," in *Can the Subaltern Speak? Reflections on the History of an Idea*, ed. Rosalind C. Morris (New York: Columbia University Press, 2010), 21–79.

5 Eng-Beng Lim, *Brown Boys and Rice Queens: Spellbinding Performance in the Asias* (New York: NYU Press, 2014).

6 For Roger Casement's diaries, see Jeffrey Dudgeon, *Roger Casement: The Black Diaries with a Study of His Background, Sexuality and Irish Political Life* (Belfast: Belfast Press, 2002).

7 Conrad, *Heart of Darkness*, 18.

8 David M. Halperin, *One Hundred Years of Homosexuality and Other Essays on Greek Love* (New York: Routledge, 1990).

9 Eliot, "Little Gidding," 50.

10 Michael Taussig, *Shamanism, Colonialism, and the Wild Man: A Study in Terror and Healing* (Chicago: University of Chicago Press, 1987).

11 Joseph Roach, *Cities of the Dead: Circum-Atlantic Performance* (New York: Columbia University Press, 1996).

12 Taussig, *Shamanism, Colonialism, and the Wild Man*, 132.

13 Macarena Gómez-Barris, *The Extractive Zone: Social Ecologies and Decolonial Perspectives* (Durham, NC: Duke University Press, 2017), 46.

14 Taussig, *Shamanism, Colonialism, and the Wild Man*, 100.

15 Walter Benjamin, "Theses on the Philosophy of History," in *Illuminations*, ed. and with introduction by Hannah Arendt, trans. Harry Zohn (New York: Schocken, 1968), 256.

16 C. Riley Snorton, *Nobody Is Supposed to Know: Black Sexuality on the Down Low* (Minneapolis: University of Minnesota Press, 2014).

17 Stefano Harney and Fred Moten, *The Undercommons: Fugitive Planning and Black Study* (New York: Autonomedia, 2013), 20.

18 José Esteban Muñoz, "Theorizing Queer Inhumanisms: The Sense of Brownness," *GLQ: A Journal of Lesbian and Gay Studies* 21, nos. 2–3 (2015): 209–10.

19 I take this phrase from my notes from a lecture José Muñoz gave in dialogue with David Eng at UCLA on February 22, 2013.

20 Taussig, *Shamanism, Colonialism, and the Wild Man*, 219.

21 Fred Moten, *In the Break: The Aesthetics of the Black Radical Tradition* (Minneapolis: University of Minnesota Press, 2003).

22 Taussig, *Shamanism, Colonialism, and the Wild Man*, 220.

23 Snorton, *Nobody Is Supposed to Know*, 29.

24 See Conrad, *Heart of Darkness*. For Roger Casement's diaries, see Dudgeon, *Roger Casement*, but also Brian Lewis, "The Queer Life and Afterlife of Roger Casement," *Journal of the History of Sexuality* 14, no. 4 (October 2005): 363–82.

25 Maya Jasanoff, *The Dawn Watch: Joseph Conrad in a Global World* (New York: Penguin, 2017), 7.

26 For more on homosexual erotic colonialism, see Lim, *Brown Boys and Rice Queens*.

27 Taussig, *Shamanism Colonialism, and the Wild Man*, 127.

28 Conrad, *Heart of Darkness*, 6.

29 Taussig, *Shamanism, Colonialism, and the Wild Man*, 11.

30 Colm Tóibín, "The Tragedy of Roger Casement," *New York Review of Books*, May 27, 2004, https://www.nybooks.com/articles/2004/05/27/the-tragedy-of-roger-casement/.

31 Jasanoff, *Dawn Watch*, 214.

32 Adam Hochschild, *King Leopold's Ghost: A Story of Greed, Terror, and Heroism in Colonial Africa* (Boston: Houghton Mifflin, 1998).

33 Tóibín, "Tragedy of Roger Casement."

34 Tóibín, "Tragedy of Roger Casement."

35 Tóibín, "Tragedy of Roger Casement."

36 Tóibín, "Tragedy of Roger Casement."

37 Oscar Wilde, *The Picture of Dorian Gray*, Edition De Luxe (New York: Brainard, 1909), 88.

38 Graf Harry Kessler, *Journey to the Abyss: The Diaries of Count Harry Kessler, 1880–1918*, ed. and trans. Laird M. Easton (New York: Knopf, 2011), 619.

39 Winyan Soo Hoo, "Soundsuits Sculptor Nick Cave Performs at the U.S. State Department's Art in Embassies 50th Anniversary Celebration," *Washington Post*, November 28, 2012, https://www.washingtonpost.com/blogs/arts-post/post /soundsuits-sculptor-nick-cave-performs-at-the-us-state-departments-art-in-embassies -50th-anniversary-celebration/2012/11/28/ab97c740-39a1-11e2-a263-foebffed2f15_blog .html.

40 José Esteban Muñoz, *Disidentifications: Queers of Color and the Performance of Politics* (Minneapolis: University of Minnesota Press, 1999), 31.

2. "A New Kind of Wildness"

1 Graf Harry Kessler, *Journey to the Abyss: The Diaries of Count Harry Kessler, 1880–1918*, ed. and trans. Laird M. Easton (New York: Alfred A. Knopf, 2011), entry for May 28, 1913.

2 Jacques Rivière, "Le Sacre du Printemps," in *The Ideal Reader: Selected Essays by Jacques Rivière*, ed. and trans. Blanche A. Price (London: Harvill), 145.

3 José Esteban Muñoz, *Cruising Utopia: The Then and There of Queer Futurity* (New York: NYU Press, 2009), 147.

4 Frank Bidart, "The War of Vaslav Nijinsky," *Paris Review* 80 (Summer 1981), https:// www.theparisreview.org/poetry/3235/the-war-of-vaslav-nijinsky-frank-bidart.

5 thomas f. defrantz, "Queer Dance in Three Acts," in *Queer Dance: Meanings and Makings*, ed. Clare Croft (Oxford: Oxford University Press, 2017), 173.

6 Kessler, *Journey to the Abyss*, 620.

7. Greil Marcus, *Lipstick Traces: A Secret History of the Twentieth Century* (Cambridge, MA: Harvard University Press, 1990).

8 Joseph Roach, *Cities of the Dead: Circum-Atlantic Performance* (New York: Columbia University Press, 1996), 3.

9 See Millicent Hodson, "Death by Dancing in Nijinsky's *Rite*," in *The Rite of Spring at 100*, ed. Severine Neff, Maureen A. Carr, and Gretchen G. Horlacher, with John Reef (Bloomington: Indiana University Press, 2017), 47–80.

10 Isadora Duncan, *Isadora Speaks: Writings and Speeches of Isadora Duncan*, ed. Franklin Rosemont (Chicago: Charles H. Kerr, 1994), 138.

11 Bidart, "The War of Vaslav Nijinsky."

12 Bidart, "The War of Vaslav Nijinsky."

13 For another queer version of *Rite of Spring* along these same lines, a queer re-performance that refuses foundations, see Keith Hennessy's *BEAR/SKIN* (2015), in which, dressed as a bear, Hennessey tries and fails to re-perform the Chosen One's solo. thomas f. defrantz writes about this piece in "Queer Dance in Three Acts," in *Queer Dance: Meanings and Makings*, ed. Clare Croft (Oxford: Oxford University

Press, 2017), 169–80. defrantz writes: "He dances and fails, trying something queer in taking on the dance for a young 'maiden,' doing queer as the extended failure of a performance" (173). *Rite of Spring* has also been remade by Bill T. Jones as *A Rite* (2013).

14 Igor Stravinsky, *Observer*, October 8, 1961, https://allthingsstravinsky.wordpress.com /quotes.

15 Bruno Latour, *We Have Never Been Modern*, trans. Catherine Porter (Cambridge, MA: Harvard University Press, 1993), 100.

16 Walter Benjamin, "Theses on the Philosophy of History" (1940), in *Illuminations*, ed. and with an introduction by Hannah Arendt, trans. Harry Zohn (New York: Schocken Books, 1968), 257.

17 Fred Moten, *Black and Blur* (Durham, NC: Duke University Press, 2017), xiii.

18 Igor Stravinsky and Robert Craft, *Expositions and Developments* (New York: Doubleday, 1962), 147–48.

19 Jenny Gilbert, "The Rite of Spring: Shock of the New," *Independent*, April 6, 2013, https://www.independent.co.uk/arts-entertainment/theatre-dance/features/the-rite -of-spring-shock-of-the-new-8563012.html.

20 Jane Bennett, *Vibrant Matter: A Political Ecology of Things* (Durham, NC: Duke University Press, 2010), 13.

21 Rivière, "Le Sacre du Printemps," 142.

22 See Robert Craft, "100 Years On: Igor Stravinsky and *The Rite of Spring*," *Times Literary Supplement*, June 19, 2013.

23 Sjeng Scheijen, *Diaghilev: A Life*, trans. Jane Hadley-Prole and S. J. Leinbach (Oxford: Oxford University Press, 2009), 68.

24 Scheijen, *Diaghilev*, 121.

25 Peter Coviello, *Tomorrow's Parties: Sex and the Untimely in Nineteenth-Century America* (New York: NYU Press, 2013), 7.

26 Daniel K. L. Chua, "Rioting with Stravinsky: A Particular Analysis of the *Rite of Spring*," *Music Analysis* 26, nos. 1–2 (March–July 2007): 69.

27 There have been multiple queer restagings of *The Rite of Spring*: most notably, Keith Hennessy's *Bear/Skin* in 2013, Bill T. Jones's *A Rite* from the same year, and Michael Clark's *Mmm . . .* in 1992.

28 Theodor W. Adorno, *Philosophy of Modern Music*, trans. Anne G. Mitchell and Wesley V. Blomster (New York: Continuum, 2004), 164.

29 Rivière, "Le Sacre du Printemps," 146.

30 So pervasive is this sense of *The Rite of Spring* as an event that its first performance has been the subject of a three-volume dissertation. See Truman C. Bullard, "The First Performance of Igor Stravinsky's Sacre du Printemps" (PhD diss., Eastman School of Music, 1971).

31 See John Culhane, "The Making of *Fantasia*," in *Walt Disney's Fantasia* (New York: Harry N. Abrams, Inc., 1983), 11.

32 Tamara Levitz, "Racism at *The Rite*," in *The Rite of Spring at 100*, ed. Severine Neff, Maureen Carr, and Gretchen Horlacher, with John Reef (Bloomington: Indiana University Press, 2017), 147.

33 Pierre Lalo, "Considérations sur le 'Sacre du printemps,'" in *Igor Stravinsky, Le sacre du printemps*, ed. François Lesure (Geneva: Minkoff, 1980), 32–33.

34 Jodi A. Byrd, *The Transit of Empire: Indigenous Critiques of Colonialism* (Minneapolis: University of Minnesota Press, 2011).

35 *Oxford English Dictionary*, accessed September 8, 2019, https://www.oed.com (log-in required).

36 *Oxford English Dictionary*.

37 Hagar Kotef, *Movement and the Ordering of Freedom: On Liberal Governances of Mobility* (Durham, NC: Duke University Press, 2015).

38 Fanny Howe, "Bewilderment," *How2* 1, no. 1 (March 1999), https://www.asu.edu/pipercwcenter/how2journal/archive/online_archive/v1_1_1999/fhbewild.html.

39 Howe, "Bewilderment."

40 Howe, "Bewilderment."

41 Fred Moten, *The Feel Trio* (Tucson, AZ: Letter Machine Editions, 2014), 65.

42 Jennifer C. James, "Ecomelancholia: Slavery, War, and Black Ecological Imaginings," in *Environmental Criticism for the Twenty-First Century*, ed. Stephanie LeMenager, Teresa Shewry, and Ken Hiltner (New York: Routledge, 2011), 164.

43 Joseph Conrad, *Heart of Darkness*, excerpted, accessed January 21, 2020, https://www.planetebook.com/free-ebooks/heart-of-darkness.pdf, 95.

44 Jodi Byrd, "Beast of America: Sovereignty and the Wildness of Objects," *South Atlantic Quarterly* 117, no. 3 (July 2018): 600.

45 Byrd, *Transit of Empire*.

46 See "Kent Monkman," accessed January 21, 2020, https://www.kentmonkman.com/installation/re2gt7n4v8maq6nolo3909rog9hdlo.

47 In the notes on this installation on Monkman's website he writes: "In his memoirs, published in 1844, *From Letters and Notes on the Manners, Customs, and Conditions of North American Indians*, Catlin speaks of this ritual unsympathetically: 'One of the most unaccountable and disgusting customs that I have ever met in the Indian country . . . and where I should wish that it might be extinguished before it be more fully recorded.'" Accessed January 21, 2020, https://www.kentmonkman.com/installation/a9xeq1s8xdyqboeo9umrn5ipidrdbi.

48 Kent Monkman, *Failure of Modernity*, e-catalog (Santa Fe, NM: Gerald Peters Contemporary, 2016), accessed January 21, 2020, http://www.petersprojects.com/kent-monkman-failure-of-modernity.

49 Fred Moten, *In the Break: The Aesthetics of the Black Radical Tradition* (Minneapolis: University of Minnesota Press, 2003), 22.

50 Ann Laura Stoler, *Along the Archival Grain: Epistemic Anxieties and Colonial Common Sense* (Princeton, NJ: Princeton University Press, 2009), 20.

51 Jack Halberstam and Tavia Nyong'o, "Introduction: Theory in the Wild," *South Atlantic Quarterly* 117, no. 3 (July 2018): 453–64, https://doi.org/10.1215/00382876-6942081.

52 June Scudeler, "'Indians on Top': Kent Monkman's Sovereign Erotics," *American Indian Culture and Research Journal* 39, no. 4 (2015): 19–32. Scudeler takes the term "sovereign erotics" from Qwo-Li Driskill, "Stolen from Our Bodies: First Nations

Two-Spirit/Queers and the Journey to a Sovereign Erotic," *Studies in American Indian Literature* 16, no. 2 (2004): 50–64.

53 Macarena Gómez-Barris, *The Extractive Zone: Social Ecologies and Decolonial Perspectives* (Durham, NC: Duke University Press, 2017); see "Introduction: Submerged Perspectives."

3. The Epistemology of the Ferox

1 In addition to Jack London's *The Call of the Wild* (1903), see, more recently, Jon Krakauer, *Into the Wild* (New York: Anchor, 1987). Krakauer's book is not a romantic fantasy of wildness, but a documentary narrative about a young man, Christopher McCandless, who dropped out of school and went off into the Alaskan wilderness on a Thoreauvian odyssey. This one ended badly, however, and McCandless starved to death.

2 J. A. Baker, *The Peregrine*, 50th anniv. ed., afterword by Robert Macfarlane (London: HarperCollins, 2017), 31.

3 Dianne Chisholm, "Biophilia, Creative Involution, and the Ecological Future of Queer Desire," in *Queer Ecologies: Sex, Nature, Politics, Desire*, ed. Catriona Mortimer-Sandilands and Bruce Erickson (Bloomington: Indiana University Press, 2010), 359–82.

4 Eve Kosofsky Sedgwick, *Epistemology of the Closet* (Berkeley: University of California Press, 1990), 8.

5 Timothy Morton, "Guest Column: Queer Ecology," *PMLA* 125, no. 2 (March 2010): 273–83, 275.

6 Catriona Mortimer-Sandilands and Bruce Erickson, "Introduction: A Genealogy of Queer Ecologies," in *Queer Ecologies: Sex, Nature, Politics, Desire*, ed. Catriona Mortimer-Sandilands and Bruce Erickson (Bloomington: Indiana University Press, 2010), 1–50.

7 Baker, *The Peregrine*, 41.

8 For more on abject, passive, and masochistic desires that constitute an assault on subjectivity itself, see Amber J. Musser, *Sensational Flesh: Race, Power, and Masochism* (New York: NYU Press, 2014).

9 Baker, *The Peregrine*, 28.

10 Helen Macdonald, *H Is for Hawk* (London: Jonathan Cape, 2014).

11 T. S. Eliot, "Burnt Norton," in *Four Quartets* (New York: Harcourt, 1943), 14.

12 Eduardo Kohn, *How Forests Think: Toward an Anthropology beyond the Human* (Berkeley: University of California Press, 2013), 8.

13 Jane Bennett, *Vibrant Matter: A Political Ecology of Things* (Durham, NC: Duke University Press, 2010).

14 Dame Juliana Berners, *The Boke of Saint Albans* (1486), quoted in Barry Hines, *A Kestrel for a Knave* (1968; reprint, London: Valancourt, 2015), Kindle ed., epigraph.

15 Hines, *A Kestrel for a Knave*, loc. 2202.

16 Macdonald, *H Is for Hawk*, 31.

17 Branka Arsić, *Bird Relics: Grief and Vitalism in Thoreau* (Cambridge: Harvard University Press, 2016).

18 Jane Bennett, *Thoreau's Nature: Ethics, Politics, and the Wild* (Lanham, MD: Rowman and Littlefield, 2002), 53.

19 Macdonald, *H Is for Hawk*, 32.

20 Sedgewick, *Epistemology of the Closet*, 23.

21 Arsić, *Bird Relics*, 10.

22 T. H. White, *The Goshawk* (1951; reprint, New York: NYRB Classics, 2007).

23 Sylvia Townsend Warner, *T. H. White: A Biography* (New York: Viking, 1967). There are numerous references to White's homosexuality—see pages 42–43 and page 86, for example. Warner also refers to White as possessing a "sadist's acute intelligence for pain" (120).

24 Macdonald, *H Is for Hawk*, 160.

25 Baker, *The Peregrine*, 15.

26 Letter by Warner to Maxwell, August 8, 1964, in *The Element of Lavishness: Letters of Sylvia Townsend Warner and Richard Maxwell, 1938–1978*, ed. Michael Steinman (New York: Counterpoint, 2003).

27 White, *The Goshawk*, 224.

28 Cited in Warner, *T. H. White*, 149.

29 Cited in Warner, *T. H. White*, 78.

30 David Garnett, ed., *The White/Garnett Letters* (New York: Viking, 1968), 182.

31 Macdonald, *H Is for Hawk*, 200.

32 Warner, *T. H. White*, 182.

33 Macdonald, *H Is for Hawk*, 33.

34 See Macdonald, *H Is for Hawk*, 45. She cites an unpublished manuscript by White titled "A Sort of Mania," which is housed at the Harry Ransom Humanities Research Center, University of Texas at Austin.

35 Michel Foucault, *The Order of Things: An Archaeology of the Human Sciences* (1966; reprint, London: Routledge, 2002), 302.

36 Peter Coviello, *Tomorrow's Parties: Sex and the Untimely in Nineteenth-Century America* (New York: NYU Press, 2013).

37 Glenway Westcott, *The Pilgrim Hawk: A Love Story* (1940; reprint, New York: NYRB Classics, 2011).

38 Edmund White, "The Loves of the Falcon," *New York Review of Books*, February 2009, https://www.nybooks.com/articles/2009/02/12/the-loves-of-the-falcon; Westcott, *Pilgrim Hawk*, xix.

39 Westcott, *Pilgrim Hawk*, 6.

40 Benjamin Liberatore, "'Casual as Birds': *Mue, Tragizein*, and Voices from the Animal Interval," unpublished manuscript.

41 Eliot, "East Coker," in *Four Quartets*, 29.

42 Westcott, *Pilgrim Hawk*, 15.

43 I found Chase Dimock's comments on a site sponsored by the University of Illinois called "Modern American Poetry." This page was devoted to Duncan's poem. Last accessed August 11, 2018, http://www.english.illinois.edu/maps/poets/a_f/duncan/falcon.htm. See also "On Robert Duncan's 'My Mother Would Be a Falconress,'"

Chase Dimock, October 23, 2013, https://chasedimock.com/2013/10/23/on-robert
-duncans-my-mother-would-be-a-falconress/.

44 Robert Duncan, "My Mother Would Be a Falconress," in *Bending the Bow* (New
York: New Directions, 1968).

45 "The Homosexual in Society" originally appeared in *Politics* 1, no. 7 (August 1944).
Revisions were made in 1959. The expanded version was first published in *Jimmy and
Lucy's House of "K,"* no. 3 (January 1985).

46 Louis Proyect, "Robert Duncan's 'The Homosexual in Society,'" *Louis Proyect: The
Unrepentant Marxist*, May 2, 2009, https://louisproyect.org/2009/05/02/robert
-duncans-the-homosexual-in-society.

47 Duncan, "My Mother Would Be a Falconress."

48 Duncan, "My Mother Would Be a Falconress."

49 Duncan, "My Mother Would Be a Falconress."

50 See Gayatri Gopinath, "Local Sites/Global Contexts: The Transnational Trajectories
of *Fire* and 'The Quilt,'" in *Impossible Desires: Queer Diasporas and South Asian Public Cultures* (Durham, NC: Duke University Press, 2005), 131–60. Gopinath writes:
"Eve Sedgwick, in her paradigm-shifting *Epistemology of the Closet*, claims the closet
as 'the defining structure for gay oppression in this century,' thereby disregarding
other possible epistemic categories or tropes of spacialization that may exist outside,
or indeed within, a Euro-American context" (145).

51 Kara Keeling, "Looking for M—: Queer Temporality, Black Political Possibility, and
Poetry from the Future," *GLQ: A Journal of Lesbian and Gay Studies* 15, no. 4 (August
2009): 572.

52 Saidiya Hartman, *Wayward Lives, Beautiful Experiments: Intimate Histories of Social
Upheaval* (New York: W. W. Norton, 2019), 193.

53 Shane Vogel, "Closing Time: Langston Hughes and the Queer Poetics of Harlem
Nightlife," *Criticism* 48, no. 3 (Summer 2006): 397.

54 Langston Hughes, "Genius Child" (1937), excerpted, accessed January 25, 2020,
https://genius.com/Langston-hughes-genius-child-annotated.

55 Hughes, "Genius Child."

56 Coviello, *Tomorrow's Parties*, 10.

57 Brent Edwards, "The Taste of the Archive," *Callaloo* 35, no. 4 (2012): 948.

58 See George Chauncey's foundational essay on the chronology of the emergence of
modern gay and lesbian identities out of the morass of sexological definition. He gives
the years 1880–1930 as definitive in terms of making the transition from discourses of
acts to those of identities. George Chauncey Jr., "From Sexual Inversion to Homosexuality: Medicine and the Changing Conceptualization of Female Deviance," *Salmagundi*, nos. 58–59 (Fall 1982–Winter 1983): 114–46. Also, George Chauncey, *Gay
New York: Gender, Urban Culture, and the Making of the Gay Male World, 1890–1940*
(New York: Basic Books, 1995).

59 Madison Moore, *Fabulous: The Rise of the Beautiful Eccentric* (New Haven, CT: Yale
University Press, 2018), xcix.

60 Henry David Thoreau, "Night and Moonlight," in *The Writings of Henry David Thoreau*, vol. 5: *Excursions and Poems* (Boston: Houghton Mifflin, 1906), 332.

61 White, *The Goshawk*, 72.

62 Finally, in making a tenuous but suggestive set of connections between Black queer wildness or fierceness and the solitary quest to become feral that marks the "lonely man in nature" narratives examined earlier in this chapter, it is surely no accident that the first Black superhero introduced by Marvel comics in 1969 was the Falcon! The Falcon, in the comic book narrative, was a man named Sam Wilson who lived in Harlem and trained falcons. One day he responds to a request for a hunting falcon from a group of men living on an island. The group turns out to be made up of Nazis, and Wilson joins forces with Steve Rogers to help the Native peoples of the island fight against the exiled Nazis. Steve is Captain America, and he encourages Sam to train with him under the name of Falcon. Sam's superpower is a control over birds!

63 For more on the history of sodomy, see Jens Rydstrom, *Sinners and Citizens: Bestiality and Homosexuality in Sweden, 1880–1950* (Chicago: University of Chicago Press, 2003).

64 Susan Crane, *Animal Encounters: Contacts and Concepts in Medieval Britain* (Philadelphia: University of Pennsylvania Press, 2013), 1.

65 Stefano Harney and Fred Moten, *The Undercommons: Fugitive Planning and Black Study* (New York: Autonomedia, 2013), 51.

66 Macdonald, *H Is for Hawk*, 232, 234.

67 White, *The Goshawk*, 212.

68 Gilles Deleuze and Félix Guattari, *A Thousand Plateaus: Capitalism and Schizophrenia*, trans. Brian Massumi (Minneapolis: University of Minnesota Press, 1987).

69 Baker, *The Peregrine*, 13.

70 T. H. White, *The Once and Future King* (New York: Penguin, 2011), chapter 13.

Introduction to Part II

1 "Dead Parrot Sketch," *Monty Python's Flying Circus*, series 1, episode 8, original air date December 7, 1969.

2 Ruth Wilson Gilmore, *Golden Gulag: Prisons, Surplus, Crisis, and Opposition in Globalizing California* (Berkeley: University of California Press, 2007), 28.

3 Jane Bennett, *Vibrant Matter: A Political Ecology of Things* (Durham, NC: Duke University Press, 2010), 54.

4 Donna Haraway, *The Companion Species Manifesto: Dogs, People, and Significant Otherness* (Chicago: Prickly Paradigm, 2003), 100.

5 Minus the bit about refraining from having sex with animals, this critique of pet owning can be found polemically and in more scholarly forms in the work of a range of authors, including Gary L. Francione and Anna E. Charlton, "The Case against Pets," *Aeon*, September 28, 2016, https://aeon.co/essays/why-keeping-a-pet-is -fundamentally-unethical; but also in Lori Gruen, ed., *The Ethics of Captivity* (Oxford: Oxford University Press, 2014).

6 Gabriel Rosenberg, "How Meat Changed Sex: The Law of Interspecies Intimacy after Industrial Reproduction," *GLQ: A Journal of Lesbian and Gay Studies* 23, no. 4 (2017): 473–507.

7 See Jens Rydstrom, *Sinners and Citizens: Bestiality and Homosexuality in Sweden, 1880–1950* (Chicago: University of Chicago Press, 2003).

8 Rosenberg, "How Meat Changed Sex," 489.

9 Zakiyyah Iman Jackson, "Losing Manhood: Animality and Plasticity in the (Neo)Slave Narrative," *Qui Parle: Critical Humanities and Social Sciences* 25, nos. 1–2 (2016): 96.

10 Jackson, "Losing Manhood," 117, emphasis added.

11 Fiona Probyn-Rapsey, "Five Propositions on Ferals," *Feral Feminisms*, no. 6 (Fall 2016): 20, https://feralfeminisms.com/five-propositions-on-ferals.

4. Where the Wild Things Are

1 George Monbiot, *Feral: Rewilding the Land, the Sea and Human Life* (London: Penguin, 2014), 9.

2 Jacques Derrida, *The Beast and the Sovereign*, vol. 2, trans. Geoffrey Bennington (Chicago: University of Chicago Press, 2011).

3 Michel Foucault, *The Order of Things: An Archaeology of the Human Sciences* (1966; reprint, London: Routledge, 2002).

4 Maurice Sendak, *Where The Wild Things Are*, 50th anniv. ed. (New York: HarperCollins, 2013).

5 Derrida, *The Beast and the Sovereign*, 33.

6 Yann Martel, *Life of Pi: A Novel* (New York: Harcourt, 2001), 17.

7 See Daniel Defoe, *Robinson Crusoe* (London: William Taylor, 1719).

8 Sendak, *Where the Wild Things Are*, n.p.

9 "Jewish Author Maurice Sendak, Creator of 'Where the Wild Things Are,' Dies at 83," *Haaretz*, May 8, 2012, https://www.haaretz.com/jewish/1.5220575.

10 Emma Brockes, "Maurice Sendak: 'I Refuse to Lie to Children,'" *Guardian*, October 2, 2011, https://www.theguardian.com/books/2011/oct/02/maurice-sendak-interview.

11 Sendak, *Where the Wild Things Are*, n.p.

12 Adriana Cavavero, *Horrorism: Naming Contemporary Violence*, trans. William McCuaig (New York: Columbia University Press, 2007).

13 Sendak, *Where the Wild Things Are*, n.p.

14 T. S. Eliot, "East Coker," in *Four Quartets* (New York: Harcourt, 1943), 29.

15 Eliot, "East Coker," 29.

16 Friedrich Nietzsche, Section 352, in *The Gay Science: With a Prelude in Rhymes and an Appendix in Songs*, trans. Walter Kaufmann (New York: Random House, 1974), 295.

17 Bruno Bettelheim, "The Care and Feeding of Monsters," *Ladies' Home Journal*, March 1969. For the quote from the *Publisher's Weekly* critique, see Nat Hentoff, "Profiles: Among the Wild Things," *New Yorker*, January 22, 1966, 38–39.

18 Selma G. Lanes, *The Art of Maurice Sendak* (New York: Abrams, 1980).

19 Mick Brown, "Yann Martel: In Search of Understanding," *Telegraph*, June 1, 2010, https://www.telegraph.co.uk/culture/books/7793416/Yann-Martel-in-search-of-understanding.html.

20 See M. NourbeSe Philip, *Zong!* (Middletown, CT: Wesleyan University Press, 2011).

21 See Christina Sharpe, *In the Wake: On Blackness and Being* (Durham, NC: Duke University Press, 2016). Sharpe writes: "I use the wake in all of its meanings and as a means of understanding how slavery's violences emerge within the contemporary conditions of spatial, legal, psychic, material, and other dimensions of Black non/being as well as Black modes of resistance" (14).

22 Lisa Lowe, *The Intimacies of Four Continents* (Durham, NC: Duke University Press, 2015).

23 Frantz Fanon, *The Wretched of the Earth*, trans. Richard Philcox (New York: Grove, 1963).

24 Foucault, *Order of Things*, 302.

25 Fanon, *Wretched of the Earth*, 33.

26 Martel, *Life of Pi*, 21.

27 The 2005 film *Grizzly Man* by Werner Herzog tries to underscore the danger of getting the human/animal and wild/intimate equation wrong. The film pieces together the last days of naturalist Timothy Treadwell, who spent many of his adult summers in Alaska living alongside a community of bears. Tragically, one summer, Treadwell and his girlfriend stayed longer than usual in the area, and when a new group of bears entered the area, they killed and ate Treadwell and his partner. The actual attack was captured by the audio on Treadwell's camera, which he had running to film what he thought would be another interesting encounter with the wild. Herzog represents Treadwell as somewhere between a fool and a mystic, and he uses the hours of footage Treadwell made himself to chart the journey he took into the wild but also to catalog the mistakes he made once there. Of all the errors that Treadwell made, including the fantasy he entertained about the bears seeing him as different from other humans—as their protector no less—this film implies that the most grievous mistake the Grizzly Man makes is that he presumes intimacy where there is only proximity, and on account of this he breaks his own rules about interactions with wildlife. These rules, as we find out during the film, depend on all kinds of factors, including hunger, seasonality, familiarity, strangeness, and recognition.

28 Kalpana Rahita Seshadri, *HumAnimal: Race, Law, Language* (Minneapolis: University of Minnesota Press, 2012).

29 Giorgio Agamben, *Infancy and History: Essays on the Destruction of Experience*, trans. Liz Heron (Brooklyn: Verso, 1993), 51–52.

30 Seshadri, *HumAnimal*, 174.

31 Alexander G. Weheliye, *Habeas Viscus: Racializing Assemblages, Biopolitics, and Black Feminist Theories of the Human* (Durham, NC: Duke University Press, 2014), 26.

32 Martel, *Life of Pi*, 382.

5. Zombie Antihumanism

1 See Elizabeth A. Povinelli, *Geontologies: A Requiem to Late Liberalism* (Durham, NC: Duke University Press, 2016).

2 T. S. Eliot, "Little Gidding," in *Four Quartets* (New York: Harcourt, 1943), 55.

3 For the demographic impact of pet owning on cities, see Heidi J. Nast, "Critical Pet Studies?," *Antipode* 38, no. 5 (November 2006): 894–906.

4 See John Berger, *Why Look at Animals?* (London: Penguin, 2009).

5 Haraway uses the term "critters" throughout her work, but see *Staying with the Trouble*, for one example: "*Critters* is an American everyday idiom for varmints of all sorts. Scientists talk of their 'critters' all the time; and so do ordinary people all over the U.S., but perhaps especially in the South. The taint of 'creatures' and 'creation' does not stick to 'critters'; if you see such a semiotic barnacle, scrape it off. In this book, 'critters' refers promiscuously to microbes, plants, animals, humans and nonhumans, and sometimes even to machines." Donna J. Haraway, *Staying with the Trouble: Making Kin in the Chthulucene* (Durham, NC: Duke University Press, 2016), 169n1.

6 Yann Martel, *Life of Pi: A Novel* (New York: Harcourt, 2001), 23.

7 Laura Marks, *Touch: Sensuous Theory and Multisensory Media* (Minneapolis: University of Minnesota Press, 2002), 34.

8 Temple Grandin, *Animals in Translation: Using the Mysteries of Autism to Decode Animal Behavior* (New York: Harcourt, 2006), 276.

9 Ryan Bell, "Temple Grandin, Killing Them Softly at Slaughterhouses for Thirty Years," *National Geographic*, August 19, 2015.

10 See Lori Gruen, *The Ethics of Captivity* (Oxford: Oxford University Press, 2014), and Anat Pick, *Creaturely Poetics: Animality and Vulnerability in Literature and Film* (New York: Columbia University Press, 2011).

11 Jason Hribal, *Fear of the Animal Planet: The Hidden History of Animal Resistance* (New York: Counterpunch, 2013).

12 See James C. Scott, *Weapons of the Weak: Everyday Forms of Peasant Resistance* (New Haven, CT: Yale University Press, 1987); Jason Hribal, "Animals, Agency, and Class: Writing the History of Animals from Below," *Human Ecology Review* 14, no. 1 (2007): 103.

13 See Julietta Singh, *Unthinking Mastery: Dehumanism and Decolonial Entanglements* (Durham, NC: Duke University Press, 2018), for a critique of mastery in colonial and decolonial contexts.

14 For more on the topic of animal rebellion, see Dinesh Wadiwel, "Chicken Harvesting Machine: Animal Labor, Resistance, and the Time of Production," *South Atlantic Quarterly* 117, no. 3 (July 2018): 527–49. Wadiwel writes: "The refinement of technologies of domination, and their response to the 'wild' resistances of animals, aims at bringing animal labor time in sync with the rhythms of productive processes. This perspective highlights the politics of time involved with animal subordination to capital, but perhaps also connects with a utopian imagining of life for animals outside of this time" (529).

15 These quotes come from a folio notebook in which White kept a journal; the entire sequence appears in Sylvia Townsend Warner, *T. H. White: A Biography* (New York: Viking, 1967), 210.

16 Kathy Rudy, "LGBTQ . . . Z?," *Hypatia* 27, no. 3 (Summer 2012): 604.

17 *The Secret Life of Pets*, dir. Chris Renaud (Universal Pictures, 2016).

18 *Flushed Away*, dir. David Bowers and Sam Fell (DreamWorks, 2006).

19 Wadiwel, "Chicken Harvesting Machine," 528.

20 Radhika Govindrajan, *Animal Intimacies: Interspecies Relatedness in India's Central Himalayas* (Chicago: University of Chicago Press, 2018).

21 *White God*, dir. Kornél Mundruczó, Viktória Petrányi, and Kata Wéber (Proton Cinema, 2015).

22 Donna Haraway, *The Companion Species Manifesto: Dogs, People, and Significant Otherness* (Chicago: Prickly Paradigm, 2003).

23 *White God* does not figure eros into the relation between humans and dogs either, but several other films do: a German film by Nicoletta Krebitz titled *Wild* (2016), for example, features a full-on sexual relationship between a young woman and a wolf. The woman wears a protective suit to have sex with the wolf and eventually leaves the human community to live with the wolf in the wild. We might add Kelly Reichart's film *Wendy and Lucy* (2008) to this genre. While Reichart does not show the girl having sex with the dog in this film, she does depict a human-animal relationship that exceeds the domestic space and that replaces human-human contact.

24 Colin Dayan, *With Dogs at the Edge of Life* (New York: Columbia University Press, 2016).

25 Haraway, *Companion Species Manifesto*, 50.

26 Dayan, *With Dogs at the Edge of Life*, 50.

27 Zakiyyah Iman Jackson, "Losing Manhood: Animality and Plasticity in the (Neo)Slave Narrative," in *Qui Parle: Critical Humanities and Social Sciences* 25, nos. 1–2 (Fall/Winter 2016): 96.

28 Georg Wilhelm Friedrich Hegel, *The Philosophy of History*, trans. J. Sibree (Kitchener, Ontario: Batoche Books, 2001), 111.

29 Calvin L. Warren, "Introduction: The Free Black Is Nothing," in *Ontological Terror: Blackness, Nihilism, and Emancipation* (Durham, NC: Duke University Press, 2018), 5.

30 *Night of the Living Dead*, dir. George A. Romero (Image Ten, 1968).

31 The title of Viet Thanh Nguyen's acclaimed book on the Vietnam War obliquely references this connection between the war and the specter of the zombie: see *Nothing Ever Dies: Vietnam and the Memory of War* (Cambridge, MA: Harvard University Press, 2016).

32 Alex Pappademas and Colson Whitehead, "When Zombies Attack! Behind Our National Obsession with the Walking Dead," *Grantland*, October 24, 2011, http://grantland.com/features/when-zombies-attack.

33 Colson Whitehead, *Zone One* (New York: Doubleday, 2011), 321.

34 Monique Allewaert, *Ariel's Ecology: Plantations, Personhood, and Colonialism in the American Tropics* (Minneapolis: University of Minnesota Press, 2013), 14. Parahumanity, Allewaert proposes, is a byproduct of the plantation system in the United States, where the production of humanism occurred alongside the enslavement of African populations. For her, parahumanity describes "a kind of interstitial life between humans, animals, objects, and even plants." Parahumanity for Allewaert is not simply evidence of the dehumanization of Afro-Americans and the colonized; it is

also a reminder that the brutal modalities of the human as a discursive form of governance were not shared by these people who were subject to its violence. And so, as Allewaert puts it: "This meant that Africans in the diaspora whether slave or maroon had especially deft imaginings of the forms of power and agency that developed at the interstices between human and nonhuman life" (7). *Ariel's Ecology* describes what Allewaert calls an emerging "minoritarian and anti-colonial mode of personhood that was largely developed by Afro-Americans" (9). These other forms of personhood were cast as parahuman even as they resisted what Allewaert calls an eighteenth-century addiction to hierarchy and accepted a notion of the body as fragmented and disorderly. Such communities, Allewaert implies, did not think about their relation to the landscape, to vegetation, and to animal life in terms of ownership or domination. The category of the parahuman implied a familiarity with fragmentation that blocked a belief in wholeness, and it held within it a different set of assumptions about bodies, mastery, becoming, and the human. Subaltern resistance for Allewaert is caught up in an ecology within which things, places, persons collaborate to resist, refuse, and categorically deny the claims of the human.

35 Julian Huxley, "Transhumanism," in *New Bottles for New Wine* (London: Chatto and Windus, 1957), 13–17.

36 See "About Long Now," accessed January 31, 2020, http://longnow.org/about.

37 See "What We Do," Revive & Restore, accessed January 31, 2020, https://reviverestore .org/what-we-do.

38 See "How Genetic Rescue Works," Revive & Restore, accessed September 26, 2019, https://reviverestore.org/what-we-do/geneticrescue.

39 Jodi A. Byrd, *The Transit of Empire: Indigenous Critiques of Colonialism* (Minneapolis: University of Minnesota Press, 2011), 221.

40 Hortense Spillers, "Mama's Baby, Papa's Maybe: An American Grammar Book," *Diacritics* 17, no. 2 (Summer 1987): 64–81.

Conclusions

1 Alfred Lord Tennyson, *Idylls of the King*, ed. Eugene Parsons (New York: Thomas Y. Cromwell, 1901), 23.

2 Tennyson, *Idylls of the King*, 10.

3 Kate Bush, "Cloudbusting," performed on *Hounds of Love* (EMI America, 1985).

4 Paul B. Preciado, *Testo Junkie: Sex, Drugs, and Biopolitics in the Pharmacopornographic Era*, trans. Bruce Benderson (New York: Feminist Press, 2008), 42.

5 Bush, "Cloudbusting."

6 Kate Bush, "The Ninth Wave: Side B," *Hounds of Love* (EMI America, 1985).

7 Kate Bush, "Hello Earth," performed on *Hounds of Love* (EMI America, 1985).

8 Christina Sharpe, *In the Wake: On Blackness and Being* (Durham, NC: Duke University Press, 2016).

9 Sharpe cites Toni Morrison, *Beloved* (New York: Plume Contemporary Fiction, 1987), 198.

10 T. S. Eliot, "The Dry Salvages," in *Four Quartets* (New York: Harcourt, 1943), 38.

11 Eliot, "Dry Salvages," 42; Eliot, "East Coker," in *Four Quartets*, 24; Eliot, "Little Gidding," in *Four Quartets*, 49.

12 Eliot, "Little Gidding," 50.

13 Eliot, "Little Gidding," 50.

Achebe, Chinua. *Things Fall Apart*. London: Heinemann, 1958.

Adorno, Theodor W. *Philosophy of Modern Music*. Translated by Anne G. Mitchell and Wesley V. Blomster. New York: Continuum, 2004.

Agamben, Giorgio. *Infancy and History: Essays on the Destruction of Experience*. Translated by Liz Heron. Brooklyn: Verso, 1993.

Allewaert, Monique. *Ariel's Ecology: Plantations, Personhood, and Colonialism in the American Tropics*. Minneapolis: University of Minnesota Press, 2013.

Arsić, Branka. *Bird Relics: Grief and Vitalism in Thoreau*. Cambridge, MA: Harvard University Press, 2016.

Baker, J. A. *The Peregrine*. 50th anniv. ed. Afterword by Robert Macfarlane. London: HarperCollins, 2017.

Barad, Karen. "Transmaterialities: Trans*/Matter/Realities and Queer Political Imaginings." *GLQ: A Journal of Lesbian and Gay Studies* 21, nos. 2–3 (2015): 387–422.

Barrett, Lindon. *Blackness and Value: Seeing Double*. Cambridge: Cambridge University Press, 1999.

Bell, Ryan. "Temple Grandin, Killing Them Softly at Slaughterhouses for Thirty Years." *National Geographic*, August 19, 2015.

Benjamin, Walter. "Theses on the Philosophy of History" (1940). In *Illuminations*, edited and with an introduction by Hannah Arendt, translated by Harry Zohn. New York: Schocken Books, 1968.

Bennett, Jane. *Thoreau's Nature: Ethics, Politics, and the Wild*. Lanham, MD: Rowman and Littlefield, 2002.

Bennett, Jane. *Vibrant Matter: A Political Ecology of Things*. Durham, NC: Duke University Press, 2010.

Berger, John. *Why Look at Animals?* London: Penguin, 2009.

Bidart, Frank. "The War of Vaslav Nijinsky." *Paris Review* 80 (Summer 1981). https://www.theparisreview.org/poetry/3235/the-war-of-vaslav-nijinsky-frank-bidart.

Brockes, Emma. "Maurice Sendak: 'I Refuse to Lie to Children.'" *Guardian*, October 2, 2011. https://www.theguardian.com/books/2011/oct/02/maurice-sendak-interview.

Brown, Mick. "Yann Martel: In Search of Understanding." *Telegraph*, June 1, 2010. https://www.telegraph.co.uk/culture/books/7793416/Yann-Martel-in-search-of-understanding.html.

Bullard, Truman C. "The First Performance of Igor Stravinsky's Sacre du Printemps." PhD diss., Eastman School of Music, 1971.

Byrd, Jodi A. "Beast of America: Sovereignty and the Wildness of Objects." *South Atlantic Quarterly* 117, no. 3 (July 2018): 599–615.

Byrd, Jodi A. *The Transit of Empire: Indigenous Critiques of Colonialism*. Minneapolis: University of Minnesota Press, 2011.

Cadden, Joan. *Nothing Natural Is Shameful: Sodomy and Science in Late Medieval Europe*. Philadelphia: University of Pennsylvania Press, 2017.

Cavavero, Adriana. *Horrorism: Naming Contemporary Violence*. Translated by William McCuaig. New York: Columbia University Press, 2007.

Chauncey, George Jr. "From Sexual Inversion to Homosexuality: Medicine and the Changing Conceptualization of Female Deviance." *Salmagundi*, nos. 58–59 (Fall 1982–Winter 1983): 114–46.

Chauncey, George Jr. *Gay New York: Gender, Urban Culture, and the Making of the Gay Male World, 1890–1940*. New York: Basic Books, 1995.

Chen, Mel Y. *Animacies: Biopolitics, Racial Mattering, and Queer Affect*. Durham, NC: Duke University Press, 2012.

Chisholm, Diane. "Biophilia, Creative Involution, and the Ecological Future of Queer Desire." In *Queer Ecologies: Sex, Nature, Politics, Desire*, edited by Catriona Mortimer-Sandilands and Bruce Erickson, 359–82. Bloomington: Indiana University Press, 2010.

Chua, Daniel K. L. "Rioting with Stravinsky: A Particular Analysis of the *Rite of Spring*." *Music Analysis* 26, nos. 1–2 (March–July 2007): 59–109.

Conrad, Joseph. *Heart of Darkness*. 1902. Reprint, Claremont, CA: Coyote Canyon, 2007.

Coviello, Peter. *Tomorrow's Parties: Sex and the Untimely in Nineteenth-Century America*. New York: NYU Press, 2013.

Craft, Robert. "100 Years On: Igor Stravinsky and *The Rite of Spring*." *Times Literary Supplement*, June 19, 2013.

Crane, Susan. *Animal Encounters: Contacts and Concepts in Medieval Britain*. Philadelphia: University of Pennsylvania Press, 2013.

Culhane, John. "The Making of *Fantasia*." In *Walt Disney's Fantasia*. New York: Harry N. Abrams, Inc., 1983.

Dayan, Colin. *With Dogs at the Edge of Life*. New York: Columbia University Press, 2016.

defrantz, thomas f. "Queer Dance in Three Acts." In *Queer Dance: Meanings and Makings*, edited by Clare Croft, 169–80. Oxford: Oxford University Press, 2017.

Deleuze, Gilles, and Félix Guattari. *A Thousand Plateaus: Capitalism and Schizophrenia.* Translated by Brian Massumi. Minneapolis: University of Minnesota Press, 1987.

Derrida, Jacques. *The Beast and the Sovereign.* Vol. 2. Translated by Geoffrey Bennington. Chicago: University of Chicago Press, 2011.

Driskill, Qwo-Li. "Stolen from Our Bodies: First Nations Two-Spirit/Queers and the Journey to a Sovereign Erotic." *Studies in American Indian Literature* 16, no. 2 (2004): 50–64.

Dudgeon, Jeffrey. *Roger Casement: The Black Diaries with a Study of His Background, Sexuality and Irish Political Life.* Belfast: Belfast Press, 2002.

Duncan, Isadora. *Isadora Speaks: Writings and Speeches of Isadora Duncan.* Edited by Franklin Rosemont. Chicago: Charles H. Kerr, 1994.

Duncan, Robert. "My Mother Would Be a Falconress." In *Bending the Bow,* 52–54. New York: New Directions, 1968.

Edwards, Brent. "The Taste of the Archive." *Callaloo* 35, no. 4 (2012): 944–72.

Eliot, T. S. *Four Quartets.* New York: Harcourt, 1943.

Fanon, Frantz. "The Fact of Blackness." In *Black Skin, White Masks,* translated by Charles Lam Markmann. New York: Grove, 1967.

Fanon, Frantz. *The Wretched of the Earth.* Translated by Richard Philcox. New York: Grove, 1963.

Foucault, Michel. *The History of Sexuality.* Translated by Robert Hurley. New York: Random House, 1985.

Foucault, Michel. *The Order of Things: An Archaeology of the Human Sciences.* 1966. Reprint, London: Routledge, 2002.

Francione, Gary L., and Anna E. Charlton. "The Case against Pets." *Aeon,* September 28, 2016. https://aeon.co/essays/why-keeping-a-pet-is-fundamentally-unethical.

Garnett, David, ed. *The White/Garnett Letters.* New York: Viking, 1968.

Gilbert, Jenny. "The Rite of Spring: Shock of the New." *Independent,* April 6, 2013. https://www.independent.co.uk/arts-entertainment/theatre-dance/features/the-rite-of-spring-shock-of-the-new-8563012.html.

Gilmore, Ruth Wilson. *Golden Gulag: Prisons, Surplus, Crisis, and Opposition in Globalizing California.* Berkeley: University of California Press, 2007.

Gómez-Barris, Macarena. *The Extractive Zone: Social Ecologies and Decolonial Perspectives.* Durham, NC: Duke University Press, 2017.

Gopinath, Gayatri. "Local Sites/Global Contexts: The Transnational Trajectories of *Fire* and 'The Quilt.'" In *Impossible Desires: Queer Diasporas and South Asian Public Cultures,* 131–60. Durham, NC: Duke University Press, 2005.

Govindrajan, Radhika. *Animal Intimacies: Interspecies Relatedness in India's Central Himalayas.* Chicago: University of Chicago Press, 2018.

Grandin, Temple. *Animals in Translation: Using the Mysteries of Autism to Decode Animal Behavior.* New York: Harcourt, 2006.

Gruen, Lori, ed. *The Ethics of Captivity.* Oxford: Oxford University Press, 2014.

Halberstam, Jack. *Female Masculinity.* Durham, NC: Duke University Press, 1998.

Halberstam, Jack. *The Queer Art of Failure.* Durham, NC: Duke University Press, 2011.

Halberstam, Jack, and Tavia Nyong'o. "Introduction: Theory in the Wild." *South Atlantic Quarterly* 117, no. 3 (July 2018): 453–64.

Hall, Radclyffe. *The Well of Loneliness*. 1928. Reprint, Ware, UK: Wordsworth Editions, 2005.

Halperin, David M. *One Hundred Years of Homosexuality and Other Essays on Greek Love*. New York: Routledge, 1990.

Haraway, Donna. *The Companion Species Manifesto: Dogs, People, and Significant Otherness*. Chicago: Prickly Paradigm, 2003.

Haraway, Donna J. *Staying with the Trouble: Making Kin in the Chthulucene*. Durham, NC: Duke University Press, 2016.

Harney, Stefano, and Fred Moten. *The Undercommons: Fugitive Planning and Black Study*. New York: Autonomedia, 2013.

Hartman, Saidiya. *Wayward Lives, Beautiful Experiments: Intimate Histories of Social Upheaval*. New York: W. W. Norton, 2019.

Hegel, Georg Wilhelm Friedrich. *The Philosophy of History*. Translated by J. Sibree. Kitchener, Ontario: Batoche Books, 2001.

Hines, Barry. *A Kestrel for a Knave*. 1968. Reprint, London: Valancourt, 2015. Kindle ed.

Hochschild, Adam. *King Leopold's Ghost: A Story of Greed, Terror, and Heroism in Colonial Africa*. Boston: Houghton Mifflin, 1998.

Hodson, Millicent. "Death by Dancing in Nijinsky's *Rite*." In *The Rite of Spring at 100*, edited by Severine Neff, Maureen Carr, and Gretchen Horlacher, with John Reef, 47–80. Bloomington: Indiana University Press, 2017.

Howe, Fanny. "Bewilderment." *How2* 1, no. 1 (March 1999). https://www.asu.edu/pipercw center/how2journal/archive/online_archive/v1_1_1999/fhbewild.html.

Hribal, Jason C. "Animals, Agency, and Class: Writing the History of Animals from Below." *Human Ecology Review* 14, no. 1 (2007): 101–12.

Hribal, Jason C. *Fear of the Animal Planet: The Hidden History of Animal Resistance*. New York: Counterpunch, 2013.

Hughes, Langston. "Genius Child." 1937. Excerpted. Accessed January 25, 2020. https://genius.com/Langston-hughes-genius-child-annotated.

Huxley, Julian. "Transhumanism." In *New Bottles for New Wine*, 13–17. London: Chatto and Windus, 1957.

Huysmans, Joris-Karl. *Against the Grain [À rebours]*. Translated by John Howard. 1884. Project Gutenberg E Book, 2014.

Jackson, Zakiyyah Iman. "Losing Manhood: Animality and Plasticity in the (Neo)Slave Narrative." *Qui Parle: Critical Humanities and Social Sciences* 25, nos. 1–2 (Fall/Winter 2016): 95–136.

Jagose, Annamarie. *Inconsequence: Lesbian Representation and the Logic of Sexual Sequence*. Ithaca, NY: Cornell University Press, 2002.

James, Jennifer C. "Ecomelancholia: Slavery, War, and Black Ecological Imaginings." In *Environmental Criticism for the Twenty-First Century*, edited by Stephanie LeMenager, Teresa Shewry, and Ken Hiltner, 163–78. New York: Routledge, 2011.

Jarenwattananon, Patrick. "Why Jazz Musicians Love 'The Rite of Spring.'" NPR's *Deceptive Cadence*, May 26, 2013. https://www.npr.org/sections/deceptivecadence /2013/05/26/186486269/why-jazz-musicians-love-the-rite-of-spring.

Jasanoff, Maya. *The Dawn Watch: Joseph Conrad in a Global World*. New York: Penguin, 2017.

"Jewish Author Maurice Sendak, Creator of 'Where the Wild Things Are,' Dies at 83." *Haaretz*, May 8, 2012. https://www.haaretz.com/jewish/1.5220575.

Kahan, Benjamin. *The Book of Minor Perverts: Sexology, Etiology, and the Emergences of Sexuality*. Chicago: University of Chicago Press, 2019.

Kauanui, J. Kēhaulani. "'Savage' Sexualities." In *Paradoxes of Hawaiian Sovereignty: Land, Sex, and the Colonial Politics of State Nationalism*, 153–93. Durham, NC: Duke University Press, 2018.

Keeling, Kara. "Looking for M——: Queer Temporality, Black Political Possibility, and Poetry from the Future." *GLQ: A Journal of Lesbian and Gay Studies* 15, no. 4 (2009): 565–82.

Keeling, Kara. *Queer Times, Black Futures*. New York: NYU Press, 2019.

Kessler, Graf Harry. *Journey to the Abyss: The Diaries of Count Harry Kessler, 1880–1918*. Edited and translated by Laird M. Easton. New York: Knopf, 2011.

Kohn, Eduardo. *How Forests Think: Toward an Anthropology beyond the Human*. Berkeley: University of California Press, 2013.

Kotef, Hagar. *Movement and the Ordering of Freedom: On Liberal Governances of Mobility*. Durham, NC: Duke University Press, 2015.

Krakauer, Jon. *Into the Wild*. New York: Anchor, 1987.

Lalo, Pierre. "Considérations sur le 'Sacre du printemps.'" In *Igor Stravinsky, Le sacre du printemps*, edited by François Lesure, 31–35. Geneva: Minkoff, 1980.

Lanes, Selma G. *The Art of Maurice Sendak*. New York: Harry N. Abrams, 1980.

Latour, Bruno. *We Have Never Been Modern*. Translated by Catherine Porter. Cambridge, MA: Harvard University Press, 1993.

Levitz, Tamara. "Racism at *The Rite*." In *The Rite of Spring at 100*, edited by Severine Neff, Maureen Carr, and Gretchen Horlacher, with John Reef, 146–78. Bloomington: Indiana University Press, 2017.

Lewis, Brian. "The Queer Life and Afterlife of Roger Casement." *Journal of the History of Sexuality* 14, no. 4 (October 2005): 363–82.

Lim, Eng-Beng. *Brown Boys and Rice Queens: Spellbinding Performance in the Asias*. New York, NYU Press, 2014.

Lowe, Lisa. *The Intimacies of Four Continents*. Durham, NC: Duke University Press, 2015.

Macdonald, Helen. *H Is for Hawk*. London: Jonathan Cape, 2014.

Marcus, Greil. *Lipstick Traces: A Secret History of the Twentieth Century*. Cambridge, MA: Harvard University Press, 1990.

Marinetti, Filippo Tommaso. "The Futurist Manifesto" (1909). In *Futurism*. New York: MoMA, 2017. Accessed September 14, 2019. https://www.moma.org/documents/moma_catalogue_2821_300062224.pdf.

Marks, Laura. *Touch: Sensuous Theory and Multisensory Media*. Minneapolis: University of Minnesota Press, 2002.

Martel, Yann. *Life of Pi: A Novel*. New York: Harcourt, 2001.

Mexal, Stephen J. "The Roots of 'Wilding': Black Literary Naturalism, the Language of Wilderness, and Hip Hop in the Central Park Jogger Rape." *African American Review* 46, no. 1 (2013): 101–15.

Monbiot, George. *Feral: Rewilding the Land, the Sea and Human Life*. London: Penguin, 2014.

Moore, Madison. *Fabulous: The Rise of the Beautiful Eccentric*. New Haven, CT: Yale University Press, 2018.

Mortimer-Sandilands, Catriona, and Bruce Erickson. "Introduction: A Genealogy of Queer Ecologies." In *Queer Ecologies: Sex, Nature, Politics, Desire*, edited by Catriona Mortimer-Sandilands and Bruce Erickson, 1–50. Bloomington: Indiana University Press, 2010.

Morton, Timothy. "Guest Column: Queer Ecology." *PMLA* 125, no. 2 (March 2010): 273–83.

Morton, Timothy. *Hyperobjects: Philosophy and Ecology after the End of the World*. Minneapolis: University of Minnesota Press, 2013.

Moten, Fred. *Black and Blur*. Durham, NC: Duke University Press, 2017.

Moten, Fred. *The Feel Trio*. Tucson, AZ: Letter Machine Editions, 2014.

Moten, Fred. *In the Break: The Aesthetics of the Black Radical Tradition*. Minneapolis: University of Minnesota Press, 2003.

Muñoz, José Esteban. *Cruising Utopia: The Then and There of Queer Futurity*. New York: NYU Press, 2009.

Muñoz, José Esteban. *Disidentifications: Queers of Color and the Performance of Politics*. Minneapolis: University of Minnesota Press, 1999.

Muñoz, José Esteban. "Theorizing Queer Inhumanisms: The Sense of Brownness." *GLQ: A Journal of Lesbian and Gay Studies* 21, nos. 2–3 (2015): 209–10.

Musser, Amber J. *Sensational Flesh: Race, Power, and Masochism* (New York: NYU Press, 2014).

Nast, Heidi J. "Critical Pet Studies?" *Antipode* 38, no. 5 (November 2006): 894–906.

Nguyen, Viet Thanh. *Nothing Ever Dies: Vietnam and the Memory of War*. Cambridge, MA: Harvard University Press, 2016.

Nietzsche, Friedrich. *The Gay Science: With a Prelude in Rhymes and an Appendix in Songs*. Translated by Walter Kaufmann. New York: Random House, 1974.

Pappademas, Alex, and Colson Whitehead. "When Zombies Attack! Behind Our National Obsession with the Walking Dead." *Grantland*, October 24, 2011. http://grantland.com/features/when-zombies-attack.

Philip, M. NourbeSe. *Zong!* Middletown, CT: Wesleyan University Press, 2011.

Pick, Anat. *Creaturely Poetics: Animality and Vulnerability in Literature and Film*. New York: Columbia University Press, 2011.

Povinelli, Elizabeth A. *Geontologies: A Requiem to Late Liberalism*. Durham, NC: Duke University Press, 2016.

Preciado, Paul B. *Countersexual Manifesto*. Translated by Kevin Gerry Dunn. Foreword by Jack Halberstam. New York: Columbia University Press, 2018.

Preciado, Paul B. *Testo Junkie: Sex, Drugs, and Biopolitics in the Pharmacopornographic Era*. Translated by Bruce Benderson. New York: Feminist Press, 2008.

Probyn-Rapsey, Fiona. "Five Propositions on Ferals." *Feral Feminisms*, no. 6 (Fall 2016): 18–21. https://feralfeminisms.com/five-propositions-on-ferals.

Proyect, Louis. "Robert Duncan's 'The Homosexual in Society.'" *Louis Proyect: The Unrepentant Marxist*, May 2, 2009. https://louisproyect.org/2009/05/02/robert-duncans-the-homosexual-in-society.

Rampersad, Arnold. *The Life of Langston Hughes*. Vol. 1: *1902–1942, I, Too, Sing America*. Oxford: Oxford University Press, 1986.

Rivière, Jacques. "Le Sacre du Printemps." In *The Ideal Reader: Selected Essays by Jacques Rivière*, edited and translated by Blanche A. Price. London: Harvill, 1960.

Roach, Joseph. *Cities of the Dead: Circum-Atlantic Performance*. New York: Columbia University Press, 1996.

Rosenberg, Gabriel. "How Meat Changed Sex: The Law of Interspecies Intimacy after Industrial Reproduction." *GLQ: A Journal of Lesbian and Gay Studies* 23, no. 4 (2017): 473–507.

Rosenberg, Jordy. *Confessions of the Fox*. New York: One World, 2018.

Rudy, Kathy. "LGBTQ . . . Z?" *Hypatia* 27, no. 3 (2012): 601–15.

Rydstrom, Jens. *Sinners and Citizens: Bestiality and Homosexuality in Sweden, 1880–1950*. Chicago: University of Chicago Press, 2003.

Scheijen, Sjeng. *Diaghilev: A Life*. Translated by Jane Hadley-Prole and S. J. Leinbach. Oxford: Oxford University Press, 2009.

Scott, James C. *Weapons of the Weak: Everyday Forms of Peasant Resistance*. New Haven, CT: Yale University Press, 1987.

Scudeler, June. "'Indians on Top': Kent Monkman's Sovereign Erotics." *American Indian Culture and Research Journal* 39, no. 4 (2015): 19–32.

Sedgwick, Eve Kosofsky. *Epistemology of the Closet*. Berkeley: University of California Press, 1990.

Sendak, Maurice. *Where the Wild Things Are*. 50th anniv. ed. New York: HarperCollins, 2013.

Seshadri, Kalpana Rahita. *HumAnimal: Race, Law, Language*. Minneapolis: University of Minnesota Press, 2012.

Seymour-Jones, Carole. *Painted Shadow: The Life of Vivienne Eliot*. New York: Doubleday, 2001.

Sharpe, Christina. *In the Wake: On Blackness and Being*. Durham, NC: Duke University Press, 2016.

Shelley, Percy Bysshe. *Mont Blanc: Lines Written in the Vale of Chamouni* (1861). Excerpted. Accessed January 14, 2020. https://www.poetryfoundation.org/poems/45130 /mont-blanc-lines-written-in-the-vale-of-chamouni.

Singh, Julietta. *Unthinking Mastery: Dehumanism and Decolonial Entanglements*. Durham, NC: Duke University Press, 2018.

Snorton, C. Riley. *Black on Both Sides: A Racial History of Trans Identity*. Minneapolis: University of Minnesota Press, 2018.

Snorton, C. Riley. *Nobody Is Supposed to Know: Black Sexuality on the Down Low*. Minneapolis: University of Minnesota Press, 2014.

Sontag, Susan. "Notes on Camp." In *Against Interpretation and Other Essays*. New York: Farrar, Straus and Giroux, 1966.

Soo Hoo, Winyan. "Soundsuits Sculptor Nick Cave Performs at the U.S. State Department's Art in Embassies 50th Anniversary Celebration." *Washington Post*, November 28, 2012. https://www.washingtonpost.com/blogs/arts-post/post/soundsuits-sculpto -nick-cave-performs-at-the-us-state-departments-art-in-embassies-50th-anniversary -celebration/2012/11/28/ab97c740-39a1-11e2-a263-foebffed2f15_blog.html.

Spillers, Hortense. "Mama's Baby, Papa's Maybe: An American Grammar Book." *Diacritics* 17, no. 2 (Summer 1987): 64–81.

Spivak, Gayatri Chakravorty. "Can the Subaltern Speak?" In *Can the Subaltern Speak? Reflections on the History of an Idea*, edited by Rosalind C. Morris, 21–79. New York: Columbia University Press, 2010.

Steinman, Michael, ed. *The Element of Lavishness: Letters of Sylvia Townsend Warner and Richard Maxwell, 1938–1978*. New York: Counterpoint, 2003.

Stoler, Anna Laura. *Along the Archival Grain: Epistemic Anxieties and Colonial Common Sense*. Princeton, NJ: Princeton University Press, 2009.

Stravinsky, Igor, and Robert Craft. *Expositions and Developments*. New York: Doubleday, 1962.

Taussig, Michael. *Shamanism, Colonialism, and the Wild Man: A Study in Terror and Healing*. Chicago: University of Chicago Press, 1987.

Tennyson, Alfred Lord. *Idylls of the King*. Edited by Eugene Parsons. New York: Thomas Y. Cromwell, 1901.

Thoreau, Henry David. "Night and Moonlight." In *The Writings of Henry David Thoreau*, vol. 5: *Excursions and Poems*, 323–36. Boston: Houghton Mifflin, 1906.

Toíbín, Colm. "The Tragedy of Roger Casement." *New York Review of Books*, May 27, 2004.

Vogel, Shane. "Closing Time: Langston Hughes and the Queer Poetics of Harlem Nightlife." *Criticism* 48, no. 3 (Summer 2006): 397–425.

Wadiwel, Dinesh. "Chicken Harvesting Machine: Animal Labor, Resistance, and the Time of Production." *South Atlantic Quarterly* 117, no. 3 (July 2018): 527–49.

Warner, Sylvia Townsend. *T. H. White: A Biography*. New York: Viking, 1967.

Warren, Calvin L. "Introduction: The Free Black Is Nothing." In *Ontological Terror: Blackness, Nihilism, and Emancipation*, 1–24. Durham, NC: Duke University Press, 2018.

Weheliye, Alexander G. *Habeas Viscus: Racializing Assemblages, Biopolitics, and Black Feminist Theories of the Human*. Durham, NC: Duke University Press, 2014.

Westcott, Glenway. *The Pilgrim Hawk: A Love Story*. 1940. Reprint, New York: NYRB Classics, 2011.

White, Edmund. "The Loves of the Falcon." *New York Review of Books*, February 2009. https://www.nybooks.com/articles/2009/02/12/the-loves-of-the-falcon.

White, Hayden. "The Forms of Wildness: An Archaeology of an Idea." In *Tropics of Discourse: Essays in Cultural Criticism*. Baltimore: Johns Hopkins University Press, 1986.

White, T. H. *The Goshawk*. 1951. Reprint, New York: NYRB Classics, 2007.

White, T. H. *The Once and Future King*. New York: Penguin, 2011.

Whitehead, Colson. *Zone One*. New York: Doubleday, 2011.

Wilde, Oscar. "The Decay of Lying." In *Intentions: The Works of Oscar Wilde*. Edition De Luxe. New York: Brainard, 1909.

Wilde, Oscar. *An Ideal Husband*. London: Leonard Smithers, 1899.

Wilde, Oscar. *The Picture of Dorian Gray*. 1891. Edition De Luxe. New York: Brainard, 1909.

Wilderson, Frank B., III. *Red, White, and Black: Cinema and the Structure of U.S. Antagonisms*. Durham, NC: Duke University Press, 2010.

Wynter, Sylvia. "Unsettling the Coloniality of Being/Power/Truth/Freedom: Towards the Human, after Man, Its Overrepresentation—an Argument." *New Centennial Review* 3, no. 3 (Fall 2003): 257–337.

Mundruczó, Kornél, 159–62
Muñoz, José, 40, 46, 49, 52, 59
"My Mother Would Be a Falconress"
    (Duncan), 100–102

Native Americans, 8, 68–71, 76, 170
nature: against, 18–21; before, 21–25; after,
    6–7, 15–17; beyond, 21–29; "crimes
    against," 15–16, 121; Foucault on, 11–12,
    81; Romantic cruel, 57; sexuality as
    natural/unnatural/postnatural, 6–7, 17
Nazism, 62, 138–39, 161, 193n62. *See also*
    fascism
necropolitics, 118
Nguyen, Viet Thanh, 197n31
Nietzsche, Friedrich, 135–36, 139, 147
Night of the Living Dead (Romero),
    164–66
Nijinsky, Vaslav, 52–53, 57–59, 62. See also
    Rite of Spring, The
ninth wave, 175–80
Nobody Is Supposed to Know (Snorton),
    39–40
nocturnal, the, 108
Not Dressed for Conquering (Doujak),
    129–30
Nyong'o, Tavia, 40

Once and Future King, The (White), 93,
    109
Order of Things, The (Foucault), 11–12,
    29, 95
Orwell, George, 159
otherness, 24–27, 38–39. *See also* Black-
    ness; racialization

parahumanity, 166, 197n34
Peele, Jordan, 117–18
Peregrine, The (Baker), 78–86, 110–11
pets: all pets as dead pets, 116; dependence,
    149; feral child as opposite of, 142;
    Jackson's "Losing Manhood: Animality
    and Plasticity in the (Neo)Slave Nar-
    rative," 122–23; love of, 155–56; Monty

Python "Dead Parrot Sketch," 115–16,
    119–20; origins of the term, 150; tor-
    toise in Huysman's *Against the Grain*,
    21, 116–17; zombification and, 119–20,
    149–51, 155–62
Philip, M. NourbeSe, 138
Pick, Anat, 154
Picture of Dorian Gray, The (Wilde),
    18–21
Pilgrim Hawk, The (Westcott), 96–100
Planet of the Apes (film; Schaffner), 159
Pollock, Jackson, 9–10
Preciado, Paul, 15, 20, 177
primitivism, 9, 49, 126
primitivity: Blackness and, 49; colonial
    notions of, 38, 41, 69; Disney's *Fantasia*
    and, 62–63; Stravinsky's *Rite of Spring*
    and, 61–66, 69; wild past and, 5, 9–10,
    52, 62, 73
Probyn-Rapsey, Fiona, 123

queerness: Bersani on, 60; Black, 49; Black
    fierceness and, 102–9; Coviello on, 106;
    death drive and, 21, 60; falconry and,
    99, 109–10; feral child and, 145; Hughes
    and, 28, 104, 106; Huysmans's *À rebours*
    and, 21; knowing, not knowing, and, 10;
    Muñoz and, 49–50, 59; postnatural and
    antinatural, 6, 43, 116; Sendak's *Where
    the Wild Things Are* and, 132; Stravin-
    sky's *Rite of Spring* and, 53–61; Thoreau
    and Huysmans on, 20; wildness and, 30,
    39, 47, 53
queer theory, 10, 13–14, 30, 39, 41, 122

racialization: animacy and, 25; animal-
    ization of the Native, 140–41; bare
    life and biopolitics occluding, 144;
    coloniality of being and, 8; eugenics,
    167, 169; the feral and, 123; freedom,
    fugitivity, and capture, relationship to,
    68; human concept and, 166; James's
    "Ecomelancholia," 68; Kahan on his-
    tory of sexuality and, 182n18; order and